Karl Friedrich Schinkel: A Universal Man

Karl Friedrich Schinkel: A Universal Man

Karl Friedrich Schinkel:
A Universal Man

EDITED BY

Michael Snodin

Yale University Press · New Haven and London   1991

IN ASSOCIATION WITH

The Victoria and Albert Museum

Published to coincide with the exhibition *Karl Friedrich Schinkel*: *A Universal Man* held at The Victoria and Albert Museum, London, July 31st to October 27th, 1991

Exhibition sponsored by BMW(GB) Ltd

Translations: We should like to thank Patricia Crampton, Anthony Vivis and Eileen Martin for translating the texts for us, and, in particular, Patricia Crampton, for overall revision of the translations.

Designed by John Nicoll

Set in Monophoto Bembo by Servis Filmsetting Ltd., Manchester

Printed in Hong Kong through Worldprint Ltd.

Library of Congress Catalog Card No. 91-50586
ISBN 0-300-05165-4 (cloth)
ISBN 0-300-05166-2 (paper)

1. Franz Krüger. *Portrait of Karl Friedrich Schinkel*, 1836. Coloured chalks, heightened with white, 318 × 255. Nationalgalerie, SMB (SZ 554).

Contents

Prefaces

BMW (GB) LIMITED is delighted to support the Victoria & Albert Museum by sponsoring the 'Schinkel' Exhibition.

It is very exciting for our company to support this extensive and diverse exhibition and we are proud to be associated with the V&A.

We hope that visitors to this exhibition will greatly enjoy the collection of Schinkel's work which demonstrates his broad vision and design skills.

As a truly European company, with headquarters in Germany and representation throughout the world, we are pleased to be associated with the great German classical architect, Karl Friedrich Schinkel.

Tom Purves
Managing Director
BMW (GB) Limited

I WELCOME VERY much this unique opportunity to introduce you to the world of Karl Friedrich Schinkel, one of the greatest figures in German art in the early nineteenth century. His achievements bear comparison with those of other great artists of similar genius: he was an architect, a designer and a painter.

Today, his neo-classical buildings in Berlin remain one of the German capital's greatest attractions. Early in his career, Schinkel visited England, Scotland and Wales, and what he saw of the early industrial cities in Britain made a deep impression on him. He developed a style of his own, derived from the Romantic movement but with a firm grounding in the Classics. It is the breadth of his vision and the refinement of his style that makes him so potent a figure today.

This exhibition brings to Britain the possessions of a number of German museums. Many of the exhibits are here for the first time and may not be seen in Britain again for a lifetime. You will find a rich array of furniture, sculpture and silver, as well as over 100 paintings and drawings, brought together under the expert guidance of the Stiftung Preussischer Kulturbesitz and the Schlösser und Gärten of Charlottenburg and Potsdam-Sanssouci, and fittingly housed in this museum founded by Prince Albert as the world's leading museum of fine and decorative art.

This exhibition is one of the highlights of British–German cultural exchange in 1991 and I am sure you will find it an enriching experience.

Baron Hermann von Richthofen
H.E. the German Ambassador

THIS IS NOT THE first time that Karl Friedrich Schinkel, outstanding architect, designer, and painter of Prussian Classicism, has come to London. His first visit took place 165 years ago, in May 1826, when he travelled through England, Scotland and Wales. Schinkel's companion on this journey was his friend Peter Beuth, with whom he had been working at home in Berlin to speed up the technical equipment of Prussian industry, which was then rapidly developing. Schinkel and Beuth had come to Britain to study the changes that the Industrial Revolution had brought about in English cities and industrial areas.

Karl Friedrich Schinkel had a second and no less important reason for his journey to England. Two years earlier, in 1824, work had started in Berlin on the first of the Royal Museums (today called the Altes Museum) near the Lustgarten, using Schinkel's plans. In London, the British Museum had been under construction for the same period, and Schinkel wanted to study the project on the spot to extend his knowledge of museum building problems. The diary he kept during his travels shows to this day how much he benefited from his contacts with architecture and building techniques in the United Kingdom.

In 1991 Schinkel makes his second visit to London. This time it is his legacy which arrives. Most of what has survived of his paintings, drawings, watercolours, furniture and other objects for daily use, and the designs themselves, is kept in the collections of east and west Berlin, and of Potsdam. As long as the division of Berlin and of Germany lasted, this precious legacy could never be shown as a whole. The exhibition in the Victoria & Albert Museum, whose planning started as early as 1984, long before the removal of the Berlin Wall, was originally meant to include only objects from East Berlin, where the bulk of Schinkel's drawings are kept, and from the Potsdam palaces. At that time the West Berlin collections seemed to be out of reach.

Now all frontiers inside Germany have gone, and both Berlin and Germany have been re-united. These developments have made it possible to include loans from the collections of the Stiftung Preussischer Kulturbesitz (Prussian Cultural Heritage Foundation) in West Berlin and the collections at Schloss Charlottenburg. All four homes of Schinkel's legacy now unite their efforts for the first time since the Second World War to make a comprehensive exhibition possible.

It gives me great pleasure that this first presentation abroad of the 'undivided Schinkel' takes place in London, the capital of Great Britain, to whom the free Berlin owes so much. Special thanks are due to the hospitality of the Victoria & Albert Museum, and to the efforts of its staff. May this exhibition herald a time of further close co-operation between the Victoria & Albert and the reunited State Museums in Berlin.

Professor Dr Werner Knopp
President of the Stiftung Preussischer Kulturbesitz

SCHINKEL, ALTHOUGH firmly rooted in architecture, was one of the great artistic all-rounders, a true 'uomo universale'. His astonishing range of activity exactly mirrors the aims, concerns and collections of the Victoria and Albert Museum, founded eleven years after his death and now the venue for the first exhibition on him ever to be held in the English-speaking world.

The idea for an exhibition at the V&A on Schinkel's work was first suggested in 1984 by Dr David Bindman, then working on the publication of the diary of his British journey with Dr Gottfried Riemann, curator of the great Schinkel *Nachlass* in Berlin. Brilliantly curated by Dr Riemann and my colleague, Michael Snodin, the original concept for the exhibition has been expanded since re-unification to include the whole range of Schinkel's activity, bringing key oil paintings and other exhibits from West Berlin to join those already selected.

Britain exercised a profound influence on Schinkel, and close Anglo-German cooperation has been the keynote of this exhibition. The Government of the Federal Republic of Germany has magnificently supported the exhibition as a cultural exchange, in response to an exhibition of 100 masterpieces in watercolour lent from the V&A, which was shown in eastern Germany in 1990. Our requests for loans from Berlin have been met with unwavering generosity by Professor Günther Schade, Generaldirektor of the Staatliche Museen zu Berlin, Professor Wolf-Dieter Dube, Generaldirektor of the Staatliche Museen Preussischer Kulturbesitz, Dr Hans-Joachim Giersberg, Generaldirektor of the Staatliche Schlösser und Gärten at Potsdam-Sanssouci and Professor Jürgen Julier, Generaldirektor of the Staatliche Schlösser und Gärten based at Schloss Charlottenburg. My personal thanks are above all due to His Excellency, Baron Hermann von Richthofen, the present Ambassador, who has given the exhibition great encouragement and support.

The two British lenders, the Royal Collection and Rainer Zietz Ltd, have made a significant contribution. We are especially grateful to Her Majesty the Queen for the loan of the KPM vase designed by Schinkel. Presented by Friedrich Wilhelm III to William IV, it depicts a miniature frigate, the 'Royal Louise', given by Britain to Prussia. There is no better symbol of the spirit of cooperation and exchange embodied in the exhibition and this book.

Elizabeth Esteve-Coll
Director
Victoria and Albert Museum

Acknowledgements

Any major international exhibition involves the skills of a great many people. The Schinkel exhibition and this accompanying book have been no exception. The Museum is indebted to a large number of curators, librarians, scholars, administrators, publishers' staff and friends in both Britain and Germany without whose efforts there would be no exhibition, and no book.

In Berlin we owe a special debt to Gottfried Riemann, curator of Sammlung der Zeichnungen, Nationalgalerie, Staatliche Museen zu Berlin, who has played the central role in this project since its inception, and to Peter Betthausen, formerly Director of the Nationalgalerie, who has unwaveringly supported it. Winfried and Ilse Baer, Helmut Börsch-Supan, Hans-Joachim Giersberg, Burkhardt Göres, Renate Möller, Werner Schade and Peter-Klaus Schuster have given unstintingly of their time and attention in areas both scholarly and organisational. A special role has been played by the British Embassy on Unter den Linden and its officers from the British Council, Michael Holcroft and Ian Frater, as well as by the interpretative skills of Liselotte Wlachopoulos and Doris Schneider.

In London we are particularly indebted to Reinhard Ehni, cultural attaché at the German Embassy. The Visual Arts Department of the British Council has been particularly important and we are grateful to Henry Meyric Hughes, Muriel Wilson and David Fuller, as well as to Claus Henning of the Visiting Arts Unit. We are indebted for scholarly advice to David Bindman and Alex Potts and for assistance and encouragement to Karin Herrmann of the Goethe Institute. The exhibition has been staged in the Victoria and Albert Museum by the Exhibitions Department, led by Linda Lloyd-Jones, with the assistance of Hilary Young and Caroline Lorentz, as well as Clare Graham of the Research Department. It has been designed by Mike Malham, with graphics by Richard Cottingham.

The illustrations in the catalogue section are reproduced by kind permission of the owners. We are also grateful to the following for their permission to reproduce illustrations. Harlan Walshaw: figs. 2, 5, 7, 8, 14, 15, 17, 18, 20, 21–3, 27, 41, 42, 43–53, 55, 57, 60; Martin Goalen: 37, 39, 40; Institut für Denkmalpflege, Berlin: 63–6, 70–86; Kunstgeschichtliche Bildstelle, Humboldt-Universität, Berlin: 62, 67–9; Nationalgalerie SMB: 1, 3, 4, 6, 9–12, 16, 19, 24–6, 54, 56, 59; Nationalgalerie SMPK: 13; Kunstgewerbemuseum SMB: 58; SSG Potsdam-Sanssouci: 61; Sotheby's: 145a; La Roche-sur-Yon, Conservation départementale des Musées de Vendée: 26a.

List of Contributors

G.B.   Gerd Bartoschek, SSG Potsdam-Sanssouci

H.B-S   Helmut Börsch-Supan, SSG Schloss Charlottenburg

I.B.   Ilse Baer, SSG Schloss Charlottenburg

Peter Betthausen, formerly Nationalgalerie, SMB

S.B.   Sibylle Badstübner-Gröger, Akademie der Wissenschaften, Berlin

W.B.   Winfried Baer, SSG Schloss Charlottenburg

H.D.   Horst Drescher, Institut für Denkmalpflege, Arbeitstelle, Berlin

P.F.   Peter Findeisen, Institut für Denkmalpflege, Arbeitstelle, Berlin

B.G.   Burkhardt Göres, Kunstgewerbemuseum, SMB

H.G.   Hans-Joachim Giersberg, SSG Potsdam-Sanssouci

M.G.   Matthias Gärtner, SSG Potsdam-Sanssouci

Martin Goalen, Bartlett School of Architecture and planning

C.H.   Christa Heese, Senator für Stadt- und Umweltenwicklung, Berlin

M.H.   Marlise Hoff, SSG Potsdam-Sanssouci

S.H.   Sybille Harksen, SSG Potsdam-Sanssouci

R.K.   Renate Kroll, Kupferstichkabinett, SMB

C.M.   Claudia Meckel, Kunstgewerbemuseum, SMB

R.M.   Renate Möller, SSG Potsdam-Sanssouci

A.P.   Alex Potts, Goldsmiths' College

P.P.   Peter Prohl, Berlin

G.R.   Gottfried Riemann, Nationalgalerie, SMB

M.U.R.-R.   Marie Ursula Riemann-Reyher, Nationalgalerie, SMB

A.S.   Adelheid Schendel, SSG Potsdam-Sanssouci

H.S.   Heinz Schönemann, SSG Potsdam-Sanssouci

M.S.   Michael Snodin, Victoria and Albert Museum

C.T.   Christina Thon, Kunstbibliothek, SMPK

A.W.   Angelika Wesenberg, Nationalgalerie, SMB

List of Lenders

(abbreviations of lenders' names are given in brackets)

Freunde der Preussischer Schlösser und Gärten, Berlin: cat. 139

Her Majesty the Queen: cat. 153

(KPM-Archiv, Schloss Charlottenburg) Staatliche Porzellan Manufaktur Berlin, KPM-Archiv, Schloss Charlottenburg: cat. 49, 50, 55, 59, 60, 71, 79, 80, 83, 96, 99, 106, 142, 144

(Kunstbibliothek, SMPK) Kunstbibliothek, Staatliche Museen Preussischer Kulturbesitz: cat. 6, 7

(Kunstgewerbemuseum, SMB) Kunstgewerbemuseum, Staatliche Museen zu Berlin: cat. 25, 39, 85, 93, 131, 132, 135, 138, 141, 147, 151

(Kupferstichkabinett, SMB) Kupferstichkabinett, Staatliche Museen zu Berlin: cat. 15, 23, 61, 133, 134, 140, 143, 148, 149, 160

(Nationalgalerie, SMB) Sammlung der Zeichnungen, Nationalgalerie, Staatliche Museen zu Berlin: cat. 3, 5, 8–14, 16–9, 21, 24, 26, 27, 29–34, 36, 38, 42, 43, 45–8, 51–4, 57, 62, 65, 66, 69, 76, 77, 81, 84, 86–92, 94, 95, 98, 100–5, 108–18, 120–30, 136, 137, 145, 146, 150, 152, 154–9

(Nationalgalerie, SMPK) Nationalgalerie, Staatliche Museen Preussischer Kulturbesitz: cat. 2, 22, 119

Rainer Zietz Ltd: cat. 145a

(SSG Potsdam-Sanssouci) Verwaltung der Staatliche Schlösser und Gärten, Potsdam-Sanssouci: cat. 1, 4, 28, 37, 40, 44, 56, 58, 63, 64, 68, 70, 72–5, 78, 82, 97, 107

(SSG Schloss Charlottenburg) Verwaltung der Staatliche Schlösser und Gärten, Schloss Charlottenburg: cat. 20, 35, 41, 67

Editor's Note

NAMES

Anglo-German literature inevitably faces the problem of names. In this book only established English versions of place names have been retained (e.g. Munich), all others being rendered in German. While approximate translations of official titles and state and other organisations have been given at their first appearance, they are essentially untranslatable and are generally given in German. Names of buildings and other features have been left in German, notably Brücke (bridge), Haus (house or building), Kirche (church), Markt (market), Palais (a town mansion, i.e. a palazzo), Platz (square), Residenz (a palace which is the seat of a court), Schloss (either a fortified, or once fortified, castle or a country house, i.e. a chateau), See (lake), Strasse (street or road) and Tor (a town gate).

THE SCHINKEL COLLECTIONS IN BERLIN

In 1842, on the orders of the king, the Prussian state purchased from Schinkel's heirs his artistic estate, consisting of drawings, models and manuscripts. Some knowledge of its subsequent history, and that of the other Schinkel collections, is essential in using the Schinkel literature. The great purchase, joined by the material of Schinkel's colleague Peter Beuth, was formed into the Schinkelsche Museum, set up in the architect's rooms in the Bauakademie. In 1931 the material was redisplayed as the Schinkel Museum in the Kronprinzen Palais. Meanwhile, the Nationalgalerie had acquired a number of important Schinkel oil paintings. Since the Second World War the collection of drawings and models has formed part of the drawings collection of the Nationalgalerie in east Berlin (Staatliche Museen zu Berlin), while the oil paintings have been housed in the Nationalgalerie, west Berlin (Staatliche Museen Preussischer Kulturbesitz), being displayed at the Galerie der Romantik at Schloss Charlottenburg. Smaller collections of drawings, chiefly of royal provenance, are kept in the Staatliche Schlösser und Gärten organisations at Potsdam-Sanssouci and Schloss Charlottenburg, and at the Kunstbibliothek. Much of Schinkel's royal furniture was lost in the Second World War, but there are good collections of furniture and other artefacts at Potsdam-Sanssouci, Charlottenburg and the applied art museums, both east and west. Museums to Schinkel have been set up at the restored Friedrich-Werder Kirche and the Neue Pavillon at Charlottenburg, renamed the Schinkel-Pavillon. At the time of writing, the future arrangement of the Berlin collections is under discussion.

ABBREVIATIONS

Dimensions are in millimetres, height, width, depth, unless otherwise specified.

All catalogue items are by Schinkel unless otherwise mentioned.

b. born
d. died
c. circa

For abbreviations of lenders see List of Lenders.

Michael Snodin
May 1991

Karl Friedrich Schinkel: A Universal Man

Peter Betthausen

According to many contemporaries, Schinkel was a man of 'Raphaelian friendliness', endowed by nature with gentleness, modesty, patience and kindliness, combined with great cultivation and a deeply rooted sense of beauty. 'The imprint of the intellect was apparent in him as in few others,' wrote Franz Kugler, Schinkel's first biographer, in 1842. 'There was a nobility and harmony in his movements, a smile on his lips, a clarity in his brow, a depth and fire in his eye . . . but still greater was the power of his word, when that which moved him inwardly came unbidden and unprepared to his lips. Then the doors of beauty opened.'[1] Hagen, the Oberbaurat of Public Works and a former colleague of Schinkel's at the Oberbaudeputation (Royal Office of Works), recalled in 1858:

> Schinkel expressed himself with simplicity, fluency and surprising clarity. It was his habit to describe the shapes of which he spoke with gestures . . . . Any criticism (of the work of others), though sometimes expressed with wit and humour, was nevertheless always clothed in mildness . . . . He was never led into violence of expression and was always a mediator . . . Schinkel's personality was the most complete image of genuine humanity.[2]

When on 12 October 1841 the coffin containing Schinkel's body was driven to the Friedrich-Werder cemetery in the Chausseestrasse, Berlin, it was followed by thousands, mourning not the 'illustrious architect', but the 'modest man': Schinkel, the human being.

He had taken thirteen months to die. Having returned from convalescence, on 11 September 1840, he had fallen into a coma and paralysis from which, apart from a few moments of clarity, he never awakened. This tragic end, expected and feared by those close to him, had a history, and directs our attention to the dark side of his being. Human experience suggests that the origin of Schinkel's disease and early death lay in a lifelong over-taxing of his mental and physical powers. Schinkel himself seems to have been fully aware of his fanatical zeal for work. He had 'much to thank' for it, as he confessed in an autobiography in 1825,[3] but was well aware of the dangers. To the French architect Jacob Ignaz Hittorf he had once spoken regretfully of the 'uncontrollable aspect of his imagination', 'against which he continually struggled', a tireless imagination which no doubt always drove him back to work.[4] Karl Friedrich Waagen, who knew Schinkel well, speaks in his biography of an 'almost cruel dominion of mind over body'.[5]

However complex the psychological background connections may have been, one thing is certain: Schinkel's obsession with work was not fuelled by ambition, or a thirst for fame. Its philosophical justification lay in an expressly Protestant, Prussian duty ethic, which is also demonstrated in the artist's personal motto:

> Our mind is not free if it is not the master of its imagination; the freedom of the mind is manifest in every victory over self, every resistance to external enticements, every elimination of an obstacle to this goal. Every moment of freedom is blessed.[6]

Schinkel was convinced that he lived in an age of profound and historically necessary revolutions. He both wished and felt obliged to support them by devoting his art to ennobling 'all human conditions',[7] by perfecting man morally through aesthetic education and in this way enabling him to humanise his relationships. A

2. The Neue Wache, Berlin (1817–18). The portico.

typical representative of German idealism, Schinkel was inspired by the belief that he could change society, as it were from the head down.

From the pursuit of these goals sprang a life's work which certainly did not affect the consciousness and practical actions of his contemporaries to the extent Schinkel had hoped, but its artistic quality lived up to the historical dimensions of the age. It represented a large-scale attempt to give the artistic milieu of rising capitalism a humane character, rooted in history, yet at the same time modern. For Prussia this life's work became the 'source from which the prevailing taste flows', as Athanasius Count Raczynski commented in 1841.[8] It made its mark on the architectural face of a metropolis in the making, and on the whole of Prussia after Frederick the Great.

All this was possible only because Schinkel put himself at the service of the state. On 19 May 1810 he abandoned his brief career as an independent architect, which had not been very successful owing to factors beyond his control, and took service under his king; he became a civil servant as an Oberbauassessor with the Königlichen Technischen Oberbaudeputation, Prussia's supreme building authority, which he served until his death, as Oberbaurat (councillor) from 1815 onwards and from 1830 as its Oberbaudirektor and chief.

For the time being, however, there was scarcely any opportunity for building in Prussia. Following the military collapse of 1806–7 and the continuing French occupation, all building in the country was at a standstill. New prospects opened up when Napoleon was finally defeated in 1815. For Schinkel this was the real beginning of his work as a civil servant and as an architect. In 1815 he was commissioned by the king to work on the Neue Wache (New Guardhouse, fig. 2) and only a few years later on the Schauspielhaus (Theatre) and Museum (now known as the Altes Museum). At the Oberbaudeputation, too, Schinkel soon had more to do than he could really manage. At the beginning of 1821 he was already feeling badly overburdened, as can be seen in a letter to the Minister of Trade and Industry, Hans Victor von Bülow, to whom the Oberbaudeputation was also responsible:

> In my view the artistic sphere, which alone appeals to me, is of such a limitless extent that a man's life is much too short for it. I feel, with regret, that in other circumstances I could have achieved still more in it, but that I am being inwardly torn apart by work which draws me away from my real purpose.[9]

The appeal was rejected. In the late 1820s, when most of his principal works had already been built, Schinkel tried once again to petition for some space for himself. On this occasion he lists all his duties – an oppressive array: first he names the artistic surveys (for churches the costing also had to be checked) of all government buildings for the Oberbaudeputation, then his own buildings, for which he was either the director or the chief supervisor, and finally the great variety of work on behalf of the royal family. Also mentioned is his work in the Technische Deputation für Handel, Gewerbe und Bauwesen (State Agency for Trade, Industry and Building Construction) as well as in the Senate of the Academy of Art, and the installation of the Museum on the Lustgarten.

As head of the Oberbaudeputation, Schinkel supervised all building work in Prussia, a task that he took very seriously (fig. 3).

3. August Günther after Schinkel. Design for a lighthouse at Cape Arkona on the island of Rügen, 1825. Ink and pencil, 642 × 424. Nationalgalerie, SMB (SM 45c.83). Although in the hand of Oberbaurat Günther, this design is clearly indebted to Schinkel, and demonstrates his wide oversight of the various activities of the Oberbaudeputation.

Between 1832 and 1835 he visited all the provinces, first Silesia, then Saxony, Westphalia and the Rhineland and finally Pomerania, East and West Prussia, the Altmark, East Pomerania and the Neumark, and set down his impressions and findings in detailed reports, of incalculable value as sources for historical research. These very strenuous journeys can be regarded as the peak of Schinkel's career as a civil servant. In 1838 he was promoted to Oberlandesbaudirektor (Supreme Director of National Public Works) – the highest title that could be bestowed on a Prussian architect.

The crucial experience at the beginning of his career as artist and

4. Schinkel. Design for a cathedral as a memorial to the Wars of Liberation, 1815. Pen and ink and watercolour, 660 × 1030. Lost, formerly in the Schinkel Museum.

civil servant was the meeting with the architect Friedrich Gilly. In 1797 the young Schinkel saw Gilly's grand design for a monument to Frederick the Great at the Berlin Academy Exhibition (cat. 5). It is recorded that the monumental temple complex so fascinated the youth that he made the instant decision to become an architect. A few months later he met Gilly and became his eager pupil. Many years later he gratefully recalled:

> It was the work of professor and building inspector Gilly, however, that exercised a particular charm on Schinkel's young mind, which made its first close encounter with art in these architectural objects treated intellectually in a quite unique manner . . . [and] with whom he passed the regrettably brief period of two years in the most intimate friendship, engaged in wonderful artistic activity and in ever more instructive communion, after which a too early death carried off this man of genius.[10]

Philosophically the young Schinkel was most influenced by Johann Gottlieb Fichte, and Fichte's unshakeable faith in the will and creative power of man in action. In Fichte's writing he encountered the concept of the duty of the individual *vis-à-vis* society and the active role of the state in the cultural education and training of the people. Schinkel's philosophy was also influenced by his childhood friend, the aesthetic Karl Wilhelm Ferdinand Solger, by Jean Paul and the Schlegel brothers.

Schinkel had writings by Fichte in his baggage when he set off on 1 May 1803 on his first Italian Grand Tour (cat. 10–13), from which he did not return (via Paris), until January 1805. For a classically trained architect like Schinkel, the study of the architecture of antiquity and the Renaissance was naturally of prime importance, but he also showed an astonishing interest in medieval and mannerist art and architecture. On his return journey he admired the great cathedrals in Prague and Vienna; in Italy itself, above all, the Romanesque arches and the unplastered brick buildings of Lombardy. The beauty and solidity of the churches and palaces in Ferrara and Bologna confirmed him in his rejection, on aesthetic grounds, of the contemporary practice in Prussia, an area poor in natural stone, of covering brick with plaster and 'wretched stucco embellishments'. However, Schinkel spent most of his time in Italy drawing. Over 400 drawings have been preserved, mainly of landscapes and buildings whose natural harmony he attempted to enhance artistically.

After his return to Berlin Schinkel earned his living in several ways. For David Gilly, the father of his late friend and teacher, he took charge of the building of Schloss Orwinsk on Warthe, designed a country house and park and incidentally assisted Gottfried Schadow by drawing the decorative details for his sculptures and was from 1809 onwards one of the first German artists to work in the completely new field of lithography. He also began to paint so-called 'optical perspective pictures', optically enhanced paintings related to those panoramas and dioramas which had originated in England at the end of the eighteenth century and were enjoying growing popularity in Prussia, as well as traditional architectural landscape paintings and, from 1815 onwards, theatre sets. His sets for Mozart's *Magic Flute* have become famous (cat. 28, 29).

Gustav Friedrich Waagen, first director of the painting gallery in the Altes Museum, was the first art historian to become interested in Schinkel's architectural landscapes, most of which were painted between 1805 and 1815. He called them 'historical' landscapes, which '[differ] essentially from all previously known types of landscape painting, in that they present us, in a beautiful and artistic form, a complete and faithful image of the conditions of life and art of a great variety of places and periods'.[11] In these paintings which might also be called 'cultural landscapes', the artist was constantly presenting the viewer with the world of antiquity and the Middle Ages, recommending both Classical Athens and the medieval Roman Empire of the German nation as social models and guides to the modernisation of conditions in Prussia and in Germany as a whole (cat. 22, 160). They were thus a look into the future, towards a society reborn of the spirit of antiquity and the Middle Ages. Schinkel was profoundly convinced that architecture was to make an essential contribution to this society. It stands at the centre of his cultural landscapes, now in classical, now in Gothic form, indicating the field of tension within which his own architectural work was also soon to develop.

In the years of the Napoleonic occupation, when the wave of patriotism rose high in Germany, Schinkel was a Romantic, filled with zeal for the Gothic, generally regarded as the national style. The most inspired artistic evidence from this part of his life are the Gothic designs for Queen Luise's mausoleum (1810) (cat. 16) – in the commentary, antique architecture is rejected as 'cold' and 'meaningless' in comparison with Gothic – and a cathedral in memory of the Wars of Liberation (1815) (cat. 21, fig. 4). Neither design was carried out. Friedrich Wilhelm III wanted a Doric temple for his wife's mausoleum. The cathedral project failed because of the exorbitant building costs, and the revival of feudal conditions in the Restoration era. Why should Friedrich Wilhelm III, whose concern after 1815 had been more than ever for his own personal interests as a German prince, support a project which would perpetuate the national spirit of the Wars of Liberation in such a monumental building?

At the same time basic changes were taking place in Schinkel's outlook. We observe a growing affinity with classical attitudes and a release from the Gothic and Romantic, a change of heart partly brought about by a sobering confrontation with the practical demands of the rapidly expanding Prussian building industry. If he then began to think and design exclusively in the classical manner, it was because he increasingly saw himself as the chief architect of the Prussian state, whose leaders preferred the systematic, stabilising and ceremonial language of antiquity to the nationalist associations aroused by the Gothic. And finally, antiquity also appealed to the bourgeoisie, to which Schinkel belonged, the ideals of which were rooted both in the national past and in the culture of Greece and Rome. Nevertheless, Gothic architecture remained one of Schinkel's lifelong sources of inspiration.

Schinkel's major works in the classical style are the Neue Wache (New Guardhouse), the Schauspielhaus (Theatre) and the Museum on the Lustgarten (the Altes Museum), all of which launched his reputation as one of the leading German architects of the nineteenth century and greatly influenced historical Berlin. Whereas the Neue Wache (cat. 42–44), with its original, clearly accentuated structure, its robust but well-proportioned plasticity, is still an echo of Friedrich Gilly's powerful sense of form, the Schauspielhaus, largely through its grid system of elements spanning and linking the entire building, makes a more open, inviting and modern impression. The Museum, now called the Altes (old) Museum, is among the earliest and most perfect of its type in Germany (cat. 48–56). Schinkel himself chose its exposed position, which had been created by filling

5. The Schlossbrücke, Berlin (1819–24). The Schlossbrücke over the Kupfergraben was an essential part of Schinkel's plan for central Berlin. In the background is the baroque Zeughaus (begun in 1695).

in a branch of the River Spree north of the Lustgarten, close to the Cathedral, Königliches Schloss and the Zeughaus (Arsenal) on the other side of the Kupfergraben channel (fig. 5). With the building of the Museum, this imposing architectural ensemble achieved perfect completion. Schinkel's building, with its extended façade of Ionic columns, added a peaceful and cheerful note to the whole and created a place of honour for the fine arts at the heart of royal Berlin.

While the foundations were being laid on the Museum site, Schinkel made his second Italian tour in the summer of 1824 (cat. 2), accompanied by Gustav Friedrich Waagen, with whom he visited

6. View of the library in the house of the architect John Nash, Regent Street, London, 4 June 1826. Pen and ink. From the British Diary. Nationalgalerie, SMB. Schinkel took particular note of the plaster casts, the models of temples and the lighting through small skylights.

7. The Friedrich-Werder Kirche, Berlin (1824–30).

8. The Friedrich-Werder Kirche. Detail.

numerous art collections in Florence, Rome and Naples carrying out research for the Berlin Museum project. The haste in which this whole extensive programme was completed was such that on this occasion Schinkel scarcely found time to draw.

Museum studies also motivated Schinkel's journey to France, England and Scotland two years later, with his friend Peter Wilhelm Beuth, Director of the Technische Deputation für Gewerbe since 1819 (cat. 109–112, fig. 6). Through Beuth, who had already visited England several times and was a zealous promoter of modern production methods in Prussian industry, Schinkel was able to see numerous factories, foundries, shipyards, gas plants and other types of industrial building, the practicality, fitness of the materials and constructional novelty of which astonished him. Yet he was disturbed by this industrial development, which seemed to him to threaten both the existence of architecture as the *art* of building, and social peace within society.[12]

These dual impressions and experiences of the English journey are the key to an understanding of Schinkel's intellectual and artistic development in the last twenty years of his life. After his return, there was, at first, an increase in experimentation, a growing struggle to go beyond classical architrave building and seek new technical and constructional methods. Schinkel wanted to found a modern architecture.

Brick played a fundamental role in these efforts. When Schinkel went to Britain he had already gained experience of this material in the Neue Wache, with its exterior walls of unplastered brick, and in the Friedrich-Werder Kirche (figs 7, 8), his first exclusively brick building. He knew the medieval brick buildings of Lombardy and North Germany, but it was not until he came face to face with the industrial buildings of London, Manchester and other British towns that he was able to see that brick was more than merely an aid to regions poor in building stone, and that both on aesthetic and on structural grounds it fulfilled the demands of modern architecture better than any other known building material. Its technical properties led Schinkel inevitably to arch and vault construction. As time went by, a number of plans, some executed, some not, were produced for functional architecture in the Rundbogen or 'rounded arch' style, for a storage building, a library and church buildings in Berlin.

Schinkel's indisputable masterpiece in brick was the building of the Allgemeine Bauschule (General School of Architecture), known as the Bauakademie (Architectural Academy) (cat. 119–123). After tentative beginnings with a house for the manufacturer Tobias Christoph Feilner (cat. 115–116) and the Neue Packhof (New Customs House) (cat. 117) Schinkel now began to tread a logical path, which showed the way beyond historicism towards a modern architecture which was developed out of the materials. He did not continue with it, partly because of the external factors which were not particularly conducive to this architecture, and partly because of the restraint he himself practised. He was a Prussian civil servant and a cautious man by nature, more of a reformer than a revolutionary. So it should be no surprise that comparatively conservative buildings were being produced at the same time as the Bauakademie. This was not simply Schinkel accommodating his client; at the end of his life he increasingly felt an inner urge to contribute to the

9. Schinkel. Design for the entrance to the Fürstliche Residenz, 1835. Pen and ink and wash, 558 × 488. Nationalgalerie, SMB (SM 40c.52).

preservation of traditional attitudes and values. His conservative outlook was expressed both in his work and in his writings:

> The new age [England] does everything lightly; it no longer believes in an established state . . . . On the other hand, the complete contempt for everything established, which they desire to replace as quickly as possible by putting another in its place, this tendency and preference for change, which ultimately allows no time for anything to be recognised and enjoyed, is a sure sign of the vanity of the age and of those who stand at its head.[13]

Schinkel's late works were mostly carried out at the behest of Crown Prince Friedrich Wilhelm (IV) and were appreciably influenced by the Prince, who was a gifted amateur. The collaboration between the two had begun twenty years earlier, first as a kind of teacher–pupil relationship, though later differences arose. The Crown Prince's arch-conservative views probably went too far for Schinkel. When one recalls Schinkel's ambiguous reaction to British capitalism and looks at the late works – the designs for a country house in the antique style, a Schloss on the Acropolis in Athens and a princely residence – and sees in them Friedrich Wilhelm's romantic yearnings to return to a time of harmonious human existence, or for a kingdom of a medieval type, one has to see them as at least partly in tune with Schinkel's own outlook.

10. Schinkel. Exterior of the Jagdschloss (hunting lodge) of Antonin near Posen (Poznan). Drawing for the *Sammlung architektonischer Entwürfe*, 1824. Pen and ink, 266 × 411. Nationalgalerie, SMB (SM 21c.106).

11. Schinkel. Interior of the Jagdschloss Antonin. Drawing for the *Sammlung*, 1824. Pen and ink, 258 × 248. Nationalgalerie, SMB (SM 21c.107). Antonin, made entirely of wood in 1822–4 for Schinkel's theatrical patron Prince Anton Heinrich von Radziwill, is one of his most extraordinary buildings. It is now a hotel.

The designs for the Fürstliche Residenz (Residenz for a Prince) (fig. 9) bring to a close Schinkel's decades of work on an architectural textbook, which was never completed. Schinkel had better fortune with another publishing enterprise, through which he hoped to influence contemporary building. From 1819 onwards, beginning with the Neue Wache, his *Sammlung architektonischer Entwürfe* (*Collection of Architectural Designs*) began to be published in twenty-eight parts. Here Schinkel followed the style of traditional architectural prints. What was new was that he also published alternative designs and – as in his building journals later on – gave his own views in the form of a commentary. The series closed in 1840 with the designs for a classical manor house for Friedrich Wilhelm.

This index is indispensable if one wants to gain anything like a complete picture of the huge range of Schinkel's architectural work.

Many of his buildings have disappeared in the 150 years since his death, including, oddly enough, almost all his forward-looking, functional buildings, although the extraordinary hunting lodge at Antonin has survived (figs 10, 11). They had to give way to other buildings, like the Neue Packhof, which stood on what today is Museum Island (and was replaced by the Pergamon and Bode Museums), or else fell victim to war and subsequent demolition, like the Feilner Haus and the Bauakademie. The image of Schinkel passed on today by the grand, classical buildings that have been preserved in Berlin and Potsdam is therefore not quite accurate.

The artist and architect was not the whole Schinkel. Although he regarded the industrial age with some scepticism, he strove to meet its challenges.

[1] Kugler 1842, p. 4 ff.
[2] Quoted from Grisebach 1981, p. 26.
[3] Mackowsky 1922, p. 26.
[4] Hittorf 1858, p. 102.
[5] Waagen 1844, p. 309.
[6] Wolzogen 1862–3, Vol. I, p. 23.
[7] Mackowsky 1922, p. 192.
[8] Raczynski 1841, Vol. III, p. 157.
[9] Quoted from Paul Ortwin Rave, 'Schinkel als Beamter', in Berlin 1981, p. 88.
[10] Mackowsky 1922, p. 25 ff.
[11] Waagen 1844, pp. 333, 337.
[12] Wolzogen 1862–3, Vol. II, p. 161; Vol. III, p. 358.
[13] *Ibid*., Vol. III, p. 371.

Schinkel the Artist

Helmut Börsch-Supan

In 1844, Gustav Friedrich Waagen, in his day arguably the greatest connoisseur of oil paintings in Germany, wrote of Schinkel's relationship to landscape painting:

> For this genre his talent developed a versatility unique in the history of art. He would undoubtedly have emerged as the greatest landscape-painter of all time, had he possessed the technique of the old masters and been able to devote his entire energies to this genre. For he combined the Nordic temperament's intensely vital feeling for simple, unpretentious delights – made so appealing to us by the pictures of Ruysdael – with Claude Lorrain's sense of magical effects of light, for which the landscape of southern Europe offers such abundant inspiration.[1]

For Waagen, Schinkel's greatness lay in his ability to rise above the parochial and to do justice to a variety of subjects from a more elevated standpoint. It is significant that, just before his physical and mental collapse on the evening of 8 September 1840, the last artistic project that Schinkel planned was a panorama depicting the history of architecture, intended to bridge vast distances of time and space. As Waagen recounts, that afternoon Schinkel had gone for a walk in the Tiergarten, during which he had met the set designer, Carl Gropius. He confided to the latter:

> the idea of creating a panorama 90 feet across to represent the most important monuments of as many countries as possible – Asia, Egypt, Greece, Rome and medieval Germany – in the context of appropriate landscapes. When Gropius maintained this was almost certainly impractical, Schinkel promised that if he was not daunted by the costs of such an enterprise he, Schinkel, would be glad to collaborate on its execution. Thus it was one of Schinkel's last notions to bring together in the form of a painting the spiritual cultures of various periods and peoples, which he had so often expressed in individual works of art, creating a large work composed of the most fascinating contradictions and similarities. And he was the man to fulfil such a promise.[2]

It is difficult to imagine how this panorama would have been achieved – in particular how Schinkel would have carried off the transitions between the landscapes associated with the buildings. Looking back over Schinkel's whole *oeuvre*, one can, however, see this project as the summation of his life's work as a painter.

Universality, surely one of the main characteristics of Schinkel's art, is exemplified not only in the multiplicity of his talents but also in his ability to think in global terms – at least, within the context of his times, for the Berlin of his day produced the explorer Alexander von Humboldt as well as Schinkel. Schinkel's escape from parochialism, from which he soared, as it were, on the wings of genius, was conditioned by the situation in Prussia, whose shortcomings were very apparent in the wake of Napoleon's victory – though this very defeat led, a few years later, to a unique artistic as well as military resurgence. His attitude to history was also determined by Prussian circumstances: the country's own lack of history produced a need to identify with the culture of other countries.

A desire to see the world from above, basic to Schinkel's temperament, is manifested in many pictures. A view from above –

12. Schinkel. *The view from the summit of Etna with the sunrise on the distant horizon*, 1804. Pen and ink and pencil, 490 × 324. Nationalgalerie, SMB (SM 6b.30).

thousands of feet below me. Vineyards clustered on the mountains, forming slopes; many hundreds of country villas, behind thick foliage, shone brightly out of the green or hid in the valleys.[3]

Except for the time of day, this description could be applied to *Morning* (fig. 13), an oil painting whose pendant, *Night*, was destroyed in 1945. Out of the darkness of the night and from the mountains, walkers in medieval costume make for an open area from which they have a view over a harbour town and the sea, stretching out in the morning light. Seen against the light, the trees – sturdy old ones as well as young ones – form a circle, intersected by the path; there is a hint of garden architecture. In the foreground, lilies with their white calyxes complement the light of the rising sun. This exemplifies the Romantic notion, which also motivated Philipp Otto Runge, that the sun, the most powerful and distant object in creation, finds a parallel in the exquisite, regular forms of plants. Schinkel captures an overall view of this tension between the infinite and the finite in space and time.

History, too, is included in this vision. Schinkel evokes it in the ruins of ancient structures lying in the grass, and in the medieval costumes. Finally, he turns his attention to the human aspect. The two women in the foreground and the two horsemen further back are accompanied by a crowd of children. The younger ones have rushed forward, and are playing under the trees. The grown-ups are intent on reaching the town; their goal is culture. Morning represents the future – and in 1813, this had a political significance. After all, this picture and its pendant belonged to one of the great Prussian generals and military reformers of the time: Field Marshal Neidhart von Gneisenau.

Of the relationship between nature and culture, Schinkel wrote twelve years later:

Landscape views are particularly interesting when we detect signs of human existence within them. An overall view of a land on which no human has ever set foot can have a quality of awesome beauty; but the viewer becomes uncertain, uneasy and unhappy because what a human being most wants to experience is the way fellow human beings tame nature, live within her and enjoy her beauty.[4]

In this approach Schinkel differs markedly from Caspar David Friedrich, who always saw God's creation and revelation in landscapes. In Friedrich's pictures, a town may be the goal of a walk, but it is also a metaphor of shelter in eternal life.

Schinkel's range as a painter was extensive. He painted easel pictures, took up the early nineteenth-century fashion for dioramas, and applied the skills acquired there to theatre set design. For his buildings the architect designed decorative murals (fig. 14) as well as large-scale pictures with many figures.

Schinkel's work as a painter touches on architecture in another respect, too. His great skill in painting was to depict an architectural project so evocatively that the client thought he was looking at something which had already been built. Schinkel always saw the aesthetic image as part of architecture's function.

He tried his hand at different print-making techniques, including

an overall view – is the goal to which he strives. One of these pictures is his drawing of an ascent of Mount Etna, made in 1804, which is accompanied by an impassioned description of his feelings at seeing land and sea lying below him (fig. 12). It is the counterpart to the experience he had in 1803 while crossing the Alps, when he suddenly saw the busy port of Trieste beneath him. Only a lowlander could have been so impressed and surprised by this perspective:

I saw the sun declining sharply as I approached the mountainside. Until that point I had no concept of the effect of such a natural scene. From that stony wasteland I was suddenly peering down on the vast surface of the Adriatic Sea, which, its waves gleaming in the evening sunlight, encircled the steep foothills many

13. Schinkel. *Morning*, 1813. Oil on canvas,
760 × 1020. Nationalgalerie, SMPK (NG 1160).

lithography, then still at the experimental stage, as well as etching. Since Schinkel liked to introduce pictorial decoration wherever it seemed appropriate, he created the most varied designs for objects and structural elements, which either border on the field of painting or can be regarded as sculpture. His starting point is always a drawing, which embodies his imagination. In his draughtsmanship, like almost all his contemporaries in Germany, Schinkel reveals himself as a classicist. He adds paint only as coloration, sometimes with a symbolic significance.

Schinkel's various painterly activities were not consistently applied in all phases of his life and art. They were determined partly by an inner law of artistic development, and partly by external pressures. Waagen thought that the balance in favour of devoting most of his studies to architecture was tipped in 1797, when the

sixteen-year-old Schinkel met Friedrich Gilly:

> The fact that the only artistic personality in Berlin at that time with whom Schinkel felt an intellectual affinity happened to be an architect thus had a decisive influence on the main artistic direction Schinkel was to take. Had this artistic personality been a sculptor or a painter, Schinkel would have just as readily made these fields his preferred areas of study.[5]

As his earliest drawings and some small gouaches testify, Schinkel was no child prodigy. Indeed, there was a disturbingly confused quality in his earliest artistic statements, though Gilly's example very quickly set this chaos to rights. The most important aspect of draughtsmanship he acquired from Gilly was mastery of perspective. He learnt how to convey convincingly the most complex

14. View of the dome of the Nikolaikirche, Potsdam (completed 1849, restored after war damage).

architectonic inventions – designs of whole cities. If art in Berlin in the early nineteenth century has an echo of the early Renaissance in Italy, it is in this passion for perspective, which we encounter in no other German landscape art. In perspective, Schinkel is articulating his formal grasp of landscape and urban space. Schinkel's skills were so highly valued that in 1807 the Academy offered him the Professorship in Geometry and Perspective, which he declined.

As rapidly as he had mastered perspective, Schinkel learnt, around 1802 and apparently without the assistance of a tutor, how to draw human figures in motion. Cities mean people; and the facility with which he invented figures enabled him to depict the people who inhabited the cities. As a classicist who thought in sculptural terms, Schinkel was more interested in expressive body posture than in the narrative element of genre painting based on observation. He would always thoroughly assimilate what he observed, and then reproduce it. To a certain extent this is true even of the drawings he made whilst travelling. He would often improve to his own specifications buildings he had seen. As he depicted them, things lost the individuality inherent in chance. In Schinkel's pictures, trees are always intact and ruins appear only rarely. This gives all the objects an ideal quality – something central to Schinkel's personal genius.

From Schinkel's journey to Italy and Sicily, begun in 1803 – and concluded in 1805 – some 400 drawings, for the most part carefully executed, have survived. They testify to the way Schinkel, schooling eye and hand, developed a way of seeing landscape. In the years that followed, he drew sustenance from these impressions in his paintings, when political conditions prevented him from working as an architect. More important than the easel paintings, which he created solely for himself and his friends, were the mechanical pictures, immediate precursors of the diorama. Through these, Schinkel tried to instruct the public in art history and geography.

It was the custom in Berlin at Christmas for confectioners and other shops to display large pictures of all manner of topical and entertaining themes – not only Christian ones – to attract the public and persuade them to buy. These pictures, which incorporated transparencies, were often peopled with figures which could move mechanically – art verging on the fun fair. Backed by Wilhelm and Carl Gropius, Schinkel participated, not merely to earn money but also to educate people, thereby raising these exhibitions to the level of genuine art. From 1808 onwards he displayed series of famous buildings and landscape scenes. In 1812, for example, he presented the Seven Wonders of the World. On several days in 1809, the presentations were accompanied by a choir. Of the forty or so 'optical perspective' pictures he designed from 1807 to 1816, only preparatory drawings and descriptions in newspapers and magazines have survived. In 1808, making use of the drawings from his Italian journey, he painted a much admired 360° panorama of Palermo. In this painting Schinkel had no compunction about replacing what he had failed to record from nature with freely invented material. With his extraordinary capacity for work, he was able to cover very large surfaces; the pictures for 1809 measured thirteen feet by twenty.

We can form an impression of the broad sweep with which Schinkel painted such gigantic pictures from a mural measuring 240 × 620 cm., painted for the Royal Inspector of Machinery and Court Master Carpenter, Glatz, and dating from 1809, now in the Nationalgalerie, SMPK. Of Schinkel's landscape decorations executed in 1813–14 for another middle-class residence, only a narrow strip survived the Second World War.[6]

The Romantic movement in Berlin reached its climax around 1810, at the time when Berlin University was founded and attracted the best minds, and the royal couple returned from exile in Königsberg. Schinkel made the acquaintance of the kindly Queen Luise, who died suddenly, in the summer of 1810. The emotions her death released were keenly felt by artists. For the queen, Schinkel designed a mausoleum in Gothic style (cat. 16), even though one had already been conceived in the form of a Doric temple (cat. 15). The Gothic architectural style, which was thought to be of German origin, was an affirmation of faith in the German Middle Ages, and, accordingly, of resistance to the hegemony of Napoleon, who took his cue from imperial Roman traditions. The religious character of Berlin art of this period also influenced Schinkel.

The most exquisite expression of this outlook is perhaps his lithograph of 1810 (cat. 17). Its lettering reinforces the union of religion and vision, nature and art, architecture and music: 'Try to express the yearning beauty of the melancholy which fills the heart as the sounds of holy worship ring out from the church. Drawn on stone by Schinkel.' The enormous tree, its trunk and branches shining through the cloak of foliage as structural elements, is positioned in front of the church as a kind of allegory, evoking echoes of the Minsters of Freiburg and Strasburg. The rose window refers both to roses as a symbol of love, and to the two sunflowers which, in turning their petals to the light, symbolise religious striving. The tombs – reminders of death, are partly Gothic and partly antique in form – and contrast with the luxuriant vegetation, a consoling allusion to nature's constant renewal of life – a notion immediately recalling the idea behind the contemporary mausoleum for Queen Luise.

The mausoleum drawings and the lithograph were shown at the same exhibition of the Berlin Academy, in autumn 1810, as Caspar David Friedrich's oil paintings, *Monk by the Sea* and *Abbey in an Oakwood*. This composition combined, in equal measure, harmony and inner inevitability, and Schinkel wanted to connect it with the concept of music, in his view the purest expression of art's divine origin. This idea appears simultaneously in the 'optical perspective exhibits' which were presented with musical accompaniment. Music repeatedly crops up as a subject in Schinkel's work, for example in his design of 1812 for a large-scale mural depicting St Cecilia for a projected reconstruction of the Choral Society building.

From 1809 onwards, the Gothic cathedral became the most important subject of his paintings. A succession of such pictures up to 1817 gives a clear idea of how his vision of Gothic art developed, moving from external observation to an ever deeper grasp of the inner workings of Gothic structure (cat. 22). Here his training as an architect came to the fore. He generally transported a cathedral from the city and placed it in an open landscape; preferably on a rocky height to demonstrate the way in which the human spirit rises above mere matter. One such picture is the drawing which shows Milan Cathedral on a height above Trieste (cat. 13). Only in one major work, of 1813, *Gothic Cathedral by the Water* – which since the

Second World War survives only in two old copies, – is a cathedral placed in a city; though, curiously, it is surrounded by buildings in completely different styles.[7] In this way, Schinkel wanted to demonstrate the superiority of Gothic art – a viewpoint which, after the Wars of Liberation, he modified in favour of antiquity.

Through his friend, the poet Clemens Brentano, Schinkel had heard of the work of Philipp Otto Runge, who had died in 1810, and he was able to see works by Caspar David Friedrich in Berlin. For these two artists, and for Schinkel, time became a central theme of pictorial invention. Schinkel preferred to approach it in pairs of pictures: morning and evening, Greek antiquity and German Middle Ages, but we can also detect this feeling for time in individual works. The sources and mouths of rivers, for instance, are metaphors for the passage of time. Interwoven with all these notions is the hope of liberation. To look back to the past is, at the same time, to envisage the future. Such polarities enabled Schinkel to use dramatic effects of light. In this he had learnt lessons from his dioramas, whose changing lighting effects added interest for the spectator. Here the artist showed he could liberate pictures from stasis, activating them into a process and dramatising them.

The Ages of Man, an important subject for Caspar David Friedrich within the theme of time, is an area Schinkel – significantly – touches on only rarely. When he does tackle it, he generally restricts himself to youth; old age and death feature scarcely at all in his *oeuvre*. His own children (born in 1810, 1811, 1813 and 1822) inspired him, especially in the years of the Wars of Liberation, which were productive for him as a painter, to create pictures which put life into perspective. As with Runge and Friedrich, Schinkel's only portraits are of family and friends. Some of the portrait drawings of his children are astonishingly close in concept to Runge's portraits of children.

The death, in 1814, of August Wilhelm Iffland, artistic director of the Königliches Theater, and the subsequent appointment to that position of Duke Karl von Brühl, who was sympathetic to Schinkel's work, gave him the opportunity to design sets for the opera and the Schauspielhaus. Schinkel had been attempting to reform set design for some years. Iffland, however, had resisted Schinkel's wish to replace the Baroque stage, with its fixed, overlapping flats, by a straightforward extension with a large-scale backcloth upstage or, at the very least, movable flats downstage to frame the action. Actors, it was hoped, would stand out strikingly against the upstage backcloth.

While still a young man, Schinkel had a highly developed feeling for the theatre, the most important institution in Berlin for education and entertainment in the early nineteenth century. The landscape descriptions from his Italian journey of 1803–4 – unlike those of the journey he undertook in 1824 – indicate how far Schinkel's vision at that time was influenced by his experiences of the stage. Everything reveals itself to him in a dramatic manner. In designing stage sets, especially those with painted architectural designs, Schinkel had the opportunity to combine the effect of words – and, in the case of opera, music – into an impressive total work of art. This new sphere of activity coincided with the start of his true architectural career after the Wars of Liberation. One activity stimulated the other, and by 1817, when the Theatre auf

15. The Altes Museum, Berlin (1822–30). View down the portico. Before 1945 the long wall above the dado carried the panoramic picture *Development of Life on Earth*. The short wall at the other end of the portico carried *Uranus and the Dance of the Constellations* (see fig.16).

dem Gendarmenmarkt burned down and a new building (the Schauspielhaus) was immediately commissioned, the theatre was of central importance to Schinkel's artistic outlook.

As early as 1802 Schinkel made his mark at the exhibition of the Berlin Academy with a well thought-of, but unexecuted, set design. Schinkel's first major achievement as a set designer was a masterpiece he never bettered, – inspired by one of the greatest of operas, Mozart's *Magic Flute* (cat. 28, 29). In his twelve set designs, Schinkel combined his knowledge of Egyptian architecture with his feeling for Mozart's music. But in the process, true to the spirit of the Romantic ethos, he sacrificed all the airy eighteenth-century grace of Papageno's world to the solemn contrast between day and night. In Schinkel's *oeuvre*, we find time and again that something new emerges almost without warning and in a state of perfection. The unfamiliar appears to have acted as a spur to his creative energy; routine is entirely foreign to his nature. He touches on this in a letter of 1840:

> Every work of art must incorporate an entirely new element, even if it is created in a well-known, beautiful style. Without this new element, it cannot fully arouse the interest either of the artist or the viewer. Yet this new element is what engages his interest in the world as it exists, highlighting the extraordinary quality of existence and thus suffusing existence with a new colour, flooding it with the charm of a vital spirit.[8]

By 1828 Schinkel had created over a hundred sets, and most of the designs for these have survived. The years leading up to the opening of the Schauspielhaus in 1821, the first major building to be

16. Schinkel. *Uranus and the Dance of the Constellations*, 1831. Body colour, 432 × 471. Design for a mural in the portico of the Altes Museum, painted in the 1840s. Nationalgalerie, SMB (SM D.8).

Athenian buildings – is the glory the city achieved after the Persian wars, presented as a parallel to Berlin's situation after the Wars of Liberation. The picture is an appeal for the city to emulate the great example of antiquity, just as Schinkel himself did as an architect.

Historical genre painting, mainly depicting the Middle Ages, was a feature of art in Berlin in the early nineteenth century. Schinkel's *oeuvre* belongs to this genre, but in quality and detail it was without parallel. What is striking is that Schinkel depicts the *process* of building construction, not the completed structure. He was concerned not so much with explaining the technical problems as with affirming his faith in the value of work, in the ethos of effort – of which he himself provided the supreme example. In 1814, in carrying out his project for a Gothic cathedral to commemorate the Wars of Liberation, he explicitly referred to this ethos (cat. 21)[11]. As the final design was lost in 1945, we can only judge it by reproductions (fig. 4).

The second major work among his figure paintings is the series of sketches he made between 1828 and 1834 for the fresco decorations to the vestibule of the Museum am Lustgarten, built between 1823 and 1830. Building the Schauspielhaus to house drama, and building this museum to house the visual arts, gave him new inspiration as a painter. The frescos were not executed until after Schinkel's death, and they were very largely destroyed in 1945 (fig. 15). Echoing the famous Stoa Poikile in Athens, they were meant to be visible to everyone from outside and to set the contents of the building – antique sculpture and modern paintings – in the context of the whole cosmos.

To achieve this, Schinkel made use of ancient mythology. The fact that these thought processes were no longer intelligible to an ordinary citizen did not bother him. He organised his figures into groups of lines full of musical feeling. In these pictures, too, Schinkel's main theme is time. In 1828 he created a sketch for a frieze-like picture, *Jupiter and the New Pantheon*. The counterpart, *Development of Life on Earth*, did not follow until three years later, along with two smaller pictures, *Uranus and the Dance of the Constellations* (fig. 16) and *The Rise of New Life and Mourning on the Tumulus*. In the latter picture, the theme of death makes its first, unmistakable appearance in his *oeuvre* as a reflection of resignation and physical exhaustion. In 1833 and 1834 there follow two more sketches with almost fervent appeals to citizens' public-spiritedness, though in the form of depictions of life in ancient times: *Self-sacrifice for Others at a Time of Natural Danger* and *Self-sacrifice for Others in Repulsing Human Brutality*. Here we can detect echoes of the Wars of Liberation, which had made such a lasting impression on Schinkel's outlook as an artist. Both pictures also provide further proof of the way Schinkel saw his artistic strivings as a mission: to fend off natural dangers and the barbarity inherent in human beings. But here Schinkel also asserts his faith in technique, or human ingenuity, and in art as a creative force that can encompass humankind.

completed to his design, were his most productive. It was not always to important works of literature or opera that Schinkel devoted his genius, though his creations were considered so exemplary that between 1819 and 1824 thirty-two of his most important set designs were reproduced in costly aquatints. 1821 also marked a caesura where his easel paintings were concerned. In 1820 Schinkel painted his last truly Romantic landscape. In the following year, he visited the island of Rügen, which had inspired some of Friedrich's most meaningful pictures, and which art connoisseurs had associated with his name ever since. As the fruit of this journey, Schinkel painted three oil paintings.[9] In contrast to the earlier landscape compositions, these faithfully reproduce what the artist observed. They are nothing less than conscious affirmations of nature's power to control an artist's vision. But they also marked the end of Schinkel's work as a landscape painter. It was not simply the fact that his increasing burden of responsibility as Prussia's leading architect deprived him of leisure; it was also his own wish to renounce landscape painting.

Instead, he took up figure painting, in two major works which displayed a symphonic breadth of conception – one of the features of his late style. In 1825 he painted a large picture, *A View of Greece in its Prime*, in which he depicts the erection of a Greek temple (cat. 160)[10]. What Schinkel has in mind – without directly reproducing

[1] Waagen 1844, p. 330.
[2] *Ibid.*, p. 420.
[3] Riemann 1979, p. 280.
[4] Wolzogen 1862–3, Vol. 3 (1863), p. 367.
[5] Waagen 1844, p. 317.
[6] Berlin 1981, 144.
[7] A copy by Wilhelm Ahlborn (Nationalgalerie, SMPK, Schinkel 1981, 176) and by Eduard Biermann in the Neue Pinakothek, Munich. Both originals were in the Nationalgalerie.
[8] Mackowsky 1922, p. 190.
[9] *A View of the Stubbenkammer* and *A View of Stettin*, once in the Nationalgalerie, were lost in 1945. Still in the Nationalgalerie, SMPK, is *The Rugard from Rügen* (Berlin 1981, 199).
[10] A copy by Wilhelm Ahlborn survives in the Nationalgalerie, SMPK (Berlin 1981, 204).
[11] Rave 1941, pp. 187–201.

Schinkel's Buildings and Plans for Berlin

Gottfried Riemann

Schinkel's rise to fame as the most important architect of nineteenth century Germany coincided with the beginning of his building activities in Berlin. He became the crucial force in the building work which began to intensify in the Prussian capital in 1815, after the final victory over Napoleon. In 1810, at the age of twenty-nine, he had become Geheimer Oberbauassessor, received his first building commissions – insignificant ones, in view of the war – and had met the king and queen. In 1815 Friedrich Wilhelm III promoted him to Geheimer Oberbaurat (councillor). This meant that he was in a position to prepare and execute in his official capacity the building commissions which in the years to come were so decisively to characterise his work in Berlin and the development of classicism in Germany.

All the demands made on him by that period – whether in the shape of splendid state or church buildings, technically executed functional buildings, or middle-class residences – were brilliantly resolved in Berlin. He made use of most of the architectural opportunities available in that period of incipient historicism, and in his own unmistakable style turned almost every one of them into a masterpiece.

The Neue Wache (New Guardhouse) (1814–15, fig. 17) stands in two senses at the very start of Schinkel's architectural life's work (cat. 42–44). With it he developed his concept of an architecture of classicist magnificence, manifested, in the years to come, in all his major works. Secondly, the building initiated his lifelong concern with the city of Berlin, to whose appearance he gave a definitive emphasis. On a unique site in the capital, opposite the Königliches Palais (Royal Palace) on Unter den Linden and between two of the most splendid Baroque buildings symbolic of the monarchy, the Zeughaus (Arsenal) and the University (the former Palais Prinz Heinrich), he erected his first important building: a guardhouse in the form of a Roman castrum, fronted by a Greek temple portico.

Despite the formal contrast, the tremendous gravity of the Doric columns combines with the closed body of the building, the walls of which are largely executed in unplastered brick, in a completely homogeneous unity. The characteristic features of the style which distinguishes all his works, large and small, from then on, were achieved at once and in full: the overall certainty of proportion, the consistency of the surface and spatial relationships and the fully reasoned significance of the details.

Schinkel was quick to recognise and attempt to grasp some of the town planning opportunities opening up for him by the impulse to expand the capital. As early as 1817, he submitted to the king the plan for a building programme in which he proposed the reorganisation of whole sections of the town, and in particular the area adjoining the Schlossinsel. At the same time he was converting the Baroque cathedral (1816–20) (figs 64, 65), beside Schlüter's Königliches Schloss, and planning the design of the Lustgarten in front of it, the most important open space in the city. The cathedral dome enabled him for the first time to realise one of his most longed-for and persistent architectural ideals.

A year or two before that, the grandiose idea had come to him of designing a medieval cathedral as 'a memorial to the Wars of Liberation' to be built before Berlin's Potsdamer Tor on the new Leipziger Platz (1814–15) (cat. 21, fig. 4). This bold project, never

17. The Neue Wache, Berlin (1817–18).

realised, was the most impressive manifestation of Schinkel's Romantic phase, which expressed – side by side with the intellectual and literary tendencies of German Romanticism – the atmosphere of national retrospection to the German Middle Ages, especially to their great architecture.

For Schinkel the adoption of medieval Gothic architecture represented the great counterweight to the intellectual and formal heritage of classical antiquity. On aesthetic grounds, above all, he felt profoundly linked with the medieval style, which was generally regarded as national. Since he had absorbed vital impressions of Gothic cathedrals between 1803 and 1805 on his cultural tour through Germany, Austria and Italy, he seized every opportunity to transform this world of forms creatively, reflecting it in his designs. The other Gothicised ecclesiastical designs, roughly contemporaneous with the great cathedral project (the Petrikirche in Kölln, 1814, and the Gertraudenkirche on the Spittelmarkt, 1819, (cat. 101,

102), both unbuilt), are important cornerstones of his architectural philosophy and life's work. Whenever he could, he seized the opportunity to use Gothic forms, as shown in the Kreuzberg Memorial (1817–21) (cat. 23), the Friedrich-Werder Kirche (1821–30) (cat. 103–106) and the Johanniskirche in the suburb of Moabit (1832–5).

Schinkel was particularly influenced in the direction of official classicism by the great state commissions which came to him soon after the building of the Neue Wache. These made a decisive contribution to his architectural work, as well as to the shaping of Berlin. Friedrichstadt, a Baroque development which included the spacious Gendarmenmarkt with two churches, the so-called French (Huguenot) Cathedral and the German Cathedral, was an area of extreme importance to the town plan, which still lacked a significant centre. With Schinkel's Schauspielhaus (Theatre) (1818–21) (cat. 45–47, fig. 18) built between the two churches, the square, the

18. The Schauspielhaus, Berlin (1818–21). The main front from the Platz der Akademie (formerly the Gendarmenmarkt).

19. The Schlossbrücke (1819–24). To the right is the
Cathedral (1894–1905) by J. Rachsdorff, which
replaced Schinkel's Cathedral. On the left, above
the trees, is the attic concealing the dome of the
Museum.

20. Schinkel. Design for the Schlossbrücke, Berlin, 1819. Ink and wash, 557 × 903. Nationalgalerie, SMB (SM 23a.64). At this stage the bridge bore its old name, the Hundebrücke (Dogs' Bridge).

21. The Schlossbrücke: Victory with a fallen warrior. The figure sculpture was carved between 1842 and 1847 by pupils and associates of Christian Daniel Rauch.

Despite their proximity to each other, there was as yet no satisfactory connection in the urban plan between the east–west axis of the officially important Unter den Linden and the Baroque Königliches Schloss to which the ceremonial avenue led. With the Schlossbrücke (1821–4) Schinkel not only created this essential link between the parts of the town separated by the Kupfergraben, a channel of the Spree, but also a significant architectural and sculptural work (cat. 49, figs 19–21). With its eight allegorical twin figure groups on the theme of war and peace, Schinkel brought about both a formal and a philosophical transition between the Neue Wache, the Zeughaus and the Schloss.

It was also this development which gave the Lustgarten its ultimate status in the town plan. With the building of the Museum (1823–30, now called the Altes Museum) one of his most important works, Schinkel gave it the crucial fourth side which had previously been missing. The Museum building (cat. 50–56), intended for a new public, was allocated the most important site in the town, directly opposite the Schloss, entirely in keeping with the advancing cultural emancipation of the middle class. In common with the Crown Prince (later Friedrich Wilhelm IV), who was fascinated by building and always making plans for Berlin, Schinkel recognised the importance and uniqueness of this location. And it is a tribute to the understanding of Friedrich Wilhelm III that he immediately accepted this brilliant solution. Although the ultimate form of Schinkel's buildings sometimes crystallised quite slowly – the marked changes in the sketches for the Neue Wache are examples of this – the design of the Museum remained unchanged and complete from the very start, and was carried out without modification.

The rectangular, cubic two-storey building, enclosing two courtyards, presents an inviting front to the Lustgarten in its monumental row of eighteen Ionic columns above a flight of steps (fig. 22). The two crucial elements of the interior are consistent with the exterior. The dome, inspired by the Roman Pantheon and forming the architectural and aesthetic central point (cat. 56), and the staircase (cat. 54, 55), which progressively opens up the view of the open space as one ascends, are both supreme achievements, not only in Schinkel's work, but in the whole field of nineteenth-century architecture. With his Museum, Schinkel created an exemplary type for the nineteenth century, in its ideal architectural form, in its classical magnificence, but also in the organisation of its contents, especially the historical polarity of the two great collections from antiquity (sculpture) and the Renaissance (painting), which were regarded as the fundamental elements of European civilisation, and to each of which one floor was dedicated.

Schinkel's lifelong work in ecclesiastical building is also evident in Berlin, in various interesting forms. As a designer fascinated by Gothic architecture, he had early on conceived a cathedral as a monument to the Wars of Liberation and plans for the Gertrauden-kirche. A real opportunity to build a new church in Berlin first arose with the Friedrich-Werder Kirche (1821–30) (cat. 103–106, fig. 23). After various classical stylistic variants had been considered, the eventual designs were in the 'medieval style', thanks to a suggestion from the Crown Prince. Schinkel was decisively influenced in this by examples of English collegiate Gothic, which had become known beyond British shores through published engravings. Its spacious

district and the whole royal city gained an architectural masterpiece beside which the previous building of the National Theatre by C. G. Langhans, builder of the Brandenburger Tor, was rendered insignificant. Schinkel's genius gave the new Theatre an incomparable form, with its broad flight of steps, its imposing façade of Ionic columns, the two main and the side pediments, and the structural grid system of the lateral elevations. It was also the first architecturally significant theatre building to be built in Germany.

A new look was also to be given to the real centre of the capital, the Lustgarten on the Schlossinsel, now called the Museumsinsel.

22. The Altes Museum, Berlin (1822–30): view from
the Lustgarten.

23. The Friedrich-Werder Kirche, Berlin (1824–30).

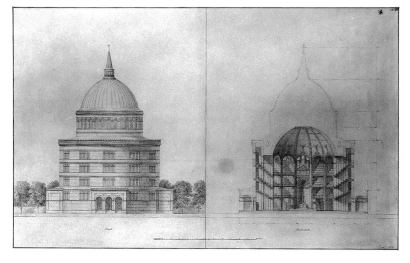

24, 25. Schinkel. Designs for cruciform and round churches from the set of five for the Oranienburg suburb of Berlin, 1828. Pen and ink and wash, 632 × 987. Nationalgalerie, SMB (SM 25.7, 25.9). They were to be built of exposed brick with terracotta details.

century church architecture. All that could be built, for reasons of economy, were the Nazarethkirche (1832–3), the Paulskirche (1832–3) and the Elisabethkirche (1830–5), modest buildings, which nevertheless demonstrate the versatility of Schinkel's ecclesiastical building in Berlin, being developed from a 'standard church' designed in 1825.

An entirely different, novel kind of building assignment came up in 1825–6, when large, modern warehouses and customs buildings were needed in the centre of Berlin. Already partially designed before Schinkel saw examples of such buildings in Britain in 1826, they demonstrate his efforts to achieve a new, constructional architectural style, free of historical reference (cat. 117). Once again at one of the key points in the city, on the northern part of the Schlossinsel and immediately beside the Museum which was then being built, Schinkel planned and built a complex of purely functional buildings: cubic, simple blocks, the largest being a five-storey brick building, adorned with serried rows of round-arched windows. Only the smaller, administrative building has classical proportions and is ornamented with a pediment on the front. As always in Schinkel's plans, the greatest attention is paid to relationship with the surrounding area. The warehouses are clearly composed with references to the other old and new buildings along the Kupfergraben: in their differing dimensions, the new buildings fit in with the blocks of the Zeughaus, Museum and Schloss. Equally important to Schinkel was the visual connection with the buildings put up along the water, so that the Friedrich-Werder Kirche and the Bauakademie were deliberately drawn into the overall image. Thus Schinkel created from the buildings spanning two centuries a composition which must have been unique in Europe, fused together by that genius for structural composition which always distinguished Schinkel's taste.

In 1827 Schinkel designed a bazaar, which was intended to stand on the Academy site beside the university, the most prestigious position on the city's main avenue, Unter den Linden. No such building had been commissioned, but the desire to combine a large number of individual shops in a new building existed in official quarters. Schinkel was completely free to follow his own ideas, and this building, which remained at the design stage, was the first example in his work of a truly forward-looking modern style, completely free of historicism (cat. 113). No earlier patterns or yardsticks in fact existed for this totally novel building assignment. On his tour in 1826 he had seen the Palais Royal in Paris and the first of the new arcades, as well as the covered markets in Paris and London and, also in London, the first warehouses. However, he came to his original formula quite independently, introducing that vital, new and fruitful phase of his development which was to continue with the Bauakademie. In contrast to the typical department store which was to develop later as a single, connected business, the idea was to combine a number of individual shops with associated flats.

The building, with its three wings set round a courtyard, is on two floors, with rows of large windows, which occupy almost the entire length and height of the building. A supporting framework of uprights and beams is only partially filled in, so that the building essentially consists only of this structural framework, visible

proportions were in fact greatly reduced, since cost and site allowed for no more than a relatively small building. Nevertheless this became one of Schinkel's most characteristic church buildings. Clarity, simplicity, balance, elegance, strictly delineated structure and mass, and the dominant tendency to the vertical, give the exterior of the building an accent which is both Gothic and classical. The interior also demonstrates Schinkel's great capacity for converting the apparently standardised character of Gothic forms into an original creation.

At the same time as the building of the Friedrich-Werder Kirche, Schinkel was commissioned to build new churches for two of the expanding northern suburbs of Berlin. Exceeding the original plan, which was for two quite small buildings, he expanded the work into five different designs (1829–33) whose monumentality greatly transcends the character of suburban churches (figs. 24, 25). Although they were never executed, these are among the most important attempts to depart from historical precedent in nineteenth externally in the continuous horizontally emphasised mouldings and the flat vertical wall sections. Despite the overall layered effect of the great window surfaces, the cubic blocks produce a light, almost weightless impression. The unification of the internal framework with the external façade is one of the leading new ideas in Schinkel's late architectural style, to which the bazaar design was the prelude. It was only a step to the rigorous grid design of the Bauakademie and the bare brick walls that filled it in.

The Bauakademie (1831–5) (cat. 119–123) represents the unwavering pursuit of this style of 'radical abstraction', as Sir Nikolaus Pevsner has called it. Once again, the site found by Schinkel for this forward-looking building is of the greatest significance within the city plan. Immediately opposite the Schloss, on the other side of the Kupfergraben and in close proximity to the Zeughaus and the Schlossbrücke, it becomes the cornerstone of Schinkel's reorganisation of this area, already regarded as the most important part of the city. The structural concept of the building itself corresponds to contemporary British industrial building, which Schinkel had seen in 1826, employing the principle of an iron framework, filled in with brick walling. Schinkel, however, was obliged to use the brick technique on its own, because cast-iron columns were still too expensive in Prussia. However, whereas the English factories were simply sober, functional buildings quite outside 'architecture' as such, Schinkel's merit was to use the new principles and the rediscovery of brick to create a building which was emphatically architecture.

The only consideration was the purpose and future use of the building. In the Bauakademie Schinkel consistently applied his principles of functional building, with the three basic elements of utility of plan, construction and decoration. The wide building, with its stratified appearance, displays four identical fronts. Each of these opens up the interior fully to the outside world, the direct result of the system of bearing uprights displaying the clear axial arrangement and the vertical thrust, and of the resting weight of the vaulted cap, expressed in the cornices, the horizontal linked layers of glazed brick and the bands of relief underneath the windows. Here the interpenetration of vertical and horizontal elements is carried to the finest point of balance, far more than in the bazaar design. Apart from the construction, the second remarkable novelty is the use of brick, which was greatly stimulated by English industrial building, whereas the use of linking terracotta elements for window areas and door frames is an adaptation of examples from the Italian Renaissance.

In his house for Tobias Feilner (1828), the manufacturer of these moulded bricks, Schinkel had already found new solutions, which he was able to expand on (cat. 115, 116). The use of brick enabled him to arrive, quite logically, at an ahistorical architecture far ahead of its time. The Bauakademie not only represents a turning-point in Schinkel's work, but also initiates the general rejection of classicism as a whole. Schinkel achieves this by abandoning historical styles in favour of new principles based on designing the building as a framework rather than a spatial concept, as was the case, for instance, in the Baroque period. As a result, the elements of this framework, linked within and without, determine the whole. In adapting the example of British industrial building, he created a model for new building techniques.

In his later work Schinkel moved consistently forward towards a new concept, dominated by the function and appearance of the building. He prepared designs for the Königliche Bibliothek (Royal Library) (1835), which was to have stood immediately beside the University but was never built (cat. 127). Its key position in the city, its imposing size, but above all its consistently purposeful modernity are the distinguishing features. Externally, the design is remarkable for its use of Rundbogenstil (round arch style), with its decisive articulating effect. Once again, the dominant internal framework points to models in industrial architecture. With logical consistency, the close sequence of narrow articulating elements on the exterior corresponds to the internal construction. The grid-like division into square compartments, produced by the interpenetration of the rows of supports and the ceilings, gives the building a solid geometrical framework.

In order to understand Schinkel's wide-ranging and varied architectural activity, it is helpful to concentrate on his work and plans for Berlin. For the Prussian capital, where Schinkel also lived, was the place where almost all the new commissions were to be carried out. They came to him as head of the highest office of public works and the country's most famous architect, who wanted to keep as much of the work as possible in his own hands. As a result, he was positively weighed down by orders.

His boundless energy and practical imagination created in and for Berlin, in particular, the buildings and projects which form the scaffolding of his work. They are principally commissions for state and city, and from private clients. Though Schinkel was not the court architect, there were also orders for the royal family. He approached this multiple workload with innate certainty, rationality and originality, as a few final examples will demonstrate.

There was a plan to convert the old Rathaus (Town Hall) (1817) for the administration of the growing capital city. Schinkel used this opportunity, as so often, to employ a completely new idea. Borrowing from the *palazzi* of the Florentine quattrocento, he intended to construct a corner building flanked by small towers. With its rusticated façade crowned at crucial points with pinnacles, this would have been one of the earliest examples of an adaptation of the Renaissance style. Like so much of Schinkel's work, it was left unbuilt owing to the continuous need for economy.

A public works order of quite a different kind, already an anachronism in the nineteenth century, was the design for pairs of gatehouses which were to stand on the Potsdamer Platz and at the end of Luisenstrasse near the Charité hospital. In contrast to the Doric temple buildings of the Potsdamer Platz (1823–4), with their imitation of four-column prostyle buildings, the buildings on the Neue Tor (New Gate) (1835–6) reveal a combination of triple round arched settings on their fronts and of window openings with linking motifs closed off flat at the top which are related to English medieval models. A crowning ring of battlements was to evoke the association with a medieval fortress, and the whole building was to be in unplastered brick.

Completely in tune with the spirit of the age, which regarded the interchangeability of styles for one and the same job as not only possible but actually desirable, it was easy for Schinkel to dress each

26. Schinkel. Design for Prince Wilhelm's Palais on
Unter den Linden, Berlin, 1832. Pencil, 343 × 532.
Nationalgalerie, SMB (SM 33.6).

building in whichever style appeared fitting. With skilful and subtle purpose, he went beyond the officially preferred, imposing classicism, to which he was naturally bound in his work for the Royal House and which represents a not inconsiderable share of the work that appeared in Berlin. For Prince Wilhelm he designed a town palace on Unter den Linden (1832) (fig. 26). Once again in a striking position, opposite the University and beside the Library, the quality of the site must have so stimulated Schinkel that he designed a great palace of bold and rigorous novelty, in addition to which the entire Library was to have been replaced by planted terraces. This is an example of Schinkel's predilection for landscaping the surroundings of his projects whenever possible.

A final example is the Palais Redern (1829) (cat. 118). In an exposed position on the Pariser Platz, at the top of Unter den Linden, the Palais Redern is typical of Schinkel's prodigious ability to use all kinds of styles while at the same time developing his own, unmistakable manner. Where a merely middle-ranking Baroque palace was to have been renovated, a completely new and unexpectedly imposing building arose, on the pattern of a Florentine palazzo.

Schinkel's work for Berlin is as universal as all his architectural work. With his tireless energy, he met almost all the demands of his age and of Berlin society. It is characteristic that the last great design he ever produced, the building plan for Moabit made in July 1840, was for the expansion of Berlin. Despite the tragic destruction of many of his buildings in the period of industrial expansion in the 1870s and during the Second World War and its aftermath, Schinkel's buildings continue to play a dominating role in the centre of Berlin.

27. The Altes Museum, Berlin (1822–30): the portico columns.

Schinkel and Durand: the Case of the Altes Museum

Martin Goalen

Introduction

It is a paradox in the writing of architectural history this century that the work of Schinkel continues to be discussed in the light of the theories of Jean-Nicholas-Louis Durand (1760–1834). Schinkel's reputation, high in his lifetime, has survived the architectural revolutions of the twentieth century undiminished, whereas Durand's theories (so wittily mocked by Gottfried Semper as early as 1834)[1] have, for many critics, come to mark a crisis in architecture – a reduction to a meaningless and mechanistic functionalism – a reduction that, to quote one critic, leads: 'to the geometry of the Bauhaus, the International Style and the Modern Movement.'[2]

An analogy between the work of Schinkel and Durand was proposed as long ago as 1922 in Sigfried Giedion's[3] formal, stylistic comparison of Schinkel's Altes Museum (cat. 48–56) with the design for a *Muséum* (fig. 28) included by Durand in his *Précis des leçons d'architecture données à l'école polytechnique*.[4] The connection has been confirmed more recently by Henry-Russell Hitchcock whose standard work, *Architecture: Nineteenth and Twentieth Centuries*,[5] discusses Schinkel's work in the chapter: 'The Docrine of J.-N.-L. Durand . . .'. More recently Nikolaus Pevsner wrote of the Altes Museum that: 'the design is clearly inspired by Durand and [it] is one of the few buildings in which the sheerness of the long colonnades so liberally put on paper by the architects of the French Revolution reached reality.'[6] Similarly, David Watkin and Tilman Mellinghof noted that: 'The plan of the [Altes Museum], including its Pantheon Hall and reticent skyline, strongly recalls a design published by Durand in his *Précis* . . . . However, Schinkel was far from sharing Durand's drably functional view of the ends of architecture.'[7]

This last remark clearly reveals a dilemma which arises in any formal comparison between the work of Schinkel and Durand;[8] an admiration for the brilliance of Schinkel appears to be in conflict with a widespread distaste for the 'mechanistic'[9] projects of Durand. This essay seeks to explore this dilemma, focusing on the building that Schinkel himself regarded as his best work,[10] the Altes Museum in Berlin.

Durand's *Précis des Leçons*

Durand's *Précis*, like the majority of architectural treatises, from antiquity and through the Renaissance, is structured on the idea of a hierarchy of building tasks which, together, form the fabric of the city: 'Just as walls, columns etc, are the elements with which one composes buildings, buildings are the elements with which one composes towns.'[11] This hierarchy of building types is reflected in Durand's plates by a hierarchy of architectural language, reaching from the monumental Roman/Corinthian colonnades of the palaces, treasuries, institutes and museums (e.g. fig. 29), through the stripped, functional, *Rundbogenstil*[12] of the markets and warehouses, to a picturesque Italianate vernacular in farms and country inns (e.g. figs 30, 31).[13]

If one compares the plates of Schinkel's *Sammlung* with those of Durand's *Précis* (some of which are indeed made by the same engraver, Charles Normand),[14] it is in the everyday buildings that the closest formal parallels can be found. Schinkel's Packhof (cat. 117)[15] is close in feeling to Durand's Market,[16] – and Schinkel's

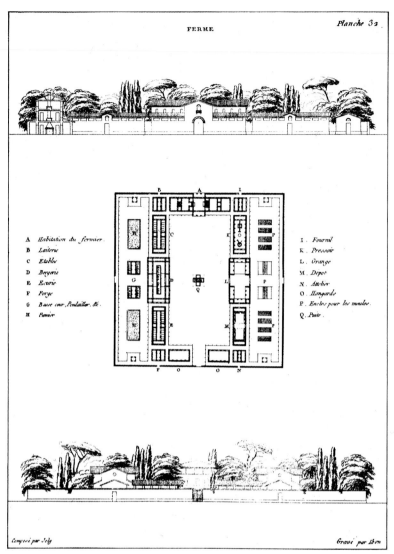

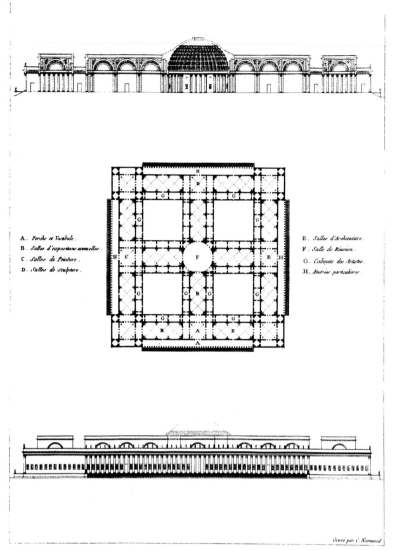

28. J.-N.-L. Durand. *Muséum*, from the *Précis*, part 3, plate 1.

29. J.-N.-L. Durand. *Marche à suivre dans la composition d'un projet quelconque*, from the *Précis*, part 2, plate 21.

30. J.-N.-L. Durand. *Ferme*, from the *Précis*, part 3, detail of plate 32.

31. J.-N.-L. Durand. *Emploi des objets de la nature dans la composition des edifices*, from the *Précis*, part 2, plate 18.

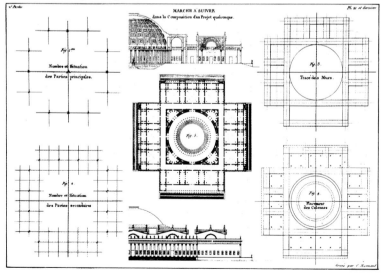

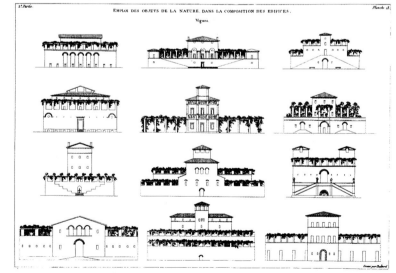

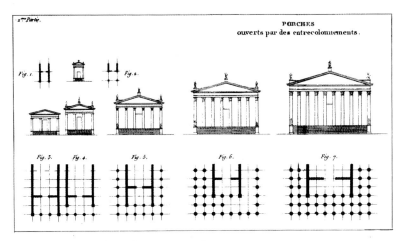

32. J.-N.-L. Durand. *Porches ouverts par des entrecolonnements*, from the *Précis*, part 2, detail of plate 8.

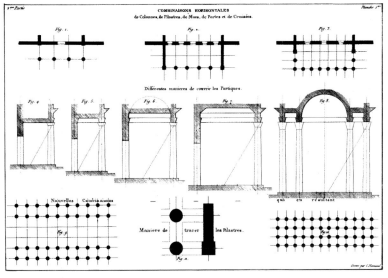

33. J.-N.-L. Durand. *Combinaisons horisontales de colonnes de pilastres, de murs, de portes et de croisées*, from the *Précis*, part 2, plate 1.

Gärtnerhaus, at Charlottenhof (cat. 76–79)[17] clearly shares its architectural imagery with Durand's plate, *Emploi des objets de la nature dans la composition des edifices* (fig. 31).[18]

Indeed, in the early nineteenth century, interest in the vernacular buildings of the Italian countryside was by no means confined to these two men. Books illustrating these humble exemplars were published in France in just the same way, and with the same intention – to provide models for contemporary production – as the great volumes describing the monuments of ancient Greece and Rome.[19] The sketches Schinkel made on his Italian journey of 1803–5 record this fascination, a fascination that decades of Northern European travellers to Italy also took home with them.

It is not Durand's systematisation of the vernacular buildings of the Italian countryside, however, that has provoked the continuing attacks on his treatise, it is his recommended method of architectural composition. Gottfried Semper, after referring to the method of the

Précis as 'worthless paper currency that this chess-board Chancellor of the Exchequer of failed ideas puts into circulation' describes it thus:

> blank sheets of paper are divided into many squares, just like an embroidery pattern or a chessboard, onto which plans of buildings arrange themselves quite mechanically . . . with them the first year polytechnical student in Paris becomes a complete architect in six months: Riding-schools, Baths, Theatres, Dance-salons and Concert-halls almost spontaneously assemble themselves onto his grids . . . and carry off the great academic prize.[20]

Figure 32 shows these graph-paper grids, which, transmitted through the pages of Joseph Gwilt's *Encyclopaedia of Architecture*, produced the teaching method of the first university course in architecture in Britain.[21] Durand's method can be summarised by reference to two further plates, the *Combinaisons horisontales* (fig. 33) and *Marche à suivre dans la composition d'un projet quelconque* (fig. 29) based on the idea that buildings are formed from the combinations of a small number of elements – walls, columns, roofs, stairs and so on – which can be assembled, horizontally or vertically, into rooms, these rooms into buildings, these buildings into towns: 'it is in this simple and natural manner, that one finds walls and columns arranged in the most beautiful buildings of Egypt, Greece and Rome, in the work of Palladio, of Scamozzi, of Serlio, and in the buildings, built or projected, of the best architects of our own day.'[22]

Durand himself stresses two aspects of his method in the summary he gives at the end of his first volume: first, the importance of, and reliance on, axiality and an underlying grid, and secondly the infinite variety to be derived from the method:

> Dealing with the basic combinations we have seen that, following the general principles of architecture, the walls and the columns, the doors and the windows . . . must each be placed on common axes. It follows naturally that rooms formed by these walls and columns and served by these doors and windows must, too, share common axes. These new axes may be combined in a thousand different ways and give birth, by their combinations, to an infinite number of different general dispositions.[23]

'The number, variety and the magnificence of the results . . . of this method',[24] Durand tells us can be seen in figure 34. His plate *Marche à Suivre . . .* (fig. 29) summarises the decisions to be made in the design of a particular building, in this case a slightly modified version of Charles Percier's *Monument destiné à rassembler les differents académies* of 1786.[25] First, he tells us, one must decide the number and position of the principal elements of the building; then the number and position of the secondary elements; then the lines of the wall are traced and, if vaults are to be used, the columns that support them. After this, one then has to determine the number of *entre-axes* (or grid squares) in each room and adjust them as necessary in relation to the whole. Nothing then remains but to choose the order (Doric, Ionic, or Corinthian) and to include the ornaments of painting and sculpture that it is judged proper to use. Thus, Durand tells us, the composition of a building can be 'an uninterrupted sequence of observation and reason.'[26]

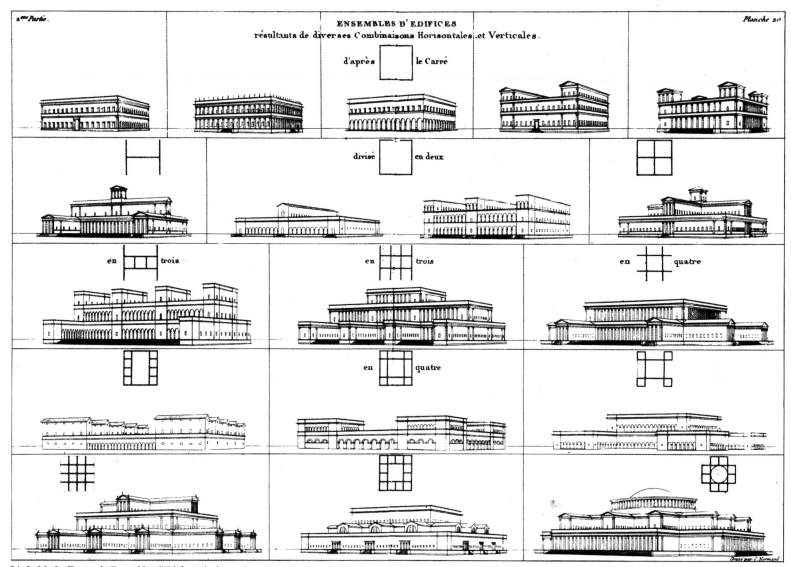

ENSEMBLES D'EDIFICES
résultants de diverses Combinaisons Horisontales et Verticales.

d'après ☐ le Carré

divisé ☐ en deux

en ☐ trois   en ☐ trois   en ☐ quatre

en ☐ quatre

Gravé par C. Normand.

34. J.-N.-L. Durand. *Ensembles d'Edifices résultants de diverses combinaisons horisontales et verticales*, from the *Précis*, part 2, plate 20.

35. The Parthenon. Plan of ceiling coffering. From Durm 1910.

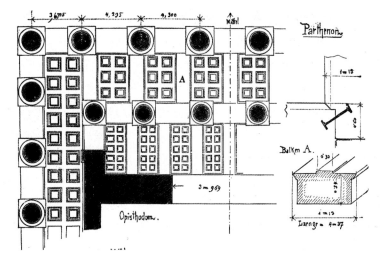

Vitruvius and the Ionic Temples of Asia Minor

The only architectural treatise that has survived to us from the ancient world is that of Vitruvius (although we know from Vitruvius himself that many were written)[27] and in spite of the apparently revolutionary character of Durand's treatise there is a revealing parallel that can be made between Durand's *Précis* and Vitruvius' *De Architectura*. The characteristic procedure of Vitruvius in dealing with any topic is to propose a scheme of classification: thus Architecture (like Gaul) is divided into three parts (Book I, c. 3), walls into two kinds (Book II, c. 8), the atria of private houses into five styles (Book VI, c. 3) and so on.

Temples also have their classificatory scheme: 'It is from the plan of a temple', Vitruvius tells us 'that the effect of its design arises', and he describes six kinds of temple plan: in antis, prostyle, amphiprostyle, peripteral, pseudodipteral and hypaethral (Book III, c. 2). This family of types (each new type in the list being a formal elaboration of the last) is exactly analogous to the progressive elaboration of wall/pilaster/column combinations shown in Durand's plate, *Combinaisons horisontales . . .* (fig. 33). Indeed in a later plate *Porches* (fig. 32), Vitruvius' types can be clearly recognised. The temple in antis (with 'two pilasters terminating the walls enclosing the shrine, and between them two columns'), the prostyle (with 'everything like the temple in antis, except two angle columns in front of the pilasters'), the peripteral ('with six columns front and back and eleven at the sides'), the dipteral (with 'double rows of columns around the sanctuary'), the pseudodipteral (with inner row of columns missing), the right half, and the hypaethral (with 'ten columns at front and back . . . and the centre open to the sky')[28] are Durand's figures 3, 4, 5, the left half of figure 6, the right half of figure 6, and figure 7 respectively.[29]

We know that Vitruvius borrowed from the (lost) writings of two Hellenistic architects of Asia Minor, Pythios and Hermogenes:

> Some of the ancient architects said that the Doric order ought to not be used for temples, because faults and incongruities were caused by the laws of its symmetry . . . . Pythios said so, as well as Hermogenes. He, for instance, after getting together a supply of marble for the construction of a Doric temple to Father Bacchus, changed his mind and built an Ionic temple with the same materials. This is not because it is unlovely in appearance or origin or dignity of form, but because the arrangement of the triglyphs and metopes is an embarrassment and inconvenience to the work.[30]

This anecdote, as well as telling us something of Vitruvius' sources, reveals a fundamental difference between the formal characteristics of temples built in the Doric and Ionic orders. The frieze running over the architrave of a Doric temple is divided by a series of vertical articulations, the triglyphs (which in origin, Vitruvius tells us (Book IV.c.2,1–3), marked the ends of roof beams). A triglyph is aligned over each column, with one half-way between, each separated by a blank (or sometimes carved) panel, the metope. This arrangement gives the characteristic bold rhythm of a Doric building. The frieze of the Ionic order, on the other hand, has no such horizontal articulation: it runs smoothly along broken only by the regular rhythm of the much smaller and more numerous dentils (marking, Vitruvius tells us (Book IV.c.2,5), merely the lines of the smallest rafters). The difference between the two orders becomes accentuated at the four corners of the temple:

> for [in the Doric order] the triglyphs ought to be placed so as to correspond to the centres of the columns and the metopes between the triglyphs ought to be as broad as they are high. But in violation of this rule, the corner triglyphs are placed on the outside edge and not corresponding to the centre of the columns. Hence the metopes next to the corner of the columns do not come out perfectly square, but are too broad by half the width of a triglyph. Those who would make the metopes all alike, make the outmost intercolumnations narrower by half the width of a triglyph. But the result is faulty, whether it is achieved by broader metopes or narrower intercolumnations.[31]

The system of the Ionic order has no such inherent problems and it is for this reason, Vitruvius tells us, that Pythios and Hermogenes preferred it to the 'embarrassment and inconvenience' of Doric. A comparison between, for example, the fifth-century BC Doric Parthenon in Athens and the fourth-century BC Ionic temple of Athena Polias at Priene (for which, Vitruvius tells us, Pythios was the architect) reveals the plastic effect of this preference: the reflected ceiling plan of the Doric Parthenon (fig. 35) shows the numerous adjustments or misalignments consequent on the narrowing of the column spacing for the corner column – the columns at Priene, however, where there are no triglyphs to disturb the regular rhythm, are all aligned on the same repeating square grid (fig. 36).[32]

What Vitrivius does not tell us, but is clear from our examples, is that this concern for the control offered by the underlying grid of the Ionic temple also gives geometrical control to another important element of the temple: the layout of the stone (or wooden) coffered ceiling. The same contrast between geometrical order on the one hand, and the accommodation to exigencies on the other, is apparent – the 'potentially correct, generalised abstractions' of the Ionic contrasting with the 'potentially active embodiments of specific kinds of force'[33] of the Doric.

This fundamental distinction in attitude is crucial when considering the relationship between Schinkel's Altes Museum and the paradigms offered in Durand's *Précis*.

The Altes Museum and the *Précis des leçons*

The first of the models offered by the *Précis* is of course the design for the *Muséum* itself (fig. 28), a comparison, as we have seen, first made by Sigfried Giedion.[34] If Durand's design is compared with the Altes Museum the most immediate formal similarities are, firstly, the presence, as a focus in the centre of each composition, of a domed

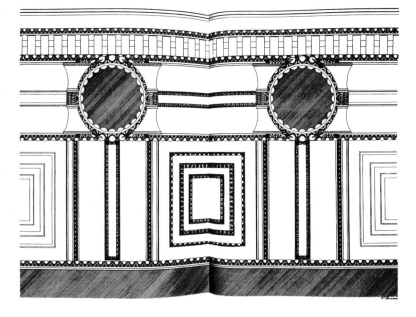

36. Temple of Athena Polias, Priene. Diagram of ceiling coffering. From Wiegand & Schrader 1904.

Pantheon-like hall, and secondly, that each composition is fronted by a long stoa-like colonnade forming an open entrance vestibule. These similarities are real but they do not take us very far into the essence of either scheme; there are closer similarities, for instance, between Durand's *Muséum* and Leo von Klenze's Glyptothek[35] in Munich where the vaulted Roman-bath halls of Durand are borrowed as the theme of the composition.

But does this sharing of compositional themes mark any closer connection? Von Klenze wrote of Schinkel that his work showed 'that one can build in the spirit of the Greeks on the barren sands of the Mark Brandenburg as well as along the banks of the Ilissos'[36] and the Altes Museum is distinguished from that of Durand by an archaeologically studied use of the Greek Ionic order. The capital that Schinkel draws so precisely in the section of the Altes Museum (cat. 53), and draws again with such intensity for the perspective of the stairhall (cat. 54), is that of the North Porch of the Erectheum on the Athenian Acropolis. Its base, however, is that of the temple of Athena at Priene, 'this type of base being more delicate and more appropriate for the Ionic order than the base which is normally used . . .'.[37]

Durand regarded the question of the detail of the orders as of little importance, a matter to be decided when all the lines of the composition had been determined. His usual mode was a generalised Imperial Roman (the endless colonnades are usually in that most characteristically Roman order, the Corinthian) as transmitted through his teacher Boullée and other French architects of the late eighteenth century.

For Schinkel, however, Greek architecture had acquired the force of an exemplar: 'if one could preserve the spiritual principle of Greek architecture, bring it to terms with the condition of our own epoch . . . then one could find perhaps the most genuine answer to our discussion.'[38] Two earlier Berlin buildings, the Neue Wache of 1815 (cat. 42–4) and the Schauspielhaus of 1821 (cat. 45–7), are united in seeking to bring the 'principle of Greek architecture . . . to terms with the condition of [the] epoch –'. Schinkel was clearly familiar with the mass of new archaeological publications both of Greece and of Asia Minor that appeared in the second half of the eighteenth century,[39] and their German successors.[40] This knowledge found expression in a combination of imaginative and analytical studies such as the drawing of the Propylaea at Eleusis for the *Vorbilder* in 1821,[41] and the painting *Blick in Griechenlands Blüte* (cat. 160)[42] of 1825. Schinkel's concern with an imaginative recreation of the forms, and a search for the principles, of the architecture of ancient Greece will be seen to be crucial in an attempt to characterise his achievement at the Altes Museum.

The Altes Museum analysed

The comparison of the Altes Museum with the *Muséum* of Durand has shown a similarity in the elements of composition, a colonnaded stoa and a central Pantheon-like rotunda, but the different exigencies of size, scale, programme and site (or lack of them in the case of Durand's *Muséum*) do not let one take the comparison further. But Durand has given us not only examples but also a method of composition; if we follow that method we should be able to propose

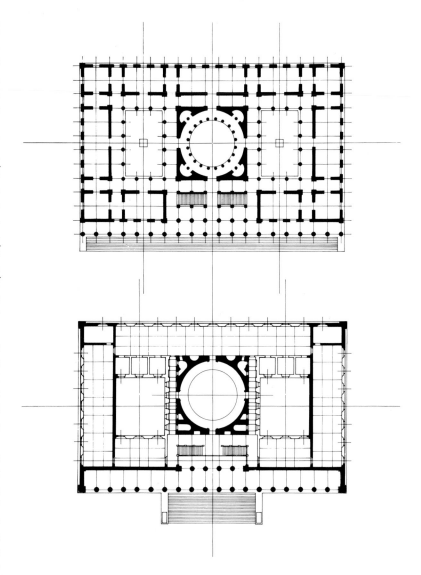

37. Plan of the Altes Museum composed in the manner of Durand (top). Analytical diagram of the Altes Museum as designed by Schinkel (bottom). (drawn by Martin Goalen)

a Durandesque composition that might distinguish more clearly the achievements of the two architects. Figure 37 shows a composition, modelled on the Altes Museum (which is shown to the same scale), but following Durand's procedures as far as possible.[43]

The first point of comparison, of course, is the question of the grid. In a building by Durand the grid is the basis for the positioning of all the walls, columns, windows and doors. In the Altes Museum, however, the rhythm set by the eighteen giant Ionic columns is not taken through the whole building. Schinkel's fourteen by twenty-one foot bays (a proportion of 2:3 in contrast to Durand's square bays)[44] which are set by the Ionic colonnade are not matched by the surrounding galleries; only at two points – on the main axis of symmetry dividing the building into two equal parts around the centre line and in the flanking connection between the receding

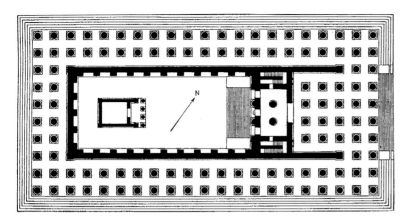

38. Temple of Apollo, Didyma; plan. After Dinsmoor 1950.

39. Anonymous engraver after Schinkel. The Altes Museum: capitals and reflected ceiling plans of portico and main staircase. *Sammlung*, plate 45, first published 1831.

The meeting of the conflicting dimensional systems of colonnade and of galleries must be resolved if clashes of architectural elements are to be avoided. At the Parthenon, as we have seen, the differing rhythms of coffering are separated by deep down-stand beams (fig. 35); here in the Altes Museum they are resolved in the long almost unbroken walls (emphasised diagrammatically in fig. 37) that form such an important aspect of the aesthetic system of the building. One is reminded of the important role the walls play in the composition of the Propylaea to the Athenian acropolis.[46]

Something that is often overlooked in the discussion of classical architecture is the importance of the actual number of columns (or divisions) in a design. Most Greek temples have six columns on their front elevations (Vitruvius' peripteral scheme)[47] – six is an even number so that there is a central opening for the entrance (and to hold the attention of the eye). On the side flanks, however, while sometimes there are Vitruvius' recommended eleven columns (giving a double square plan), there is almost invariably an odd number (with no central opening – enabling the eye to glide along the flank without being halted in its passage). Temples with more columns than six, such as the Parthenon with eight, or the hypaethral temple at Didyma with ten, acquire different characteristics to those with six. Vincent Scully has argued, from tests on visual perception, that: 'almost everyone can perceive six of any given units at once, without needing to count them . . . . Only the exceptional can perceive eight'.[48] From this he draws a fundamental distinction between the two sorts of metaphor at work in Greek temples: first, and characteristically in the Doric order, a temple can be seen as a freestanding sculptural body, where the six columns can instantly be perceived as a single unit. Secondly, and characteristically in the

40. Anonymous engraver after Schinkel. The Altes Museum: reflected ceiling plan and section of the Sculpture Gallery. *Sammlung*, plate 48, first published 1831.

staircase hall and the side galleries – do we retain that sense of infinite axial linking, of *enfilade*, so important to Durand.

It is clear that much adjustment to the exigencies of conflicting systems is going on in the plan of the Altes Museum – just that adjustment we have already seen in the comparison of the Doric Parthenon with the Ionic temple of Athena at Priene. In the Altes Museum, as in the Parthenon and at Priene, an important element of the building is the coffering of the ceiling which plays such an important role in Schinkel's perspective of the staircase hall (cat. 54): the ceiling of the sculpture galleries, too, is described in detail in the commentary to the plates of the *Sammlung*.[45] It is no accident that Schinkel includes drawings of these elements in the plates of the *Sammlung* (figs 39, 40). They are as crucial in the articulation of the building as the profiles of the order.

Ionic order, a temple can be seen as a spreading grove of columns, too numerous to be measured at once by the eye. The 'sheerness of the long colonnades' of Durand has already been commented on: he clearly tries to impress with his colonnades, complaining of Ste. Geneviève that 'the number of columns fails to convey magnificence just as the size fails to convey grandeur',[49] and offering his own scheme to correct these faults.

Schinkel also tells us that his stoa-like screen with its eighteen Ionic columns is intended to impress:

> the site required a very monumental building. Therefore I preferred one giant order rather than two individual expressions for the two main stories . . . . The building surrounded on all sides by the Ionic entablature or the Ionic columnar hall, with Ionic pilasters at the four corners, forms a simple yet grand main structure into which the two floors are inserted in a subordinate manner.[50]

Schinkel then offers us one reading of the Altes Museum as an Ionic temple, a spreading grove of columns, held at the corners, like that of the temple of Apollo at Didyma, mentioned before as an example of the hypaethral type, and described with the temple at Priene in the 1769 volume of *Antiquities of Ionia*. But if we look further we find that the rhythm of the Ionic colonnade is not uninterrupted – the central columns have been stressed by a whole series of events. First the plinths (carrying equestrian statues) framing the flight of steps are aligned with the central *eight* columns, leaving *six* columns freestanding between them. Secondly, behind these six columns a further *four* set back, marking out the presence behind those columns of the Pantheon-like two-storey rotunda, marked in turn at roof level by the square enclosure of the dome: 'defining the centre of the building' and accordingly 'decorated in a special way'.[51] This central emphasis is reinforced by the diagonals of the two ascending flights of stairs leading to the gallery of the rotunda, 'so constructed that on arriving at the upper landing, which forms a balcony, the view between the columns on to the square is presented . . .'.[52]

The twin notions of a spreading temple/grove (or stoa) and a centralised Pantheon seem to be subtly held in balance in the Altes Museum. This notion of balance, of an overall framework within which independent elements are held, is the key explanation for the differences between the Altes Museum and our Durandesque invention. If we turn back to Figure 37 we see that the central Pantheon-hall has been slipped back from the central axis of the plan, thus enlarging the entrance hall and linking with an asymmetrical circulation system through the galleries. The space created by this displacement is described by Schinkel in one of his most beguiling images (cat. 54), showing the two-storey porch with its double row of giant Ionic columns. Double staircases return on themselves to the centre of the plan to form the central balcony, which is on an axis with the tall rotunda behind and which looks forward through the rows of columns over the surrounding city. This conception of a part of the building that is at once outside the entrance doors (though sheltered by the roof), and looks out over the city through a perspective screen of columns at a height where the metaphorical connection between columns and trees[53] seems dramatically strengthened is similar to Peruzzi's *Sala delle Prospettive* in the Farnesina in Rome, where one seems to look out through painted columns to an idealised vision of the city spread beneath.[54] It is worth remembering that Schinkel, like Peruzzi, was a painter and a designer of stage scenery.[55]

In the Altes Museum Schinkel has succeeded in focusing our attention on a series of scenes, each of which has an independence of its own, but each of which contributes to a cumulative effect. Looking at the plan of the Museum (especially in contrast to those of Durand) one can trace the manipulation necessary to set those scenes: just as one can read in the reflected ceiling plan of the Parthenon (especially when compared with that of Priene, or of Didyma) a struggle between a sculptural ideal on one hand and geometrical rule on the other.

The Altes Museum and the Temple of Apollo at Didyma

There is one final connection that should be made. It is to a type that has been illustrated already – Vitruvius' hypaethral temple – the example that stood at the peak of Vitruvius' formal development of the temple types, and that was drawn by Durand (fig. 32). A particular example of it, the temple of Apollo at Didyma in Asia Minor, has already been mentioned. We have seen that Schinkel took the detail of his Ionic order from the Erectheum and from Priene. Neither of these buildings, however, offers the diagonal perspectives of receding columns within the shelter of the roof as found in the giant Ionic temples of Asia Minor, at Samos, Ephesus and at Didyma. It is worth noting, too, that between the first drawing of the Ionic capital of the Altes Museum (cat. 53), and its construction (fig. 40), it acquired the curling buds, characteristic of the order at Didyma, luxuriously unwinding from its volutes.

The plan of the temple at Didyma (fig. 38) is dipteral, that is to say it has two surrounding rows of columns, with ten columns on its front. The centre six columns are marked out by the position of the steps and behind, flanked by two antae finishing the lines of the flanking cella walls, are three further receding rows of columns. The centre is also marked by an opening higher than the floor level so that further progress has to be by way of two ramped and vaulted passages against each side of the cella walls. From these vaulted passages one emerges into the open centre courtyard, planted, according to Strabo, with a laurel grove, within which is a tiny prostyle Ionic temple.

Facing this temple, which one has just passed, is a flight of steps leading up to the place where one must assume the oracle made its appearance. Vincent Scully, always sensitive to the emotional impact of buildings, describes the experience of the temple as follows:

> Didyma . . . is remarkably complete. The whole fabric of the temple is calculated to set up a baroque drama of basic sensations in the mind of the observer . . . . shelter and coolness in [the] grove, the taste of death in the dark restriction of [the] caves, release from the darkness once again into the trapped sunlight of the court with its whispering leaves. Finally, and unexpectedly, there was . . . the promise of [Apollo's] epiphany [at the head of] the stairs.[56]

It seems to me that what is being described is very close to the experience engineered by Schinkel at the Altes Museum: in each case there is a series of focused experiences following a path up and through a grove of columns. A grove of columns that is, in the case of Didyma, organised exactly according to the axial, gridded, column/wall/pilaster system, described by Vitruvius (and codified by Durand in his *Précis*). Schinkel however leaves us, in the plan of the Altes Museum, the traces of his struggle in bringing the 'principle of Greek architecture . . . to terms with the conditions of the epoch':[57] using the Greek orders 'as much as the complicated nature of the building would admit'.[58]

A preliminary version of this essay was presented in the summer of 1989 as a lecture given in conjunction with an exhibition of my architectural work for Professor Ahrends's series 'Process to Form' at University College London. I am most grateful to Peter Ahrends and to our colleague Jeremy Melvin for their kindness in arranging the exhibition and lecture. Study of Schinkel's work in East Berlin and of the temples of Asia Minor was made with the benefit of a grant from the Hayter Travel Fund of the University of London.

1   In the preface to Semper 1834, partly quoted in Szambien 1984, pp. 182–3, English translation in Semper 1989, p. 46.
2   Pérez-Gómez 1983, p. 311. Similar views can be found, e.g. in Wittkower 1962, p. 153 and footnote, or Veseley 1985.
3   In Giedion 1922, p. 73 and plates 46, 48; p. 144 and plates 90, 91 and 92.
4   Durand 1817–19. This edition is cited here. Szambien 1984 p. 198 gives a bibliography of the many later editions.
5   Hitchcock 1971, Chapter 2.
6   Pevsner 1976, p. 127.
7   Watkin and Mellinghof 1987, p. 96.
8   Veseley 1985 displays this difficulty with particular force.
9   Durand himself speaks of 'the mechanism of composition'; Semper, see note 1, turns the phrase back against Durand.
10 In a letter to Sulpiz Boisserée.
11 'De même que les murs, les colonnes, etc., sont les éléments dont se composent les villes' Durand 1817–19, vol. II, part 3, section 1, p. 21.
12 For which see Hitchcock 1971, p. 55ff.
13 Durand 1817–19, part 3, plate 32.
14 Szambien 1989, p. 93 and p. 120, note 12.
15 *Sammlung*, plate 154.
16 Durand 1817–19, part 3, plate 13. Also see plate 16 in *Formule graphique appliable aux édifices publics voutés* in Durand 1821.
17 *Sammlung*, plate 169. Also, e.g., plate 66, *Lusthaus near Potsdam*. The Charlottenhof Gärtnerhaus could be said to offer a parable of architectural development, from the rustic shepherd's hut on the left of Schinkel's engraving and the open penthoused roofs of the Roman Campagna to the sophisticated completeness of the tiny Ionic temple on the right.
18 Durand 1817–19, part 2, plate 18 and see also part 3, plate 32: *Ferme*.
19 E.g. Clochar 1809, Seheult 1821; the phenomenon is discussed in Montclos 1976, pp. 23–6.
20 Semper 1834.
21 That of Professor Donaldson at University College, London. Professor Donaldson's examination papers and prospectuses of the 1840s relied both on Durand and Gwilt as set texts.
22 Durand 1817–19, part 2, section 1, p. 77.
23 *Ibid.*, part 2, section 3, p. 91.
24 *Ibid.*, p. 92.
25 For which see Middleton 1982, p. 14, ill. 4/5.
26 Durand 1817–19, part 2, section 3, pp. 90–9.
27 Vitruvius 1931–4.
28 *Ibid.*
29 Durand also gave Vitruvius' temple typology in plate 2 of Durand 1799–1801.
30 Vitruvius 1931–4, Book IV, Chapter 3. On Hermogenes see Robertson 1969, pp. 153–7.
31 Vitruvius 1931–4, Book IV, Chapter 3. For a discussion of the 'corner triglyph problem' see e.g., Robertson 1969, pp. 106–12.
32 For Priene see Wiegand and Schrader 1904. Plate x gives a reflected ceiling plan.
33 Scully 1969, p. 198.
34 Giedion 1922. See note 3.
35 Giedion (*ibid.*) compares Klenze's Glypothek with Durand's *Muséum*, plates 90, 91. For a discussion of Léo von Klenze (1784–1864) as a pupil of Durand see Szambien 1984, pp. 128–8.
36 Cited in Pundt 1972, p. 2.
37 *Sammlung*, text to plates 37–48.
38 From Wolzogen 1862–3, quoted in Veseley 1985, p. 30.
39 See Wiebenson 1969.
40 E.g. Gentz 1803–6 and Hirt 1809.
41 And also shown on plate 29 of Gentz 1803–6.
42 Alhborn's painting of 1836, after Schinkel, is reproduced in colour in Szambien 1989, pp. 20–1.
43 Although not, unfortunately, obeying Durand's injunction 'that the axes of the different rooms ought never to be the same as that of the columns . . .' Durand 1817–19, Vol. II, p. 18. To follow this rule the rooms would have to be three *entre-axes* wide, not two, and the grid dimension reduced accordingly. Durand describes this sort of adjustment (*ibid.*, part 3, p. 98).
44 Hitchcock 1971, note 3a, p. 595 attributes to this 'the lack . . . of the more satisfying proportional relationships seen in the projects of the late eighteenth century'.
45 See cat. 56.
46 See plan in Stuart and Revett, 1787, Vol. II, Chapter 5, pl. II.
47 See the table 'Chronological list of Greek temples' in Dinsmoor 1950.
48 Scully 1969, p. 52, p. 175 and p. 235, note 14.
49 Durand 1817–19, Vol. I, p. 22.
50 *Sammlung*, descriptive text accompanying plates 37–48.
51 *Ibid.* See also Schinkel's engraving of the main front of the Altes Museum, *Ibid.*, plate 39.
52 *Ibid.*, descriptive text accompanying plates 37–48.
53 The experience of the now destroyed tree-walk at Battersea funfair was one of the closest to that of the staircase hall of the Altes Museum. One was lifted gradually up to the crown of the trees, where branches unfolded like Ionic volutes.
54 Pundt 1972, p. 155.
55 Watkin and Mellinghof 1987 also point to the model of the Treppenhaus at the monastery of St Florian in Austria, for which see Korth 1978, plates 45ff.
56 For Didyma see Wiegand 1941.
57 See above, note 37.
58 Schinkel discussing the Schauspielhaus in the *Sammlung*, descriptive text accompanying plates 7–18.

Royal Residences on the Havel

Hans-Joachim Giersberg

Schinkel's buildings in Potsdam, especially the royal residences he designed, can only be understood in relation to the history and traditions of this city and its landscape. Schinkel's earliest recorded encounter with Potsdam testifies to this. In 1798, the seventeen-year-old exhibited a small picture in body colour of the city 'at sunrise, in front of the Babelsberg Mountains'. As yet, it is not royal buildings which interest him but towers and houses near water in a hilly landscape. The essentials, however, have been grasped.

Since the second half of the seventeenth century, Potsdam, a city well known beyond the frontiers of Prussia even then, had been the Hohenzollerns' second residence after Berlin. Not only Electors and subsequent kings would stay here, generally in summer; here, too, other members of the royal family built their houses and had the adjacent gardens laid out.

With its large Königliches Schloss and City Palaces, Berlin was the administrative capital of Prussia. Potsdam, only a few hours away by horse, offered the opportunity of a life apart in delightful surroundings. The course of the river Havel, which broadened out into several lakes, fringed with wooded hills, and the flat stretches of meadow and farming land between, presented a rich variety of artistic subject matter, offering ideal conditions for creating a mutually enriching union of architecture and landscape. These special natural features, as well as the profusion of game in Potsdam Forest, were the main reasons why the Elector of Brandenburg, Friedrich Wilhelm, the 'Great Elector' (ruled 1640–88), built the first new Schloss in the city on the banks of the Havel some time after 1660, with a zoo and broad avenues leading to new pleasure palaces. Thus began the development of Potsdam, ancient but insignificant, into a cultural metropolis with a European reputation. The intensity with which this goal was pursued varied from century to century, depending not least upon each monarch's interests and artistic ambitions. At all events, they always knew how to attract the country's most important artists to Potsdam.

From the outset, the idea was to see the city and the landscape in conjunction. The Great Elector, strongly influenced by Dutch ideas, was to develop this concept to the full; only the contributions of the garden designer, Peter Joseph Lenné, and the architect, Karl Friedrich Schinkel, in the first half of the nineteenth century, were – in equal measure – comparable. By the time the Great Elector died in the Potsdam Stadtschloss in 1688, the residence on the Havel had become not only an artistic centre, but also an established seat of the Hohenzollerns which in later years was often to take precedence over Berlin.

Under the following Elector, Friedrich III (ruled 1688–1713), who in 1701 became the first Prussian king, as Friedrich I, the Potsdam residences were principally the scene of magnificent festivities – such as the meeting, in July 1709, with the Kings of Poland and Denmark.

Friedrich Wilhelm I, known as the 'Soldier King' (who reigned from 1713 to 1740) also lived and died in Potsdam. His gaze, however, was always fixed on extending the city to accommodate his soldiers, and his interest in the surrounding countryside was restricted to its opportunities for hunting.

Potsdam resumed its artistic importance during the reign of Friedrich II (ruled 1740–88) known as Frederick the Great. The

41. The Havel and the woods of the Neuer Garten, Potsdam, seen from Schinkel's 'Grosse Neugierde' ('great curiosity') pavilion at Glienicke (1835–7).

42. The Kavalierhaus, on the Pfaueninsel (1824–6).
In this antiquarian exercise for Friedrich Wilhelm
III, Schinkel linked the heightened façade of a late
Gothic house from Danzig to an enlarged and
refaced building of 1804 already on the site.

conversion of the Stadtschloss into a winter residence and the construction of the Schloss and grounds of Sanssouci as a summer residence, intended as a 'source of relaxation, and domestic life, for the enjoyment of nature and the Muses', together with an impressive expansion of the city, transformed the soldier king's 'Sparta' into an 'Athens'. As if on a general's elevated command post, the 'philosopher of Sanssouci' resided in his Schloss, which, like a belvedere, offered the vista of the broad Havel landscape. In 1786 the Berlin publisher and man of letters, Friedrich Nicolai, described this as follows:

The area around Potsdam is as beautiful as any in flat and sandy terrain can be. Leading to most gates are avenues; and further beyond, most of the lakes are bordered by forests, bushy hills and vineyards. From some of the nearby mountains, one has superb, varying views towards the city across the Havel, which is very broad here; over several lakes, various villages, the Royal Gardens, forests, pleasure palaces and houses, some of which also cluster on hillocks.

In view of all this, it was only natural that Friedrich Wilhelm II, nephew and successor of the great king (ruled 1786–97), should, in turn, construct his own refuge in the immediate vicinity of Potsdam. This consisted of the Neues Garten and the Marmorpalais (Marble Palace) by the Heiligen See, a lake connected to the Havel by a short canal. Whilst the architecture changed in style from Baroque to classical, the garden layout moved from the French pattern of geometric order to 'free' landscaping on the English model. The

Neues Garten, with its accompanying touch of sentimentality, shows this development most clearly.

By the end of the eighteenth century, Potsdam had already become a city of royal houses and gardens enclosed behind fences and walls, but also already revealing tendencies, in keeping with Electoral ambitions, to spread out into the surrounding countryside.

Friedrich Wilhelm III, (ruled 1797–1840), focused his interest on rural Paretz, near Potsdam, and on the Pfaueninsel, on the Havel (fig. 42) and on the Neue Pavillon at Schloss Charlottenburg (figs 43, 44). He 'paid only scant attention to the Royal Gardens; restricting himself to maintaining what already existed without overstepping the budget'. In any case, the events of 1806–15 scarcely permitted major artistic enterprises.

It is a sign of happy historical circumstances when congenial artistic personalities are given the necessary conditions to fulfil their ideas in creating something uniquely great. The development of Potsdam and its environs as a centre of architectural and horticultural arts in the nineteenth century is intimately bound up with the names of Peter Joseph Lenné and Karl Friedrich Schinkel. In decades of collaboration, they succeeded in realising the goal of the seventeenth century: transforming the 'Isle of Potsdam' into a 'paradise'.

'The magician who created this paradise out of a wasteland is Lenné,' wrote the Berlin author, Ludwig Rellstab: 'And thus, we always find his name linked to that of Schinkel. Schinkel, as we have said, built Potsdam; Lenné transformed it from sandy wastes and pine groves to a valley of temples full of gardens of delights worthy

43. The Neue Pavillon, Schloss Charlottenburg (1824–5) now called the Schinkel-Pavillon. Built at the order of Friedrich Wilhelm III, to replicate the Villa Reale Chiatamone near Naples.

44. The Neue Pavillon, Schloss Charlottenburg (1824–5).

45. The Casino, Schloss Glienicke (1824–5): the Casino was Schinkel's first work for Prince Karl at Glienicke.

of Armida.' During this period, the fruits of their labour were visible everywhere, and were widely admired.

The period begins with Lenné's appointment to Potsdam in 1816 – Schinkel's work for the city started in 1820 – and ends with the deaths of the great garden and landscape designer, and of Schinkel's pupils, August Stüler (1800–65), and Heinrich Ludwig von Arnim (1814–66). Between those dates lies almost half a century of ceaseless creativity which found constant encouragement, support and, indeed, collaboration from the Crown Prince, later to become King Friedrich Wilhelm IV. Friedrich Wilhelm III often took a sceptical view of his son's projects, which more than once turned out to be unrealistic; his thriftiness forced restraint upon both architect and garden designer.

Lenné's work in Potsdam began with changes to the Neuer Garten. He broadened its small-scale layout into large, interconnecting landscaped areas, fanning out over the surrounding countryside in several different vistas. The same applies to his work in Klein-Glienicke, to the east of Potsdam on the opposite side of the Havel, which at that time belonged to Prince Hardenberg. In 1824 Prince Karl, eldest of Friedrich Wilhelm III's four sons, became the owner of Klein-Glienicke. Lenné was later employed by him, and with Ludwig Persius as collaborator, the Prince commissioned Schinkel to convert or rebuild the Schloss, along with other buildings including the Casino and the Jägerhof (Hunting Lodge) in the grounds (cat. 57–60, figs 45–8).

Crown Prince Friedrich Wilhelm had undoubtedly given firm guidelines for such a project; as early as 1823 he had sketched out rough ideas for a residence on a peninsula south-west of Potsdam on a direct axis with Schloss Sanssouci. Schinkel drew up the plans for a palace called Belriguardo, which was to rise in ancient classical style from a mighty substructure. Gardens with other buildings, flights of steps and viaducts were intended to surround the palace. Here Schinkel first used the pediment and column designs he was later to employ in the Schauspielhaus and the Altes Museum in Berlin. At the same time, Belriguardo is an essential preparatory study for Schinkel's later projects for a palace on the Acropolis in Athens (1834), and Orianda in the Crimea (1838) (cat. 154–159). After Friedrich Wilhelm IV ascended the throne in 1840 the project was revived, but very soon it was again abandoned, since it vastly exceeded the financial resources available.

Around 1825, while Friedrich Wilhelm was dreaming of a grand residence, Schinkel designed 'an elegant summer house [Lusthaus] in the vicinity of Potsdam' probably inspired by the Crown Prince's ideas. He published his plans in 1826, in Part 9 of the *Sammlung architektonischer Entwürfe*, with the following explanation:

An elegant summer house which, in a location near one of the lakes of Potsdam, was intended to enhance, in a picturesque way, a bleak part of the landscape; another specification was to enable the four co-owners of the building to forgather in the evening round the tea-table in the salon. Encircled by vine bowers and a small garden area, here, in particular, enjoyment of the agreeable landscape overlooked by these bowers was to be enhanced in every way. Each of the four co-owners has a study alongside the salon, reached through niches in the side of the room. Chandeliers, which produce a strong light for evening illumination, are

46. Schloss Glienicke (1824–32). The main front.

47. Schloss Glienicke (1824–32). Detail.

48. Schloss Glienicke. The Pavilion ('Grosse Neugierde') (1835–7).

hung in front of these niches; they light both the salon and the four studies when their doors are open. Stairs lead to a platform, from which one can look across the landscape from an even higher vantage-point.

The building, a variant on the theme of an Italian 'Casino', with flat roofs, terraces, staircases and pergolas, was designed as a meeting-place for the 'four co-owners': the Crown Prince (the future Friedrich Wilhelm IV), and the Princes Karl, Wilhelm (the future King and Kaiser Wilhelm I), and Albrecht. This accounts for the layout of the ground plan, with a large communal salon and four smaller studies. Schloss Glienicke was already under construction for Prince Karl (figs 45–48), and two other princes were planning their properties at this time. Although we have no documentary evidence, sketches by the Crown Prince for an English Gothic country house ('Villa Alberti') in a mountainous riverscape indicate a firm intention to create a summer residence for the youngest prince, too. Neither this building nor the communal summerhouse was ever built.

While all this planning was going ahead in early 1826 Schinkel was given a delightful commission: the conversion of Schloss Charlottenhof (fig. 49) into a summer residence for Crown Prince Friedrich Wilhelm and, from 1829 onwards, the construction of the Römische Bäder (Roman Baths), with the Gärtnerhaus (Court Gardener's House) as its central point. As with Glienicke, from an eighteenth-century country house Schinkel was able to create a villa in the best classical architectural style, with admirably harmonious

proportions. The Potsdam architects Boumann, Büring and Gontard had already lived there, and its name came from the previous owner, Charlotte von Gentzkow. In the architecture of the Schloss itself, and even more in the layout of the surrounding gardens, the Crown Prince was influenced by engravings of Renaissance schemes, especially at the Villa Albani, published by the French architects Percier and Fontaine, as well as by reconstructions, described by Pliny, of ancient country houses (cat. 69–75). Schinkel's own knowledge and experience of architecture in Italy must also have played a part. This is again evident, though in a different form, in the Römische Bäder (cat. 76–82). Once more, as in the case of Schloss Glienicke and Schloss Charlottenhof, Ludwig Persius was responsible for their execution (figs 50–52). After Schinkel's death in 1841, Persius, who died only four years later, was the king's leading architect. Further development towards a Romantic style of classicism is revealed mainly by his ability to group structures together in a picturesque manner and to relate them to the landscape – usually planned by Lenné. The Italian villa style, evident first in the Römische Bäder, became dominant in Potsdam architecture during the 1830s and 1840s.

Lenné transformed the area around Schloss Charlottenhof into a landscaped garden, with widely radiating views to connect it with the eighteenth-century buildings in the park. It was a new concept. Not situated near water – as had possibly been intended with Belriguardo, or like his royal brothers' buildings – it was a jewel of architectural and horticultural art, adjoining the grounds at Sanssouci designed for Frederick the Great, for which Lenné had already produced modified specifications.

Schloss Babelsberg was the third royal summer residence to be created in the vicinity of Potsdam (cat. 94–97). Prince Wilhelm had shown an interest in the site, facing across the Havel towards his brother's property in Klein-Glienicke, as early as 1826. He was encouraged in this by Lenné, who saw not only a chance to link it up with its 'brother Schloss', but a further opportunity to embellish the Potsdam landscape. The hilly area envisaged lay between the weaving and spinning colony of Nowawes (now called Babelsberg), established by Frederick the Great, in the south, and, in the north-west, the Havel, where it broadened out into the Tiefer See. The first plan Schinkel drew up from ideas the Crown Prince had sketched out was not accepted by the King. But Prince Wilhelm did not give up. In 1829 he wrote to his sister Charlotte, the Russian Tsarina Alexandra Feodorovna: 'Yesterday we took tea at Babelsberg, where, later on, appropriate castles in the air were built for me; I shall, after all, venture another assault upon his Majesty, for the magnificent location promises a beautiful outcome to the project.' But it was another five years before a start could be made on constructing the Schloss and its grounds. Meanwhile, following a sketch by Princess Augusta of Sachsen-Weimar, Persius had designed a cottage along English lines. But as with all the other princes' houses on the Havel – and their city palaces in Berlin – it was Schinkel who was given, in 1833, the commission to build Schloss Babelsberg; he presented the plans in October of that year. Princess Augusta probably again had a decisive influence on the choice of the English Gothic style, with Repton's idealised design of 1816 for a castellated country house the determining factor – though we must

49. Schloss Charlottenhof (1826–33). The entrance front.

50. The Römische Bäder, Charlottenhof (1829–40), from the west.

51. The Römische Bäder, Charlottenhof. The
Teepavillon (1830) and arcaded hall (1833) from the
lake.

52. The Römische Bäder, Charlottenhof (1829–40).
The great arbour.

also remember Schinkel's visit to England in 1826.

In spite of all the deliberate, Romantic-looking irregularities – towers, battlements, gates and terraces – the overall structure conveys an impression of repose, not least because it blends ideally into the hilly landscape. In spring 1834 a start was made on the construction, but because of a shortage of money this was only half finished by autumn 1835. Work could not be continued until 1844, and was not completed until 1849, though the building's increased formal role led to changes in Schinkel's design. Nevertheless, Babelsberg is among Schinkel's most important neo-Gothic buildings, its picturesque effect contrasting above all with classical Glienicke (cf. cat. 59).

For Lenné, Babelsberg may have been the last opportunity finally to put down on paper his idea for an overall plan for the island of Potsdam. From at least 1822 he had been concentrating his efforts on comprehensively landscaping the area. This was the year he visited England, where, at Eaton Hall in Cheshire, he saw the possibility of 'drawing whole landscapes into a plan for embellishing sites'; and he suggested something similar for the 'busiest routes in the environs of the royal residences of Berlin and Potsdam'.

With his 'Plan for Embellishing the Environs of Potsdam', drawn up by Gerhard Korber, Lenné presented in 1833 his vision of a 'garden paradise' (in Rellstab's phrase), in which not only the older eighteenth-century gardens but also the new royal residences on the Havel would have their place.

The Electors' notions of what Kopisch called a 'harmoniously connected whole' matured into a work of art which retained and incorporated the achievements of two centuries. Garden designers and architects played their part, as did the various princes, whose notions and interests, inclinations and imagination crucially influenced the artistic development of the city and its surroundings. Schinkel and Lenné realised the idea which, according to Haeberlin, 'has enhanced Potsdam and Sans-Souci, together with the beautiful stretch of country around them into one of the most exquisite and welcoming cities in the monarchy'.

Schinkel's Architectural Theory

Alex Potts

A Great Labyrinth

Schinkel's attempt to elaborate a systematic theory of architecture was an ambitious lifetime project, but it always remained unfinished business. Theorising about architecture functioned for him as a working through of certain large structural problems that he could never quite resolve, but to which he constantly felt impelled to return. The period between about 1810 and 1840, during which Schinkel drafted his notes for an *Architektonisches Lehrbuch* (Architectural Textbook) was an important one for re-conceptualising architectural practice in Europe. For the more progressive theorists, architectural style could no longer be rationalised on the same basis as it had been in post-Renaissance theory. It began to seem necessary to re-explore the relation between architectural style and the functional and technical aspects of building, and to open up for re-examination the traditional paradigmatic status of the antique as a model of architectural style.

Schinkel was not a fluent writer, and made it clear that his architectural theory, far from being entirely discursive, gave a central role to direct visual demonstration.[1] His text functioned in part as annotation and verbal accompaniment to an elaborately conceived series of architectural diagrams (see fig. 54 and cat. 124–6). At the same time, he clearly took the formulation of his ideas very seriously, and brought considerable sophistication to bear on the problems of devising an effective architectural aesthetic for his times. He was clearly conversant with the new theoretical perspectives on art and culture emerging in German idealist thought of the period. Indeed his writing on architecture can be seen as part of this larger rethinking of the relation between aesthetics and history, and its problematising of the role of the antique as an exemplary model for modern artistic practice.[2]

A passage from a relatively late draft of Schinkel's theoretical introduction dating from about 1835 is worth quoting at length because it brings into focus the basis upon which he diagnosed the unsatisfactory condition of modern architectural style. Here Schinkel highlighted concerns that were to recur again and again in the analysis of modern architecture during the nineteenth century, namely a highly critical view of the apparently arbitrary and eclectic imitation of past styles, and a desire to fashion a new art for modern times that would be a compelling equivalent to the classic work of the past, and not just a revival or imitation of it:

> I observed a great vast store of forms that had already come into being, deposited in the world over many millenia of development among very different peoples. But at the same time I saw that our use of this accumulated store of often very heterogeneous objects was arbitrary. Every particular form is possessed of a distinctive charm, further heightened by the dark presentiment of a necessary motif, be it historical or constructive, the use of which will lead you astray. You think it will endow your work with a special appeal . . . what in its primitive manifestation in an ancient work produced a highly gratifying effect was often positively disagreeable to me when employed in new works of the present day. It became particularly clear to me that the source of the lack of character and style from which so many new buildings seem to suffer is to be found in such arbitrariness in the use [of past forms].

53. The Nikolaikirche, Potsdam (1832–49).

It became a lifetime's task for me to gain clarity on this issue. But the more deeply I penetrated into the matter, the greater the difficulties that stood in the way of my efforts. Very soon I fell into the error of pure arbitrary abstraction, and developed the entire conception of a particular work exclusively from its most immediate trivial function and from its construction. This gave rise to something dry and rigid, and lacking in freedom, that entirely excluded two essential elements: the historical and the poetical.

I pursued my researches further, but very soon found myself trapped in a great labyrinth . . .[3]

The accumulated riches of the past offered a glut of desirable models of imitation for the modern imagination to pick and choose from, and modern constructional methods made it all too easy to copy these at will and indulge in decorative overloading.[4] Style had become arbitrary, lacking in any solid rooting in the practical demands and values of its time, or in the constructional processes of building. Style in other words was alienated, was no longer part of an integrated totality as it had been in the great periods of art in the past, particularly that of ancient Greece.

The terms of reference for a critique of modern architectural practice here were rather different from those current in post-Renaissance art theory. In the latter, the central problem was usually identified as a corruption of taste caused by departure from the true and simple classic principles of antiquity, encouraged by modern luxury. In Schinkel one finds a new more historicising perspective. This had both a cultural aspect – namely that the straightforward imitation of a past artistic style was essentially problematic in a modern-day context – and a technological or constructional one, which saw modern architectural practice as alienated from the simpler, more determined relation between decorative form and building techniques that held in earlier societies. The cultural historical perspective played the leading role in Schinkel's diagnosis of modern architecture, just as it did in the critiques of modern culture advanced by contemporary German writers and philosophers. The technological perspective was secondary, and did not gain ascendancy until rather later once industrialisation came to be seen as a major issue – that is once the perceived breakdown of the wholeness and integration associated with traditional societies was seen in economic rather than purely cultural terms. Nevertheless,

technological constructional concerns were central to Schinkel's theory of architecture.

Truth to Materials

Schinkel used a schematic classification of basic constructional processes as the framework for elaborating the principles of architectural design. For him, establishing a necessary connection between methods of building and stylistic beauties of form and detail was the central generative principle of architecture. But if at one level he conceived of architecture in material constructional terms, that is as the elaboration of a formal language appropriate to different methods of creating solid built structures, architecture for him was also an art, and as such by definition something that transcended the merely material and technical.

In his fullest elaboration of the basic forms of architectural design sketched out around 1825, a demonstration of 'the rational production of everything that remains hidden to the eye of the beholder in a completed piece of architecture', he focused on two fundamental points – 'construction of the enclosing walls (with their openings)' and 'construction of the ceilings (with their requisite supporting devices)'.[5] Wall construction and roof construction (see fig. 54 and cat. 124) were thus identified as generating the basic vocabulary of architectural form, and not, as in conventional architectural treatises, the theory of the orders. Architectural design derived from an understanding of the basic units of construction, such as pier and arch, column and beam, wall and vault, and could not be codified as a set of fixed formulae established once and for all by classical precedent: 'timid repetitions of certain designs in architecture current at a certain period can never be a particular merit of new architecture'. This attempt to justify the language of architecture on a new rational constructive basis links Schinkel with a number of his contemporaries, including the famous French architectural theorist Durand.[6]

Where Schinkel is particularly illuminating is in bringing out the ethical imperative implicit in such an aesthetic. At its simplest, this took the form of a commitment to avoid false appearances or 'masquerade'. Architectural detailing and design, the art of architecture, must never hide the larger structural forms: 'any masking or hiding of the construction is an error'. There was also the more exacting commitment to creating a necessary, non-arbitrary relation

54. Schinkel. Diagram for the introduction to the *Architektonisches Lehrbuch*, the so-called 'Long Sheet', *c*.1825. Pen and ink, 335 × 1493. Nationalgalerie, SMB (SM 41a.42).

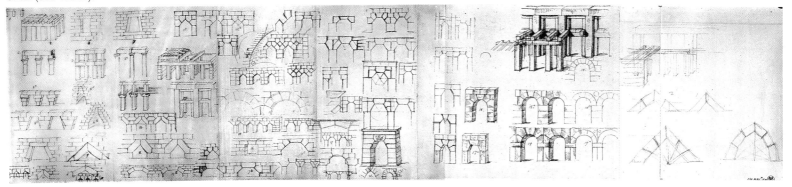

between style and construction. Construction in this sense included building materials as well as basic building processes: 'any fully perfected construction in a particular material has its own definite character and could not rationally be executed in the same way in another material'.[7]

At work here is a version of an ethic of truth to materials, though without the absolute imperative it acquired in later discussions of architecture and design, and certainly not given the leading role it had in Semper's theories. Schinkel shared with earlier Enlightenment theorists such as Laugier a concern with schema of architectonic construction. He remained closer to this tradition than he was to the more design-orientated preoccupation with properties of materials, and the processes of shaping and forming these, that began to take a hold on discussions of architecture towards the middle of the nineteenth century. Like other theorists of the Romantic period, he insisted that artists should endow their work with a generic character appropriate to the materials they used, and not force the latter into the mould of an abstract idea. In practice, however, this meant little more than seeking some rational correlation of architectural design and building materials. It did not involve cultivating an approach to design that would be true to the inner character of the materials used, as might later be found in an arts and crafts aesthetic.[8]

If for Schinkel a kind of functional constructivism was a guiding principle of architectural style, he was at the same time insistent that purely functional and technological concerns be subordinate to the art of designing architectural form. Architecture for him was at one level categorically different from mere building. It was concerned 'to make the serviceable, the useful, the appropriate, beautiful'. Building as such, the merely technical preoccupation with 'the appropriate, the efficient, the solid, the useful', was not to be conflated with the understanding of 'the elements of beauty', the distinctive concern of the architect.[9] In other words, he was no out-and-out functionalist.

Part of what was at stake in his insistence on the primacy of the artistic aspect of architecture over mere building was an ethic of freedom that played a key role in German aesthetics of the period. Art was seen as a reworking of the material world that in the final analysis had to achieve freedom from the contingencies and constraints of physical circumstance, even as it operated in conformity with the distinctive character of the materials it was using:

> Mere need does not give rise to beauty, nor does every accidental utilitarian factor have to be taken into account to endow something with character, otherwise chaos results. Only someone who moves freely above (material) need will be capable of beauty, provided that in his freedom he still endows the object with the characteristic aspect that makes it individual.[10]

What Schinkel meant by endowing an object with its characteristic aspect was the act of transforming what was merely contingently specific about it into a typifying whole, giving it a clearly delineated character that had a general cogency, the quality of a law-like necessity. Freedom of architectural design, then, involved not just liberation from material constraint, but also submission to some higher imperative.

At its simplest, this freedom was the antithesis of slavery, whether slavery to rules, or to material circumstance. At the same time, it was a freedom that voluntarily operated in conformity with the imperatives of a superhuman reason: 'Freedom consists in the first place of ethical feeling: to submit oneself freely to a higher law on the basis of reason or poetic feeling is something sublime and beautiful.' To this freedom was reserved the right to modify any given inherited law in the light of changed circumstance and fashion a new higher law to replace it. Such was the true freedom of the artist, asserting independence of the contingent rules that traditionally bound artistic practice, while endowing the operations of art with a fundamental necessity.[11]

Schinkel's notion of the freedom exemplified in the fashioning of a work of art did not always have this Hegelian dialectic quality of a freedom of idea or spirit mediated by engagement with the material world. Early on in his career, when political circumstances in Prussia after the defeat by Napoleon precluded work on major building projects, he was for a time seduced by the idea of a sovereign subjective freedom of the kind put forward in the philosophy of Fichte, who was lecturing in Berlin at the time. This was a freedom realised in the abolition of any constraint placed on individual subjectivity by the material world or by human institutions and conventions. It was in a sense the fantasy of a subjective empowerment that would render irrelevant any mediating tension or contradiction between the individual and his larger political, social, cultural or material environment.

In a manuscript entry on the concept of the monument dating from around 1814, Schinkel called for an approach to architectural design in which the free expansion of the artist's conception or idea would have total primacy over the functional and material aspects of building:

> In matters of art, it is not a question of asking what previously known useful things can be brought to the task. Rather a pure idea of the entire formation of the work arises in the soul of the architect. This idea is produced entirely from within himself, quite independently of the existing world. He feels the most profound destiny of the building immediately in his own being. Only at this point does the question arise: what are the means necessary to realise such an idea produced in total freedom?[12]

For this fantasy of a total freedom of artistic conception, the quasi-immaterial forms of the Gothic, rather than the more solid rational forms of the classical, seemed most appropriate: 'The decoration of the Goths serves a free-working idea, that of the antique a category of experience'.[13] Momentarily, the architect's conception was liberated from the functional aspects of architectural design. The imagination at work here was more that of the theatrical set designer and graphic artist than the architect. Conjuring up pictorial images suggestive of the idea of freedom had taken precedence over speculating on the nature of the freedom that might be exercised in the process of designing a building. The appeal of such a fantasy of untrammelled freedom of conception never entirely paled for Schinkel. Later on it re-emerged in his preoccupation with the idea of a monument that might allow an architect freedom to affirm his (certainly not her) ideal vision of an integrated aesthetic whole, uncompromised by the complexities and contradictions of social relations in the modern world.

Modernity and the Greek Ideal

The ethics of freedom in Schinkel's aesthetic was bound up with another significant tension besides that between the free-floating idea-like quality of artistic conception and the constraints of function and construction. Also at issue was a tension between the artist's freedom of invention and the restrictive weight of tradition. At its simplest, the latter kind of freedom demanded that a modern architecture be new and liberate itself from slavish adherence to established models, however fine the latter might be. Schinkel's insistence on the new was itself quite unusual in an early nineteenth century context. But the demand as such was less interesting than the particular theoretical inflection he gave it.

His discussion drew heavily on the tradition of cultural historical analysis elaborated in German idealist thought of the period. When he speculated on how modern art might relate to classical precedent, he envisaged the problem less as one of artistic theory than as one about the general development of human culture. He took it as axiomatic that cultural forms could not be fixed within given bounds, but were constantly changing and renewing themselves. A new art, to be compelling, would have to possess a distinctive style of its own. By insisting on the necessary historical difference between the art of classical antiquity and that of the present, Schinkel problematised the paradigmatic role of classical precedent in traditional art theory more fully than he would had he simply called for a liberation of modern architectural practice from adherence to past models.

An early manuscript note by Schinkel attacking the dogmatic classicism of *Die Baukunst nach den Grundsätzen der Alten* (Architecture According to the Principles of the Ancients), a treatise published by Ludwig Aloys Hirt in 1809, argued that slavish imitation of classical architectural form was unworthy of the 'continued development of mankind'. In a turn of phrase reminiscent of Hegel, he made the point that perfection in architecture could not be limited to the particular forms of architecture evolved by one nation, but rather that 'the perfection of architecture as a whole may well be precipitated in the endless succession of time'.[14] A valid contemporary artistic practice, while in some sense emerging out of past practices, had to be unconditionally different from these: all significant art was to be a new departure, the work of a freely creative genius.

Later this Romantic modernism was mediated considerably. Even so, Schinkel always insisted that a truly historical understanding of architecture was the antithesis of the close imitation of past forms. The latter marked the end of history, rather than a proper awareness of the historical past. To engage in a slavish imitation of the work of the old masters was:

in no way historical, but rather opposed to the historical. History has never copied earlier history, and when it has done so, then such an act is not to be accounted part of history, but rather in it history in a manner of speaking comes to a complete halt. The only truly historical act is one that introduces in some way an extra, a new element, into the world, from which a new history is produced and hatched forth.[15]

In the context of the earlier nineteenth century, an architectural aesthetic that advocated a systematic break with the classical models of the past would not, in the long run, have been viable. Indeed, after his early fascination with Gothic architecture as offering a more expressive and spiritual alternative to the antique ideal (see cat. 16, 21), Schinkel himself became increasingly convinced that Greek antiquity provided the most compelling available model of a fully realised architecture. How this model might function as a workable basis for modern architectural practice, however, remained a problematic issue. Schinkel's perspective here was very much in line with that of the more progressive German aesthetic theory of the period.[16] The general thrust of such analysis was not to advocate rejection of the Greek ideal as a valid inspiration for modern times, or to call for a radically new art of the future, but rather to rethink the role that antique models might be able to play within modern culture.

In Schinkel's cultural historical speculations, the ideal of continuous renewal and new departure operated in conjunction with the ideal of art and culture as an integrated totality. A fully realised art was the product of a whole culture, and possessed a 'lawfully self-contained character'[17] that made its style necessary rather than arbitrary. In common with his contemporaries, he held the Greek ideal to be the prime instance of a fully integrated art, standing in marked contrast to the arbitrary and fragmentary character of the modern. At this level, then, the classical ideal functioned as an object lesson for present architectural practice, even while the ready availability of such a model for direct imitation was also part of the problem: reliance on past forms was what precluded the formation of a cogent new style. The status of classical precedent as a model for modern architectural practice was, for Schinkel, of its very nature deeply contradictory.

In early nineteenth-century Germany, particularly in the circles around Goethe, it was becoming conventional wisdom to envisage the Greek ideal less as a source of models to imitate than as an example of a truly whole art and culture. The point was not to copy the particular forms of Greek art, but to fashion a modern equivalent to the Greek achievement. The Greek ideal, in Schinkel's words, was to be conceived as 'a reference point and point of departure . . . from which an artistic culture of consequence could be continued'.[18] Greek art had this exemplary status because it was thought to be the product of a uniquely harmonious, integrated and free society, as yet unburdened by the structural contradictions of the modern world. Nature and human institutions were not alienated from one another, nor was there a conflict between the interests of the individual and society. Ancient Greece fostered 'an enhanced enjoyment of life [both] for the individual and for the people in general'. For Schinkel it was the Utopia that had realised his ethical ideal of freedom – 'the most felicitous state of freedom within the law'.[19] Greek culture was thus simultaneously defined as the very antithesis of modern culture and as the best inspiration for the realisation of truly cogent and integrated art in modern times. How was this tension to be negotiated? It was always by way of some structural compromise.

When Schinkel asked the question: 'Every epoch had left behind

55. The Altes Museum (1822–30). The stairs from the colonnade.

its own style in architecture – Why should we always only build after the style of another period?'[20] the solution he proposed was at one level a fairly elitist and academic one. He advocated a creative reworking of past traditions to produce a new style that:

> will not as a result so stand out from all present and previous styles that it is like a phantasm, striking and comprehensible to everyone. On the contrary, the element of the new will be barely perceptible, and its greater merit will lie in the cogent use of a multitude of inventions made over the course of time, that previously were not capable of being brought together in an artistically convincing way.[21]

This utopian prospect of a new style that would still be in perfect harmony with tradition, that would be novel yet seem to grow naturally out of the best of past precedent, parallels at the level of aesthetics the political ideology of the Prussian state for which Schinkel worked.[22] This ideology favoured a cultural and technical modernisation, but one that would be guided from above, so it would not challenge the basis of the established social and political order. The contradictions and limitations of such an ideology are obvious to us now, and had certainly reached the point of crisis by the time of the revolutions of 1848. In some areas of Prussian state policy during the earlier Restoration period, however, it did operate with a degree of credibility. In its architectural form it served Schinkel well when he was establishing his reputation as a public architect with a blend of modernising rational functionalism and traditional classicism. Schinkel also echoed something of this official ideology in his particular openness to new building technology – indeed he took it as a fundamental aesthetic principle that:

> No object that has the quality of being solid, and of being formed and remodelled to fulfil a purpose, should be banished from architecture, for whatever can advantageously be used for creating structures contributes to the variety of architecture . . . and can always provide the basis for forging a style.[23]

At the same time, Schinkel recognised that the working compromise of a modernising classicism was deeply problematic. The calm and proportion epitomised by ancient Greek architecture was, according to Schinkel, made possible by the predominance of these qualities in Greek culture as a whole. This situation stood in marked contrast to that in modern culture: 'the modern period, with its pressing enterprises directed to the existence of the individual, does not attain reflectiveness and is absorbed in anxious activity'.[24] What real hope was there that the moderns could fashion a viable equivalent to the Greek ideal? At one point Schinkel suggested that, if previously an integrated artistic style had followed in the wake of major political developments, the reverse might prove to be true in the modern world. Echoing something of the promise held out by Schiller's theory of aesthetic education, he suggested that a successfully cultivated art might point the way ahead to the 'flourishing of a new mode of behaviour in the world'.[25]

More consistent with his general theoretical outlook is a rather different formulation of the problem found in some manuscript notes that do not appear to relate specifically to the treatise on architecture. Here he started from the assumption that a modern architecture that aspired to being an unalienated and significant whole on the model of ancient Greek work necessarily went against the grain of modern social formations. A properly realised modern recreation of the Greek ideal would thus have to function as a challenge and lesson to modern times. As mankind moved further and further from a primitive unalienated state, as its activities became more disparate and uncentred, architecture necessarily took on this same character. Architecture could only stand out against this state of affairs when it was freed from immediate functional demands, that is when it became pure monument. An architecture that was not merely subject to surrounding circumstances, but transcended them and had an improving effect on them, could only be realised:

> by way of the monument, that throughout every period of culture must actually always retain the solid simple character, that throws down its roots in the primitive circumstances of humankind, and issues forth as the very summit of its highest flowering.[26]

In this formulation, a modern architectural equivalent to the Greek ideal functioned rather like the remaining historical fragments of this ideal: it was necessarily utopian, a momentary cancellation of the alienation, fragmentation, and individualism of modern times. It could play this role by virtue of being a pure monument, at one remove from the day to day functioning of modern society.

This recourse to the monument as a resolution to the problem of fashioning a modern equivalent to the Greek ideal finds an echo in Schinkel's own *oeuvre* in his late utopian plans for vast palace complexes (cat. 154–159). These absolutist fantasies, set on hilltops with commanding views, quite literally at one remove from the city or the working countryside, were models of a fictionally integrated artistic and social order that echoed the implicitly totalitarian echoes of the monument. Unable to negotiate with the daily realities of the modern world, they stood above and ostensibly dominated them. In this return to pure architectural fantasy, the ageing Schinkel sought to deny the contradictions and complexities of the modern social order by grafting on to the latter the monumental symbol of traditional monarchical power, more ambitious in scope than any actually realised in the past. If this kind of project was not even seen as workable by the Tsarist court of Russia, it was much more in tune with the fantasies of the conservatively inclined Crown Prince of Prussia, the future Friedrich Wilhelm IV.

Schinkel's late megalomaniac projects were clearly at one level politically reactionary returns to the ethos of Versailles, in which even the public functioning of the outlying city, and not just of the court, would be absorbed within the palace precincts. But they are not all that unmodern either. The monumentalising fantasy they embody can be seen as an attempt by the architect to impose a manageable order on the modern world by way of an architectural plan. Schinkel's late project for 'the residence of a ruler who in all respects stands at the pinnacle of culture and arranges his surroundings accordingly'[27] (fig. 56) shares an element of aesthetic megalomania with Le Corbusier's City of Tomorrow. Both projects are in Schinkel's terms pure monuments, ideal images of a harmonious and

56. Schinkel. Complete elevation for the Fürstliche
Residenz, 1835. Ink and wash, 297 × 2000.
Nationalgalerie, SMB (SM 40c.51).

synchronised totality. At the same time these monuments masquerade as blueprints for a totally integrated social order, whether
imposed by princely or bureaucratic fiat.

Schinkel's theoretical analysis of the prospects for modern
architecture is most interesting where it confronts the contradictory
imperatives shaping his conception of architectural design. A
recognition of the structurally unresolvable problems he faced is
implicit in the fragmentary form of his analysis. As one reads
through the various drafts he made of his theories for the textbook
on architecture, the resolutions he proposes do not emerge as final,
but as responses to constantly reiterated questions that never find a
fully satisfactory answer. At times, he is quite explicit that the social
and political conditions of modern architecture of necessity make it
aesthetically impure and heterogeneous, and that its artistic significance in part arises out of these historical impurities:

> Mankind's [social] relations never acquire an absolutely pure
> form that conforms to the perfect laws of reason. There always
> remain many residues of imperfect development and of political
> statutes designed for particular, mostly egotistical, ends. As a
> result, architectural projects too admit of no pure solution, and
> have to take on a significant historical dimension. Wisely used,
> the latter is a source of interest and can even form part of a work's
> beauty and poetry – used badly, it gives rise to the baroque and
> the tasteless.[28]

At the same time, there is the insistent fantasy of an aesthetic
integration that would somehow cancel out or transcend historical
contingency, would somehow force the uneven and irrational aspect
of social relations into the mould of a law-like whole. Ancient
Greece is the embodiment of this ideal. It is a fantasy with which
Schinkel cannot dispense if he is to continue in the conviction that
the architect ought after all to be able to create an aesthetically
convincing whole out of the material needs and technological
capabilities of modern society. The Greek ideal functions as the
counterpart to his constantly recurring unease over the endemically
disparate, eclectic and arbitrary nature of modern architecture. It is a
necessary fiction, a myth that both compensates for and at the same
time intensifies his worry that the modern architect might be
precluded by circumstance from ever fashioning a truly integrated
style:

> Where the historical does have to play a role, you do best to use
> forms that recall the very great periods when this historical
> element was fully formed.[29]

In Schinkel's case this myth was not a nostalgic one, as it was for so
many of his German contemporaries. It operated in tandem with an
explicitly modernising myth that set great store on the engendering
of new architectural forms in response to the ever-changing
technologies and social relations of the modern world[30]. The tension
between these two mythic ideals, one offering the vision of a
powerfully integrated totality rooted in the past, and the other of
inexhaustible renewal and development promised by the present,
happened in the case of Schinkel's architectural practice to be a
peculiarly productive one.

1 Peschken 1979, pp. 55, 114.

2 Schinkel's familiarity with Fichte's ideas is clearly documented. See Peschken 1979, p. 24.

3 *Ibid.*, p. 150. Compare also the earlier formulation, *ibid.*, p. 115 ('jetzige Zeit ist aber tief versunken . . .').

4 Compare also *ibid.*, p. 117.

5 *Ibid.*, p. 54.

6 *Ibid.*, p. 54. On Durand, see Middleton 1982.

7 Peschken 1979, pp. 114–15.

8 For Schinkel's fullest account of his ideas on the subject, see pp. 115–16 (from just above 5[24] to the end of the section). Compare also *ibid.*, p. 57–8, 66.

9 *Ibid.*, pp. 57–8.

10 *Ibid.*, p. 49. For a general discussion of the conception of freedom found in German theorising about the visual arts in the period, see Podro 1982 p. 6ff.

11 Peschken 1979, p. 119 (III, 15). The wider political resonances of such a notion of freedom as it emerged in eighteenth- and early nineteenth-century aesthetics are discussed in Eagleton 1990.

12 Peschken 1979, p. 34.

13 *Ibid.*, p. 36; see cat. 21. For other examples from this phase of his career, see Schinkel's description of his Gothic version of a monument to Queen Luise (Berlin 1981, p. 56; cat. 16), and the lettering on his print of a Gothic church behind trees (cat. 17).

14 Peschken 1979, p. 29.

15 *Ibid.*, p. 149. For further discussion of this aspect of Schinkel's theory, see Behr 1984.

16 Among the more prominent writers whose perspective on artistic aesthetics and classical precedent closely resembled Schinkel's were Goethe, with whom Schinkel was in direct contact, and Hegel and Wilhelm von Humboldt, both of whom were working in Berlin at the time when Schinkel was elaborating his ideas for a treatise on architecture.

17 Peschken 1979, pp. 57–8.

18 *Ibid.*, p. 58.

19 Berlin 1981, p. 644 (from Schinkel's description of the picture *Blick in Griechenlands Blüte* (1825); see cat. 160) and Peschken 1979, p. 57. Compare also *ibid.*, p. 114.

20 Peschken 1979, p. 146.

21 *Ibid.* Compare also *ibid*, p. 58, and the late formulation, *ibid.*, p. 150.

22 For a recent discussion of the political contradictions of modernising ideology in Germany of the period, see Mah 1990, p. 3 ff.

23 Peschken 1979, p. 116.

24 *Ibid.*, pp. 70–1.

25 *Ibid.*, p. 71.

26 Wolzogen 1862–3 (Vol. III, 1863), pp. 371–2.

27 Peschken 1979, p. 151. This project was designed as the final section of Schinkel's planned architectural textbook (see also Berlin 1981, pp. 242–7). The plan for a palace at Orianda is similar in conception (cat. 154–59). For a discussion in English of these late projects, see Clelland 1980, pp. 106–13.

28 Peschken 1979, p. 117.

29 *Ibid.*

30 *Ibid.*, p. 2.

57. The Schlossbrücke, Berlin (1819–24). Detail of cast-iron balustrade.

Art and Industry

Angelika Wesenberg

In 1881 the Berlin Kunstgewerbemuseum (Museum of Applied Art) moved to its new and splendid premises, built by Martin Gropius and Heino Schmieden. Julius Lessing, author of the *Festschrift* published on the occasion, described the roots of that institution:

> The *retrospective view* to which this endeavour brings us, naturally turns our eyes towards the measures taken, in the same sense as today, two generations ago in Prussia – earlier than in other *Länder* – in the effort to educate the people's taste for art and industry, and which are indissolubly bound up with the names of *Beuth* and *Schinkel* . . . . When in 1821 Beuth founded the Gewerbe Schule [College of Trade] – from which the present Technische Hochschule [Technical College] has now grown – an ample part was allotted to the encouragement of the applied arts. The modelling, foundry and tooling workshops, the pattern school, the collection of casts of Pompeian bronzes connected with that institute, the publication of the splendid *Vorbilder für Fabrikanten und Handwerker* [*Examples for Manufacturers and Craftsmen*], also begun in association with Schinkel in 1821, the foundation of art colleges in the provincial capitals, all Schinkel's work for the beautification of the internal furnishing of residences, his readoption of visible brickwork and terracotta relief, his promotion of the zinc casting industry, silversmithing, weaving and knitting – all are within the field of the applied art of today and all are steps on the selfsame road that we are now travelling.[1]

This assessment is just as accurate today. The problematical and at that time still undemarcated relationship between the traditional crafts and industry, which was expanding rapidly and increasing in technical potential, was nowhere more intensively considered and directed in the early nineteenth century than in Prussia. The two friends, Peter Beuth and Karl Friedrich Schinkel, played a decisive role in this complicated process of reorientation, leading the reform movements that continued throughout the century.

From the late eighteenth century onwards, the new problems of 'art and industry' led to an ever greater interest in Britain and its highly developed industries, which served as an example in both a positive and a negative sense. Prussian trade and industrial art reforms throughout the nineteenth century were closely linked with British efforts – the Gewerbe-Institut (Institute of Trade), the Victoria and Albert Museum and the Kunstgewerbemuseum in Berlin are staging posts in a single journey: in 1821, in his inaugural address to the Association for the Encouragement of Trade and Industry in Prussia,[2] Beuth named the Society for the Encouragement of Arts, Manufactures and Commerce, which had existed in England since 1754, as the model for its foundation.[3] All his efforts to achieve a modern industry and art industry in Prussia found their first, very visible expression two decades later, in the 1844 General German Exhibition of Trade and Industry in Berlin.[4] It is quite conceivable that Prince Albert (of Saxe-Coburg-Gotha), was stimulated by the great success of this exhibition to begin to formulate the plan for the Great Exhibition that was staged in London in 1851.[5] But the industrial art at the 1851 Great Exhibition did not please everyone. The shock at so much blatant crudity combined with technical refinement spurred on the efforts towards design reform in Great Britain. Land in South Kensington was bought from the huge financial profits of the Great Exhibition and in 1857 the first museum devoted to the applied arts, now the Victoria and Albert Museum, was built there, furnished with purchases from the Great Exhibition as its basic stock. From the start the museum worked in accordance with a didactic concept based on seeing and teaching, like that of the early Prussian institutions. In its turn, the museum at South Kensington became the pattern for a series of new foundations. In 1866 a memorandum by Dr H. Schwabe, *Die Förderung der Kunst-Industrie in England und der Stand dieser Frage in Deutschland* (Encouragement of the Art Industry in England and its Status in Germany), commissioned by the Prussian Crown Princess, was published in Berlin. In 1867 the Prussian Gewerbemuseum (Museum of Trade and Industry) was founded, and in 1881 it was given the new museum building.

The Influence of Schinkel and Beuth on Industrial Art

Karl Friedrich Schinkel was undoubtedly the architect with the greatest impact on industrial arts and crafts in the first half of the nineteenth century. His influence, transmitted through his pupils and his own designs, reached far into the second half of the century. Schinkel's importance arose from his administrative positions, which enabled him to pass on to craftsmen a constant flow of major commissions for work on the interiors of several buildings, as well as from his wide-ranging activities as a designer.

Beuth's specific opportunities to exert an influence were his senior posts in the Ministry for Trade and Industry, in the Technische Deputation für Gewerbe (State Agency for Trade) and in the Association for the Encouragement of Trade and Industry in Prussia. All his work was carried out in close collaboration with Schinkel.

Schinkel and Beuth enjoyed a direct and close relationship with both fine and applied art, which was expressed in their private collections and in their intimate links with numerous artists and craftsmen. Whereas Schinkel's excellent knowledge of the artistic branches of industry was based principally on the practical interests of an architect who was also working on the interiors of buildings, Beuth's interest in this field was more general. As a considerable connoisseur and collector of the art of the past, he was as concerned with the revival of historic forms and techniques as with new materials and processes. Many prize competitions promoted by the Gewerbeverein (Trade Association) and experiments at the Gewerbe-Institut (Institute of Trade) derive from his inspiration.

In 1854, soon after Beuth's death, the art historian Gustav Waagen, who knew both men well, took the long friendship between Beuth and Schinkel and their joint work on behalf of art and industry as the subject of his address to the annual Schinkel Festival. He defined the contribution made by each, describing the way in which Beuth succeeded, despite the huge range of work he had to do:

by means of extensive reading of all new phenomena in any way remarkable throughout Europe, both in the industrial and in the architectural and fine arts fields, in taking note of these and on the basis of his records, viewing them himself. Through his link with Beuth, Schinkel thus enjoyed the extraordinary advantage of

constantly expanding his knowledge of Greek, Roman, Romanesque, Gothic, Arabic, Renaissance and modern art, and thereby achieved a rare universality of outlook. However, Schinkel possessed to a degree unknown to me in any other architect the quality of penetrating into the spirit of the art of the most varied nations and eras, and assimilating it in such a way that he was able to work in that spirit himself.[6]

In the same commemorative address, Waagen traced the aesthetic development of both men by looking at the genesis of Beuth's own collection of objects and the artistic work of Schinkel. Before and during the Wars of Liberation, Beuth shared the enthusiasm of Schinkel and many contemporaries for so-called Old German art. While Schinkel made studies and designs in the German Gothic style, Beuth had a copy made of the Virgin and Child from Stephen Lochner's Cologne Cathedral picture (now in the Nationalgalerie, Berlin), acquired examples of German painting from the fifteenth century and collected engravings of that era, by Schongauer and Albrecht Dürer in particular. After the Wars of Liberation the friends once again turned to antiquity and the Renaissance,

58. Covered cup from the collection of Peter Beuth, *c*.1842. Latticinio glass in white blue and red, h.330. Made by the Gräfl. Schaffgottsch'sche Josephinshutte Schreiberhau. Kunstgewerbemuseum, SMB (inv. no. 1976,230).

surrounding themselves with Greek art, with plaster casts of statues, with cameos, coins and other small *objets d'art*. Beuth collected engravings after the paintings of the great Italians, especially Raphael, and had a few ancient statues cast in bronze at the Gewerbe-Institut.

Beuth later added various contemporary craft objects to his collection. Some of these were the first fruits of his quite special concern for the applied arts. Beuth possessed two niello works in the Italian style by the Berlin goldsmith Carl Wagner, several glasses from the Josephine glass foundry, worked in the old Venetian latticinio technique (fig. 58), a medallion of cast zinc and a terracotta figure with a matt black surface made in imitation of ancient ceramics.[7]

Schinkel's work for applied arts can be found throughout his creative life, from 1800 to 1840. The versatility of his ideas, both stylistic and technical, can be seen in his many design drawings: strict classicism side by side with the Romantic neo-Gothic style, the first examples of the revived Renaissance style and new constructional forms. In general his applied art designs may be said to have arisen from an historical outlook, schooled in antiquity and the Renaissance, which nevertheless respected modern requirements and manufacturing processes.

Schinkel made designs for objects in almost all materials: even before his first Italian tour in 1803 he worked for the Eckartstein faience factory in Berlin, as was noted by Franz Kugler.[8] He supplied designs for receptacles and, according to Kugler, painted the ceramics himself. He drew a regular income of 300 thalers at Eckartstein.

A few years later, in 1808, he produced the pen and ink and wash drawing for a stove for the Höhler and Feilner factory (fig. 59). His friendly collaboration with Tobias Feilner lasted until the latter's death in 1839.

He maintained this early interest in ceramic forms. Two plates from the *Vorbilder für Fabrikanten und Handwerker* illustrate a tureen and other vessels which would be equally suitable for manufacture in pottery or porcelain (cat. 136). According to the text volume of the *Vorbilder*, they are distinguished by the fact that although 'intended for our requirements, they employ Greek forms'. There are also some designs made directly for the Royal Porcelain Factory, showing ceremonial vases and memorial pieces for the Lalla Rookh Festival organised in Berlin in 1821 (cat. 142, 144, 153). At the Great Exhibition of 1851, two candelabra in porcelain after Schinkel's design were among the principal exhibits.[9]

In the 1820s and 1830s Schinkel designed a large number of objects for the Royal Iron Foundry. He was also responsible for about half the designs in the eight numbers of the *Magazin von Abbildungen der Gusswaren aus der königlichen Eisengiesserei zu Berlin* (*Magazines of Illustrations of Cast-iron Ware from the Royal Iron Foundry in Berlin*), published from 1815 to 1833, each of which contains eight plates with descriptions. Some of the designs published in the *Vorbilder* were also in iron, considered the most up-to-date material because of its close association with industrialisation (cat. 140, 141)

Schinkel's name was intimately linked with the new technique of casting zinc in imitation of a great variety of materials. He was the

59. Schinkel. Design for a stove for the Höhler and Feilner Manufactory, Berlin, 1808. Pen and ink and wash. Nationalgalerie, SMB (SM 37c.167).

initiator of a prize competition run by the Association for the Encouragement of Trade and Industry, and at his instigation Moritz Geiss received the prize in 1838.[10] The twenty-one-part catalogue of cast zinc products from the firm of Geiss was not published until after Schinkel's death, but many of its items had been designed by him. Geiss's explanatory foreword is accompanied by a short paper by Schinkel, drawn up in 1840, in which the possibilities of zinc casting are assessed. This report contains Schinkel's ideas, seldom so

60. The Römische Bäder, Charlottenhof: the arcaded hall (1833), with an iron bench made by the Royal Iron Foundry after a design by Schinkel. The table is made of cast zinc.

clearly formulated, on the question of the imitation of materials in the crafts:

> We already see large statues in imitation of antiquity in the workshop of Herr Geiss in Berlin, executed with extreme purity, to which a marvellous colour can be given by means of a copper deposit . . . great expense is saved on restoration . . . . Ornaments for buildings can be made in the simplest way by taking a mould of the originals and casting them in zinc, by which one avoids a tedious process in stone which does not encourage taste . . . [zinc] also has the advantage of far less weight . . . . The many advantages this metal offers for architectural furnishings, outdoor vases and for other objects such as candelabra, basins, etc., where it is also less liable to damage than stone . . . will in future make it indispensable to architecture, at the same time as constantly expanding the range of architecture.[11]

While Schinkel's designs for glass, lighting fittings and textiles are of a somewhat incidental character, the designs for silver form an important area of his work (cat. 137, 138, 145, 151). These were mostly executed by the Berlin goldsmith George Hossauer, to whom Schinkel and Beuth were also related. Hossauer was an enterprising personality, of the kind imagined and encouraged by the Prussian trade reformers, an artist and entrepreneur who was full of fire and enthusiasm and open to new methods, materials and techniques.[12]

Among Schinkel's designs are many for furniture, mainly intended for specific locations in new or rebuilt royal residences. Schinkel's furniture designs and actual pieces demonstrate particularly clearly the broad stylistic range of his work, made not only in wood, but also in iron, tin, zinc, stucco and various types of stone (fig. 60) showing an unconventional attitude to materials and tradition. From 1835 to 1837 *Schinkels Möbel-Entwürfe, welche bei Einrichtung prinzlicher Wohnungen in den letzten zehn Jahren ausgeführt wurden* (*Schinkel's Furniture Designs, Executed in the Last Ten Years in the Furnishing of Princely Residences*), published by Ludwig Lohde, appeared in five parts, with a total of 16 plates. Through this publication and some plates of furniture designs in the *Vorbilder*, Schinkel's styles gained popularity with the middle classes, and variations on them continued into the 1860s.

In 1871 the address at the Schinkel Festival took as its theme Schinkel's significance to applied art. The speaker, Carl Grunow, architect and first Director of the Berlin Kunstgewerbemuseum, did not discuss the individual designs, but concentrated on Schinkel's general concern with the artistic and technical development of the crafts linked to the interior. Names and firms were mentioned: Feilner's stove and terracotta factory, Geiss's zinc foundry, Gabain's silk-weaving mill, Wanschaff the cabinet-maker, Hiltl, the decorator, the painters Asmus and Rosendahl, Hossauer the goldsmith. All of them, Grunow wrote, 'were recruited by him and received instruction, stimulus, employment and training to a previously unknown level of technical skill and artistic use of form'.[13]

Schinkel and Beuth in the Context of Prussian Trade Policy

Schinkel and Beuth's efforts to develop the applied arts in Prussia were part of a larger intellectual concept: the importance to Germany of disseminating British ideas of economic liberalism taught by Adam Smith, which supplied the theoretical foundations for Prussian economic reform. The reforms of the craftsman's trade instigated by Freiherr von Stein while he was a minister from 1804 to 1806, were continued to a lesser extent after his fall by Hardenberg and in the 1830s by the disciples of Stein. A political Restoration did begin in 1814 but, once started, the process of civil change in the socioeconomic field tended to continue. The reforms could be held up, but they could not be stopped. The central component of Prussian trade reform was a very strong emphasis on professional and general education.

Peter Beuth was connected with almost all the institutions for the encouragement of craft and industry in Prussia. With his personal enthusiasm for art, he brought together the artistic branches of the various trades and gave them special encouragement. In addition he was certainly an early theorist of arts and crafts, in which connection his close friendship with Karl Friedrich Schinkel was of special significance.

After studying law, taking a post in Bayreuth and spending some time as a senior civil servant in Potsdam, Beuth came to Berlin in 1810 to join the office of State Chancellor Hardenberg and was first a member, then leader of the Committee for Reform of Taxation and Trade. In 1818 he took over the Ministry's Department of Trade and Industry.

In July 1819 Beuth became director of the Technische Deputation für Gewerbe, the state agency for trade and industry founded in 1811, and reorganised that hidebound and inactive department. Schinkel became its adviser on all aesthetic matters. The Technische Deputation maintained a series of collections and workshops which were systematically expanded by Beuth and later joined the Gewerbe-Institut (Institute of Trade) and Gewerbeverein (Trade Association) under one roof. Beuth devoted himself in particular to expanding the library and to the collection of drawings and engravings. Straube records from the files of the Ministry of Trade and Industry a quantity of books ordered by Beuth, many from London.[14]

The publication of the *Vorbilder für Fabrikanten und Handwerker* (*Examples for Manufacturers and Craftsmen*) from 1821 onwards (cat. 133) was of far-reaching significance; the title alone underlines its didactic intentions. The *Vorbilder* were first distributed as single engravings and only later collected in two portfolios and supplied with a commentary. This is now probably the chief record of relationship between art and industry in this phase of the socioeconomic revolution. Beuth and Schinkel collaborated closely on this outstanding project, probably composing the commentaries together. The printing used for this volume of *Vorbilder* was also to set new standards. In 1824 Beuth authorised the acquisition of a printing press for books, a lithographic press and a press for prints, delivered from Edinburgh for the model collection,[15] but undoubtedly used for the *Vorbilder*. The copper engraving workshop of the Technische Deputation possessed two ruling machines for engraving the plates, one imported from London, the second copied in Berlin.

In 1821 Beuth founded the Gewerbeverein, or Association for the Encouragement of Trade and Industry in Prussia, which was to be very effective. Its members included not only craftsmen but also men from trade, the administration, art, science and politics and, soon after its foundation, Alexander and Wilhelm von Humboldt, Stein, Bülow, Gneisenau, Thaer and Krupp. The Gewerbe-Institut, or Institute of Trade, also founded by Beuth in 1821, became one of the first advanced professional educational colleges for craftsmen in Prussia. In 1831 Beuth also became leader of the Allgemeine Bauschule (General School of Architecture), which later became the Bauakademie (Architectural Academy).

The Königliche Gewerbe-Institut

Schinkel's work for the Gewerbe-Institut deserves special mention. He had special responsibility for the design of craft objects produced in the various workshops of that institution by both teachers and pupils. Most of these objects ended up in the Royal residences; some came to the Ministry of Trade and Industry, or remained in the Institute's collections. Today his designs and the objects produced are very hard to identify. Some pointers are provided by the *Verzeichnis des Schinkelnachlasses* (*Index of Schinkel's Cultural Heritage*), by Alfred von Wolzogen. A few of the drawings for craft objects listed there were in the possession of the Gewerbe-Institut, where they could have come only for conversion into engravings or as designs for one of the workshops. Indeed, Wolzogen mentions some which were realised at the Gewerbe-Institut. For instance, Boy, who taught woodwork and carving, made an ivory box for Crown Princess Elisabeth. In the same woodworking shop, a prie-dieu and a small sewing table designed by Schinkel were made for the Crown Princess, as was furniture for Beuth's new official residence in the building of the Institute (cat. 130). The wooden plinths for two sculptures of Amazons by August Kiss, who taught engraving and chasing at the Institute from 1830, are also by Boy from designs by Schinkel. The spear-throwing Amazon was formerly in the Schinkel Museum; the falling Amazon was sent as a gift from Friedrich Wilhelm III to the Crown Princess in Potsdam. The cylindrical plinth with the carved relief of a procession of Amazons has been preserved.

Glass objects made at the Gewerbe-Institut are known only from the written record. Wolzogen mentions drawings by Schinkel for a vessel and a glass chandelier for Beuth. One well-known work from the metal workshop that has been preserved is the so-called Beuthschale (cat. 131, 132), a table decoration made of oxidised silver, which Beuth received as a gift from the Gewerbeverein.

In 1830 Beuth and Rauch set up a facility for bronze casting, which became the most important of all the workshops in the Institute. One of the first large bronze works produced here was the fountain, to Schinkel's design, for the new courtyard of the Institute, which had received several new extensions (cat. 146). Today this is in the vestibule of Schloss Charlottenhof in Potsdam (fig. 75). From drawings by Schinkel we know of other works by this workshop: a mirror and a decorative casket for the Crown Princess; a table with a bronze central leg and round marble top which was a gift to the Crown Princess from the Gewerbeverein in 1836 and is now also in Charlottenhof (fig. 61).

61. Round table, 1836. Cast bronze with a coloured marble top, h.800. Designed by Schinkel and made in the Gewerbe-Institut. It has occupied its present position in the vestibule of Charlottenhof since at least 1839. SSG Potsdam-Sanssouci.

In 1855 the Gewerbe-Institut was still sure of its ground as a formative influence: at the Paris International Exhibition of 1855 it displayed the *Vorbilder der Bauausführunger des Preussischen Staates* (*examples of Building Projects of the Prussian State*) and bronze busts of Beuth and Schinkel.[16] The bust of Schinkel had been carved in 1819 by Friedrich Tieck (cat. 1); in 1846 Rauch presented the model of Beuth's bust to the pupils of the Gewerbe-Institut for execution in bronze.

The great significance of Schinkel and Beuth to the development of applied art in Prussia was also summed up by Waagen, in the famous Festival address of 1854: 'The aesthetic element, the understanding, the beauty and variety of forms in architecture, as well as in tectonic objects, have finally been brought to a level of which we here previously had no conception.'[17]

1 Berlin 1881, p. 1 ff.
2 Verein für Beförderung des Gewerbefleisses in Preussen.
3 Mieck 1965, pp. 35–7. Straube 1933, pp. 54–7.
4 Allgemeine Deutsche Gewerbe-Ausstellung.
5 Hamburg 1977, p. xv.
6 Waagen 1854, col. 301.

7 The objects referred to, as well as others from the Beuth Collection, formerly part of the Beuth-Schinkel Museum, are now in the Kunstgewerbemuseum, SMB. Also see Berlin 1980, 475–87.
8 Kugler 1842, Supplement, p. 138.
9 Lübke 1851, p. 42.
10 Berlin 1846, p. 131ff.

11 Geiss 1849. Berlin 1846, p. 131. Eggers 1856, p. 117ff.
12 Wesenberg 1987, pp. 213–40.
13 Grunow 1871, p. 5.
14 Straube, op. cit., pp. 34, 35, notes 47, 48.
15 Ibid., p. 36, note 49.
16 Berlin 1856, p. 425.
17 Waagen 1854, col. 303.

62. The Schauspielhaus, Berlin (1818–21). the main front from the Gendarmenmarkt (now the Platz der Akademie), *c.*1920. The statue is of Schiller (cat. 45–7).

63. The Schauspielhaus, Berlin (1818–21): the
Concert Hall, c.1910. The Hall, adorned with busts
of composers, occupied one of the wings of the
building, with offices and workrooms in the other.
The interior of the building was lost in the Second
World War and reconstructed with one main
concert hall (cat. 45–7).

64. Berlin Cathedral, exterior (1820–2). Schinkel's cathedral was adapted from a building of 1747–50 by Johann Boumann. The angels were made in copper after models by Friedrich Tieck. The building was demolished for the present cathedral (1894–1905) by J. Rachsdorff.

65. Berlin Cathedral, interior (1820–2). Demolished 1893.

66. Schloss Tegel (1820–4), *c.*1900. Tegel was built for Wilhelm von Humboldt, as a modification of a seventeenth-century house. It was chiefly intended for Humboldt's collection of antique sculpture.

67. The Lustgarten, Berlin, *c*.1935. On the left is the
Altes Museum and ahead is the Nationalgalerie
(1866–7) by Schinkel's pupil Friedrich August
Stüler. The Cathedral is on the right.

68. The Altes Museum, Berlin (1822–30). View of the front, *c*.1930. Visible in the portico are the mural paintings designed by Schinkel and executed after 1841 (cat. 50–6).

69. The Altes Museum, Berlin (1822–30). View of
the main front, *c*.1900 (cat. 50–6).

70. The Altes Museum, Berlin (1822–30). View of the gallery of antique sculpture on the ground floor, *c.*1900 (cat. 50–6).

71. The Crown Prince's Apartments in the
Königliches (Berliner) Schloss (1824–7): the
Sternsaal (Star Room), *c.*1940. Destroyed.

72. The Crown Prince's Apartments in the
Königliches (Berliner) Schloss (1824–7): the
Teesalon (Tea Salon), *c.*1940. In the 1920s the
Teesalon was restored to its original state but
without the monumental fixed furniture. Destroyed
(cat. 64–6).

73. The Crown Prince's Apartments in the
Königliches (Berliner) Schloss (1824–7): Princess
Elisabeth's private drawing-room, *c.*1900. On the
right-hand wall are Caspar David Friedrich's *Monk
by the sea* and *Abbey in an oakwood*, now in the
Nationalgalerie, SMPK (cat. 68).

74. Schloss Glienicke: the Casino (1824–5), *c*.1910.

Schinkel's Buildings in Photographs 1890–1940

75. The vestibule at Schloss Charlottenhof, showing the fountain designed by Schinkel in 1829 and made in bronze in 1831 by the Gewerbe-Institut. It was put in Charlottenhof in 1843.

76. Prince Karl's Palais, Berlin (1827–8): the great banqueting hall or gallery, *c*.1920. Destroyed (cat. 83–6).

77. Prince Albrecht's Palais, Berlin (1830–3): the
lower part of the cast-iron staircase, 1921. The walls
were blue and blue-grey with the ornament in red;
the glass wall lit a service stair. Destroyed (cat.
87–91).

78. Prince Albrecht's Palais, Berlin (1829–3). The upper part of the staircase, 1921. The pediment sculpture is a reduced copy of that on the north façade of the Schauspielhaus. Destroyed (cat. 87–91).

79. Prince Albrecht's Palais, Berlin (1829–3); the
great banqueting hall or ballroom, 1921. Destroyed
(cat. 90).

80. Prince Albrecht's Palais, Berlin (1829–33): the 'brown room', 1921. Later nineteenth-century alterations have obliterated Schinkel's decoration except for the door and overdoor and the furniture (cf. cat. 92). Destroyed.

81. The Bauakademie, Berlin (1831–6), *c*.1900 (cat. 119–23).

82. The Bauakademie, Berlin (1831–6). The entrance front, *c*.1900. The statues are (left to right): Peter Beuth (its director, by August Kiss), Schinkel (its architect, by Friedrich Drake) and Albert Thaer (the Professor of Agriculture at the University, by Rauch). Destroyed (cat. 119–23).

83. The Bauakademie, Berlin (1831–6). The entrance front, *c*.1900. The left-hand doorway led to the Bauschule (School of Architecture), the right to the offices of the Oberbaudeputation, and later to the first Schinkel Museum. Destroyed (cat. 119–23).

84. The Bauakademie, Berlin (1831–6). The right-hand entrance, c.1900. The terracotta decoration was made by August Kiss; the doors show celebrated architects. This ensemble was saved during the demolition of the building (cat. 119–23).

85. Schloss Glienicke: Pavilion, the so-called 'Grosse
Neugierde' ('great curiosity') (1835–7), *c*.1910.

A Universal Man

1.

Christian Friedrich Tieck (1776–1851)

Inscribed: *Carl. Friedr: Schinkel. Fried. Tieck a. v. fec. 1819*

Marble, h. 670

SSG Potsdam-Sanssouci (71. GKIII 396)

Tieck was a pupil of Gottfried Schadow and spent some time in Pierre David d'Anger's studio in Paris. He evidently found what he sought, as he was faithful to classicism for the rest of his life. Although he was closely associated with Romantic circles in Berlin through his poet brother, Ludwig, his uncompromising classicism marked him out as a maverick in the Berlin School. The Biedermeier cult of monumental art passed him by. Thanks to his friendship with Goethe, the Humboldts and the Schellings and his close association with Rauch, his supremely gifted studio-colleague, as well as Schinkel himself, Tieck spent many years working on major projects such as the Weimar Schloss, the Schauspielhaus in Berlin (contemporaneous with this bust), the Crown Prince's apartment in the Königliches Schloss in Berlin and Scharnhorst's Tomb. His special gift as a portraitist was the ideal harmony of features he achieved in the people he portrayed; the modelling of the hair is especially important here. Completed early in their collaboration, it is the first noteworthy portrait of Schinkel, capturing perfectly the restrained power of this supremely gifted architect.

It became the standard image, being reproduced in plaster, patinated zinc and biscuit porcelain. Another marble version (Nationalgalerie, SMB) was placed on permanent display in the Altes Museum in 1842 on the orders of Friedrich Wilhelm IV.

Lit.: Berlin 1980, 213a; Berlin 1981, la.

M.G.

2.

Franz Ludwig Catel (1778–1856)

Oil on canvas, 620 × 490

Nationalgalerie, SMPK (A.11 284)

On 23 October 1824 Schinkel notes in his diary of the second Italian tour: 'Quite early, before 7 o'clock, I went to Catel, who wanted to paint me into a little portrait showing a room in Naples from whose open window one can see the sea with the island of Capri and the trees under the window from Villa Reale, just as when I lived there.' Schinkel had lodged there from 5 September until the end of the month, but was in Rome when he wrote this note.

It sounds as if it had been Catel's idea to paint this portrait in an inner room. Schinkel wrote to his wife five days later from Florence: 'Catel is also painting a little picture for me, with my figure in it: it is my window in Naples with a view over the sea and Capri. This is to be your Christmas present, though unfortunately it will not now arrive in good time.'

Catel, a Berliner who had worked with Schinkel in 1805–6 on the illustrations to Ernst Friedrich Bussler's *Verzierungen aus dem Alterthum* (1806–29), had gone to Italy in 1811 and thanks to his disciplined method of work had become a successful landscape painter there. The view from the window frame occupies the centre of the picture. Schinkel is pushed to the edge, and the counterweight on the other side is represented, as Adolf Greifenhagen has established, by a panathenaian prize amphora and a shallow bronze bowl with handles, which in 1827 came to the Antikensammlung in Berlin from the collection of Von Bartholdy, Prussian Consul-General in Rome; there is also an Augustan bronze pedestal with lamp. The picture documents Schinkel's special quests on this second Italian tour: nature and antiquity.

Lit.: Greifenhagen 1963; Berlin 1981, 4; Berlin 1986, pp. 64–5.

H.B.-S.

King Friedrich Wilhelm III (1770–1840), who succeeded his father Friedrich Wilhelm II in 1797, had married Princess Luise of Mecklenburg-Strelitz (1776–1810) in 1793 and in 1824 contracted a morganatic marriage with Auguste Countess of Harrach (1800–73), who was elevated to the rank of Princess of Liegnitz.

In view of the crisis of the Prussian state which had become apparent in the defeats of Jena and Auerstädt in 1806, he allowed a number of important democratic concessions to be wrested from him. However, after 1815 he did not fulfil the constitutional pledge he had given, and instead, supported by the 'Holy Alliance', attempted to restore the absolutist system. His unassuming character, tending towards thriftiness, coincided with the demands made by the recovering economy of Prussia. This placed limitations on many of Schinkel's public plans, since his entire work fell within the reign of Friedrich Wilhelm III. Corresponding to the relatively few personal requirements of the king, the number and extent of buildings carried out for him by Schinkel was modest.

Lit.: Berlin 1980, 328.

G.B.

3.

KING FRIEDRICH WILHELM III WITH HIS SONS ON HORSEBACK.   after 1825

Franz Krüger (1797–1857)

Black chalk heightened with white, 634 × 485

Nationalgalerie, SMB (SZ 3)

In the foreground is the king on horseback, immediately behind him to the left Crown Prince Friedrich Wilhelm, to the right on a grey, Prince Wilhelm (1861 King of Prussia, 1871 German Kaiser); in the background Princes Karl and Albrecht.

Here the painter uses for a royal family portrait the kind of 'portrait with entourage' that he liked, a democratised form of the Baroque portrait of a military commander with his staff. The larger variant exhibited at the Berlin Academy of 1828 (SSG Potsdam-Sanssouci) is enriched by a view of Schinkel's Kreuzberg monument.

4.

Franz Krüger (1797–1857)

Oil on canvas, 620 × 400

SSG Potsdam-Sanssouci (GKI 5673)

The eldest son of Friedrich Wilhelm III and
Queen Luise, Friedrich Wilhelm (1795–1861)
became king in 1840. Unable to rule during his
last years, his brother and successor, Prince
Wilhelm, reigned as Regent from 1859. He
married Princess Elisabeth of Bavaria in 1823.
Of all his brothers and sisters Friedrich
Wilhelm was the most artistically gifted, a
talent developed almost exclusively in the
architectural field, making innumerable
sketches for plans expressing his inexhaustible
and at times excessive imagination. Many of
his architectural ideas were starting-points for
Schinkel's projects and are often indissolubly
linked with him, since the Crown Prince saw
Schinkel as his teacher and generally listened to
his advice. When Schinkel died shortly after
Friedrich Wilhelm IV ascended the throne, this
restraining authority disappeared. However,
political developments and finally the king's
illness soon put a stop to his ambitious plans.

In spring 1846 Friedrich Wilhelm IV
commissioned Krüger to paint his portrait for
the Königsberg astronomer Friedrich Wilhelm
Bessel, who wanted him portrayed 'in an
informal manner . . . wearing my frock coat
unbuttoned, leaning on my table, just as I
usually receive friends in my study' (letter
from the King to Bessel, dated 16 February
1846). Bessel received the picture shortly
before he died on 17 March 1846 and
bequeathed it to his native city, Minden,
where it remains. The present replica in
Schloss Sanssouci belonged to Queen Elisabeth.

From 1824 to 1826 Schinkel converted for
Crown Prince Friedrich Wilhelm the rooms in
Königliches Schloss which Frederick the Great
had occupied in the eighteenth century (see
cat. 64–68). Among them was the late Gothic
Erasmus Kapelle, which he converted into a
study cum library. All that remains of the
Gothic-style furniture Schinkel designed is a
document cabinet, of the type shown in the
portrait (Schloss Charlottenburg).

Lit.: Berlin 1980, 300; Berlin 1981, 240.

G.B.

Architectural Education

5

PERSPECTIVE DESIGN FOR A MONUMENT TO
FRIEDRICH II IN BERLIN.   1797

Friedrich Gilly (1772–1800)

Signed and dated bottom right: *Fr. Gilly, 1797*

Ink and body colour, 596 × 1352

Nationalgalerie, SMB (SZ n.5)

When in September 1797, at the age of sixteen, Schinkel saw this plan for a memorial temple at the Berlin Academy Exhibition, which also showed designs for Friedrich's monument by Langhans, Schadow, Hirt and Gentz, tradition has it that this sight awakened his resolve to devote himself to architecture.

The idea of a commemorative monument, already conceived in the king's lifetime, was constantly revived after Friedrich's death in 1786. In 1787 Hans Christian Genelli and Johann Gottfried Schadow supplied early designs for an architectural monument, together with portraits of the king. In 1791 there were further projects, and in 1796–7 the competitive designs of Langhans, Hirt, Gentz and Gilly formed the climax of these ideas.

The most important, and forward-looking, was the monumental design for a Doric temple by Gilly. In its boldness and well-considered effect it is, together with his design for a Berlin theatre (1799–1800), the most characteristic expression of Gilly's architectural ideas and, at the same time, the most impressive plan for a monument of its day. The principal elements of the design are the monumental structure of the Potsdamer Tor on the left, with the round arched entrance to the broadly planned space, externally octagonal but internally oval. On this stands the peripteral Doric temple on top of a tall and massive stepped base. The plan was to have a seated figure of the king inside in the cella, in the plinth of the mausoleum together with the coffin.

Neither this nor any of the other projects was realised. When the idea of the monument was revived once again after 1820, a series of designs by Schinkel was produced for various sites in Berlin, as well as the later design for a memorial temple on the Mühlenberg at Potsdam. These too remained unbuilt, until C.D. Rauch's equestrian statue on Unter den Linden completed the long history of the project.

Lit.: Berlin 1980, 11, 12.

G.R.

6.

Signed and dated lower right: *Schinkel inv. et fec. 98.*

Pen and black and grey ink over pencil, grey and black wash, heightened with white, 193 × 238.

Scale on the lower edge.

Kunstbibliothek, SMPK (Hdz 5877)

The three-storey, nine-bay house stands on a slight rise before trees; the image is enclosed by a ruled border. A cellar storey at the base carries the tall ground floor, which was originally intended to be shown with banded rustication. The coursing is still visible under the dark areas of the rectangular windows, which were added later to correspond to the rest of the fenestration. Nearly all the window openings are plain. The central section is accentuated by the door framed in trapezoidal and rectangular blocks, the flat niche above with a balcony railing and decorated window and the triglyphs above.

The drawing was owned by Ludwig Schumann, a friend of Schinkel in his youth, and it is Schinkel's earliest known architectural design. The influence of his master David Gilly was first pointed out in 1863 by Alfred von Wolzogen, who had seen this sheet in the collection of Ferdinand von Quast, at Schloss Radensleben. Wolzogen commented: 'The design is entirely in Gilly's manner and could be thought to be from his hand if no further identification were given.'

It is surprising that Schinkel should place this urban house type in a landscape setting. Equally unusual is the use of the curved plank roof for a relatively small building. With its economical use of timber, this system was actually evolved for large rooms. The drawing was presumably an exercise reflecting the basic principles of David Gilly. Gilly's treatise *Über Erfindung, Construction und Vorteile der Bohlen-Dächer* (On the Invention, Construction and Advantages of Curved-Plank Roofs; Berlin, 1797) appears to have been as influential here as was his general style in which simplicity and surface quality takes precedence over sparsely applied decoration.

Lit.: Wolzogen 1862–3, 3 (1863), p. 402ff., No. 1; Rave 1962, p. 196, repr. p. 197; Berlin 1981, 17.

C.T.

7.

The top drawing inscribed lower centre: *Entwurf zu einer Garten partie* (Design for a garden). Lower right: *Schinkel inv. 1800*

Pen and black ink, 189 × 123 (cut at one side)

Kunstbibliothek, SMPK (HdZ 5880)

In the two drawings on this sheet nature, both landscaped and untouched, forms the main motif, while only fragments of the buildings appear through the dense foliage of the trees. In the upper drawing, the 'Design for a Garden', the trees form a semicircle, creating a dark frame for part of a palace-like building which appears as *point de vue*, bathed in light, as if at the end of a tunnel. The dense foliage half conceals the pedestals for garden sculptures. Shadowy figures are mounting a staircase, which is indicated by parallel strokes and leads to a terrace. Of the fleetingly sketched building in the centre only a five-bay columned portico and the adjacent windows of the ground floor, with their triangular gables, are visible. These features recall Schloss Wörlitz, although differing in detail, but a connection cannot be substantiated, as the depiction is too sketchy. The drawing is an example of one of Schinkel's favourite motifs, the dark, framing landscape directing the gaze deep into a brilliantly illuminated area in the centre of the picture.

The other drawing shows a ruin with trees growing over it, probably the round corner tower and adjoining wall of a castle in brick. We only see the upper storey, which is broken by pointed arch windows and arcades and the tent-like tower roof. The lower storey is hidden behind dense crowns of trees and a cottage. The brickwork of the window frames, arcades and upper storey of the tower is shown in very fine penwork. The contrast between the lower cottage and the towering castle is based on a vignette by Friedrich Gilly showing the Marienburg Hochmeister palace on the title-page of the *Sammlung nützlicher Aufsätze und Nachrichten, die Baukunst betreffend*, 1797, vol. II (Collection of Useful Essays and Information regarding Architecture). The style of drawing was probably also influenced by Gilly's work; a pen-and-ink drawing by Gilly of 1799, *Canal leading to a Palace Park* in the Märkisches Museum, Berlin, is very similar in its handling of stroke and line.

The sheet originally belonged to Ludwig Schumann and it was acquired by Ferdinand von Quast for Schloss Radensleben from Rathenow's Berlin collection in 1869.

Lit.: Wolzogen 1862–3, 2 (1862), p. 342, No. 15; Berlin 1981, 131.

C.T.

8.

PERSPECTIVE DESIGN FOR A HALL WITH COLUMNS,
BY THE SEA.   1802

Signed and dated bottom right: *Schinkel, 1802*

Pen and ink and pencil, 272 × 405

Nationalgalerie, SMB (SM 20c.178)

A hilly coastal landscape is seen through the
screen of columns. While the hall and its
architectural and decorative elements bear the
stamp of Schinkel's own original ideas – his
early work showing increasing independence
with each design – the furniture styles are still
largely based on Gilly's designs, in their turn
indebted to French models.

Lit.: Berlin 1980, 37.

G.R.

9.

DESIGN FOR A SCHLOSS IN KÖSTRITZ. PERSPECTIVE
OF THE MAIN FRONT.   1802

Signed and dated bottom right: *Schinkel inv.*
1802

Pen and ink and watercolour, 413 × 543

Nationalgalerie, SMB (SM 20a.242)

The striking design for a spacious castle in
Köstritz (in Thuringia), produced in 1802–3
for Count Heinrich XLIII of Reuss-Schleiz-
Köstritz, combines all the characteristics of the
young Schinkel's unique style. This conversion
and expansion of older buildings, planned but
never executed, comprises a long, three-storey
main building, unified on the garden front by
a series of round arches and a two-storey
columned balcony. The main front is flanked
by wings which in their raised corner blocks
still exhibit the massiveness of Gilly's style.
These are balanced by features, such as the
columned portico and subtly diversified
structural elements. The staircase is
characterised by the contrast between the blank
lower walls, the upper surrounding arcades and
the deeply recessed coffering of the ceiling.

Lit.: Berlin 1980, 38–40.

G.R.

10.

THE BOHEMIAN MOUNTAIN RANGE AT TWILIGHT.

c. 1805

Bodycolour, 215 × 353

Nationalgalerie, SMB (SM 2.2)

Schinkel first travelled through Bohemia in 1803, aged twenty-two, on a great cultural tour, whose goal was Italy. Among the hundreds of drawings he brought back from his two-year tour were sketches of the Bohemian central mountain range. This picturesque view, painted after his return, is based on one of these (not preserved). It shows the two principal mountains of the Bohemian range, the Milleschauer and the Kletschen. Schinkel describes the scenery in a letter: 'A steep drop allows one to enjoy behind this place the prospect of a rich valley which soon rises again on the opposite side and ascends to the far mountains, where peaked tops in countless numbers form a broad theatre' (22 June 1803, Riemann 1979, p. 19ff.). The view described must have made such an impression on him that he coloured the drawing, something he rarely did with his pen-and-ink sketches of the time. In those years Schinkel swung between seeing himself as more of a painter or more of an architect – most of his landscape paintings were, however, done before 1815 and his skill as a painter and his Romantic outlook became highly developed.

The monumental aspect of the mountain range, the silhouette of the pine forest, the brilliant phenomena of the evening light are early Romantic features, reminiscent of the landscapes of Caspar David Friedrich. Friedrich discovered the same subject some years later; his *Bohemian landscape with the Milleschauer* of 1807–8 (Gemäldegalerie, Dresden) depicts the Bohemian mountains from almost exactly the same spot.

G.R.

11.

A VIEW FROM THE WINDOW OF MY LODGING IN
ROME, ST. PETER'S IN THE DISTANCE. 1803

Inscribed at the bottom: *Veduta di Roma da mia
Locanda in Monte Pinso presso la chiesa di St.
Trinita dell Monte 1. Villa Pamphili; 2.
Fontana presso St. Pietro dell Monte; 3.–13.
[Numbers given without further details];
14. Castelle St. Angelo; 15. St. Pietro; 16. Il
Vaticano; 17. St. Carlo al Corso; 18–19.
Mausoleo Augusto; 20. Piazza di Spagna*

Pen and brown ink, 295 × 488

Nationalgalerie, SMB (SM 4.56)

While in Rome Schinkel wrote to Count von
Reuss-Schleiz-Köstritz (see cat. 9): 'I have
found a lodging above the great works of art.
From the height of the Monte Pincio my
window overlooks the western part of the city.
Thousands of palaces, surmounted by domes
and towers, spread out before me. In the
distance St Peter's and the Vatican, in a straight
line behind it the Mons Janiculus, crowned by
the pinewood of the Villa Pamfili [sic]. Almost
outside my door I step on to the huge steps of
the church of St Trinitá del Monte, which
leads from the heights to the Piazza d'espagna
[sic] clinging to the foot of the hill.' The sights
have been numbered. The title is taken from
Schinkel's inventory of his best Italian
drawings.

Lit.: Berlin 1980, 46.

G.R.

to have changed a Baroque cupola on the detached tower (shown in a print of 1761) into a late medieval spire. This evidence tends to suggest that Schinkel carried out the drawing for his unexecuted publication of views of Italian medieval architecture, projected in 1805. Several elements in the drawing lived on in Schinkel's work: the fluttering flag is probably the first of the many to adorn his cathedral towers (cf. cat. 22). The drawing is also the first expression of that fascination with detached church towers expressed in the Gertraudenkirche design of 1819 (cat. 101, 102).

Lit.: Berlin 1980, 68.

M.S.

12.

VIEW OF PALERMO CATHEDRAL.   *c.* 1805(?)

Inscribed lower right: *la Cathedrale di Palermo*

Pen and ink and pencil on light blue paper, 547 × 335

Nationalgalerie, SMB (SM 6b.67)

This oblique view of the west front of the cathedral and the detached great western tower has long been believed to have been drawn on the spot by Schinkel or at any rate worked up from sketches. In fact it is directly derived from an engraving after a drawing by Jean Luis Desprez of the late 1770s in the Abbé de Saint Non's *Voyage Pittoresque ou description des royaumes de Naples et de Sicile*, (vol. IV, part I, 1785, pl. 57). Schinkel has emptied Desprez's scene of its lively *staffage* of a royal parade, leaving only the fluttering flag and the canopy over the west door. In the process the shadows have been rearranged and strengthened giving the architecture the emphasis on simple masses characteristic of his worked–up Italian views. It has become entirely his.

    When Schinkel arrived in Palermo the cathedral had just undergone a remodelling, which significantly altered the exterior from that shown by Desprez, who himself appears

The Romantic
Impulse

13.

DESIGN FOR A THEATRE SET, A CATHEDRAL ON AN
EMINENCE ABOVE A LARGE TOWN BY THE SEA.
After 1804

Pen and black and grey ink and pencil,
336 × 572

Nationalgalerie, SMB (SM 23c.83)

The title is taken from a note by Schinkel
referring to this ideal composition, but no
trace can be found of its actual use as a theatre
set, in spite of its strongly scenographic
character. The cathedral is that in Milan and
the town is Trieste, which led to a later title
for the drawing: 'Large composition showing
where Milan Cathedral should be placed'.
 Around 1813–15 Schinkel used the theme of
the Gothic cathedral on an eminence above a
town and above water in several paintings,
with variations in the composition: *Gothic
cathedral by the water*, 1813; *Gothic church on a
cliff by the sea*, 1815; and *Medieval city on a river*,
1815 (cat. 22), all at the Nationalgalerie,
SMPK.

Lit.: Berlin 1980, 78.

G.R. and M.S.

14.

DESIGN FOR A GOTHIC FIRE–SCREEN. Probably *c.* 1815

Inscribed, upper right: *Die Verzierungen werden
 golden so wie die ganzen Füße; der Grund
 hinter den Laubstengeln und Blättern erhält eine
 dunkle schmaltblaue Farbe.*
*Das Basrelief auf der blauen Fläche dürfte nur sehr
 flach seyn damit die kleineren Stengel und die
 flacheren Laubpartien nur mit Gold gemahlt zu
 werden brauchten.*
(The ornamentations and the whole of the feet,
 to be golden; the ground behind the stalks
 of foliage and the leaves to be coloured
 dark smalt blue.
The bas-relief on the blue surface should be
 only very slightly raised, so that the smaller
 stalks and the flatter sections of foliage
 would need only to be painted gold.) and
 with numbers, notes and scale.

Pen and ink, 556 × 333

Nationalgalerie, SMB (SM 37c.176)

The fire-screen was commissioned by Count
Heinrich XLIII of Reuss-Schleiz-Köstritz for
Schloss Köstritz, to display an historically
fascinating series of twenty-eight small oil
paintings from the Prince's collection of Old
German Art: portraits of the people involved

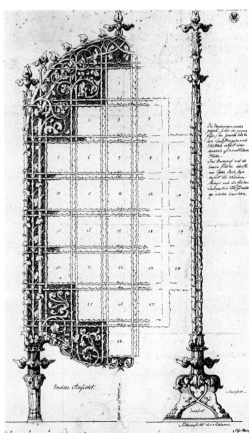

in the story of the kidnapping of the Saxon Princes in 1455.

It is unlikely that the young Schinkel would have created a neo-Gothic screen of this kind during his first visits to Köstritz in 1802 (see cat. 9). We should probably place it in the context of the new wave of nationalistic favour around 1815. In 1817, in Prince Friedrich's Palais in Berlin, Schinkel furnished a 'Gothic' armoury.

B.G.

15.

INTERIOR VIEW OF QUEEN LUISE'S MAUSOLEUM IN
    CHARLOTTENBURG.   1812

Johann Erdmann Hummel (1769–1852)

Ink and watercolour, 442 × 516

Kupferstichkabinett, SMB (KK120–1986)

A mausoleum was to be erected in the park of Schloss Charlottenburg for the queen, who had died on 18 July 1810. On the basis of a sketch by the king, Schinkel designed a Doric prostyle memorial temple which was executed by the Hofbauamt (Court Office of Works) under the direction of Heinrich Gentz. The building of the interior went on until 1812. Christian Daniel Rauch made the marble sarcophagus for the queen, and in the autumn of 1811 his plaster model was temporarily erected and left in place until May 1815. The watercolour shows the view from the portico of the mausoleum into the finished Hall of Remembrance, with the plaster model of the sarcophagus. The watercolour, from the collection of King Friedrich Wilhelm III, exists in one variant in Schloss Charlottenburg and in another in the Nationalgalerie (without the tomb). At the Märkisches Museum, Berlin, is an earlier interior project by Schinkel, with the sarcophagus sideways on; another version is at Charlottenburg. Schinkel's sandstone façade was removed in 1828 and replaced in granite and further modifications took place after 1840, but Schinkel's lamp survives *in situ*.

Lit.: Berlin 1980, 100–103; Berlin 1981, 21, 269.

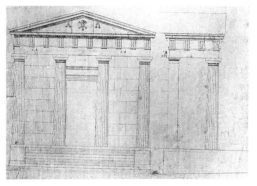

15a. Anonymous hand after Schinkel. Elevation of the portico of the mausoleum in Charlottenburg. Pen and ink and pencil. 381 × 532. SSG, Schloss Charlottenburg.

R.K.

16.

EXTERIOR PERSPECTIVE DESIGN FOR A MEMORIAL
CHAPEL FOR QUEEN LUISE.   1810

Watercolour, 715 × 514

Nationalgalerie, SMB (SM 54.3)

From the same period as the Doric scheme
(cat. 15) comes Schinkel's ideal design of a
Gothic-style three-transept memorial chapel,
which, in tune with the patriotic spirit of the
age, he saw as a medieval, Romantic, companion
piece. Schinkel's architectural interest in the
Gothic started in 1810, reaching its first peak in
1814 with the designs for a medieval cathedral
as a monument to the Wars of Liberation (cat.
21), and the plans for the Gothic rebuilding of
the Petrikirche, the parish church of Berlin-
Kölln. This drawing, together with a ground
plan and interior view, was shown in the
Berlin Academy of 1810. Schinkel's
interpretative catalogue note far transcended its
stated aim, becoming a short treatise on the
principles of architecture in which he strongly
asserted the superiority of Gothic over the
architecture of antiquity.

Lit.: Berlin 1980, 104, 105; Hamburg 1982,
4.4–6.

G.R.

17.

Lettered below: *Versuch die liebliche sehnsuchtsvolle Wehmuth auszudrücken welche das Herz beim Klange des Gottesdienstes aus der Kirche herschallend erfüllt, auf Stein gezeichnet von Schinkel.* (Try to express the yearning beauty of the melancholy which fills the heart as the sounds of holy worship ring out from the church, drawn on stone by Schinkel.)

Pen lithograph, 487 × 343

Nationalgalerie, SMB (SM 54.1)

This print is one of Schinkel's most important graphic works and one of the earliest examples of lithography in Berlin, which began in 1809 with the foundation of Georg Decker's Institute of Lithography.

It also expresses perfectly the Romantics' search for the complete work of art uniting harmoniously all the manifestations of man and nature, architecture and religion, poetry and music. The text Schinkel has inscribed beneath his composition shows the interrelation of all these elements, as he conjures up the intense emotions released by the sounds ringing out from the church. The lithograph shows figures scaled down as they walk between the gravestones or descend the church steps. High above them, behind tall leafy trees, rises the west front of a great Gothic church, whose rose window finds a natural counterpart in the large petals of the sunflowers, facing the light as they bloom by a gravestone near some roses.

Schinkel has given the church, which shimmers through the tree-tops, a symbolic relationship to its natural surroundings – both glorify God. The great church or cathedral, a recurring theme in Schinkel's work, also symbolises love of liberty and national energy, of particular importance during the Napoleonic occupation. In style, Schinkel's architecture echoes both Italian cathedrals and the Minsters of Strasburg and Freiburg.

Similar ideas inspired Schinkel's Gothic design for Queen Luise's burial chapel which was projected at the same time. According to Schinkel, he intended to combine plant forms evoking life's ceaseless renewal with musical sounds which for him embodied the purest manifestation of divine inspiration in art.

Schinkel developed the graphic style of this lithograph during his first journey to Italy. We see a similar style in several large drawings made of scenes from the Salzkammergut (cat. 18). This and other lithographs were shown in 1810 at the Autumn Exhibition of the Berlin Academy.

Lit.: Berlin 1980, 93; Berlin 1981, 157.

M.U.R.–R.

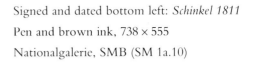

18.

WATERFALL AT GASTEIN.

Signed and dated bottom left: *Schinkel 1811*

Pen and brown ink, 738 × 555

Nationalgalerie, SMB (SM 1a.10)

In 1803, on his great Italian tour, the young
Schinkel had already become familiar with the
landscape of the Alps, but many of the
drawings of that journey were still hampered
by youthful awkwardness. It was not until he
encountered Joseph Anton Koch and his
landscape art in Rome that Schinkel found
inspiration for the monumental drawings of his
Sicilian impressions, some of which were not
produced until his return to Berlin.

After a stay in the Salzkammergut in Austria
with his wife Susanne in 1811, and his recent
experience of the mountains, he was able to
develop his drawing style still further. First
came sketches, of which some twenty have
been preserved, which he composed in Berlin
into a number of large pen-and-ink drawings:
they are among the most important of
Schinkel's achievements as a draughtsman
during these years. His landscape interpretation
tends entirely to the large scale and, typically,
evidence of human existence is added to
nature.

The majestic scenery which unfolds around
the *Waterfall at Gastein* is enriched by the
works of man: the group of Alpine buildings –
an inn with its outhouses – and the bridge
crossing the waterfall. The Alpine house is of
special interest in relation to Schinkel's
architectural outlook: the dual aspect of
technical construction and aesthetic perfection
must have captivated him. Study sketches,
designs and even completed buildings bear
testimony to this, as does his later, admiring
observation of 1836 (letter to his brother-in-
law Wilhelm Berger, in Mackowsky 1922,
p. 183).

Schinkel's landscapes of 1811 stand at the
start of the artistic discovery of the
Salzkammergut, where in the next two
decades a great part of the Romantic discovery
of landscape by German artists was to take
place.

Lit.: Berlin 1980, 91; Berlin 1981, 166.

G.R.

19.

PORTRAIT OF THE ARTIST'S WIFE, SUSANNE.

c. 1810–13

Pencil and black and grey wash, 850 × 595

Nationalgalerie, SMB (SM D.7)

The considerable size and delicate execution of
this drawing give it a particularly meaningful
painterly quality. We see the full-length
standing figure of the young woman in front
of the balustrade of a balcony which opens out
behind her like a window on to a landscape; to
the right we see the façade of a Gothic
cathedral with leafy trees, and to the left the
sea and horizon.

Schinkel's wife was born on 5 October 1782
in the mercantile seaport of Stettin. She was
called Susanne or Susette after her mother,
whose family had Huguenot roots. In the late-
Gothic balustrade of the balcony Schinkel has
stylised the pairs of mouchettes, on the
woman's right and left, into an 'S', and shaped
into a heart the leaf-shaped ornaments at the
base of the wall which firmly frames the figure
on both sides of the picture. Schinkel softens
the harshness of the stone window opening
with some climbing ivy which 'wreathes' the
standing figure. These Romantic touches
clearly express Schinkel's deep love for his
young wife, so evident in the letters he wrote
to her when they were apart.

They married on 17 August 1809. Married
life was financially uncertain until 1810, when
Wilhelm von Humboldt helped Schinkel gain
the post of Oberbauassessor. Susanne had four
children by Schinkel: Marie and Susanne in
1810 and 1811, their only son Karl Raphael in
1813, and after nine years the youngest
daughter Elisabeth, who married Alfred von
Wolzogen, later Schinkel's first biographer.

We assume that Schinkel has drawn his
young wife in the early stages of one of her
first three pregnancies, though he probably
wanted to convey a Romantic image of her
whole existence, rather than simply to capture
a faithful likeness. In a similar vein, Friedrich
Schlegel, writing in the magazine *Europa* in
1803, had called for 'symbolic' portraits. By
relating the background landscape
meaningfully to the portrait as a two-way
mirror, Schinkel intended to release the sitter's
features from the limitations of the portrait.

Thus we see Susanne standing in a long,
dark, very simple dress, her head slightly bent,
her left hand resting on her body under her
breast. In the girlish face the eyes are lowered,
like those of Gothic madonnas, pensive,
dreamy, reflecting calm contentment.
Radiating stillness and confidence, she looks
the very embodiment of hope. Schinkel seems

to be expressing his own emotions about her
pregnancy, and it is tempting to assume that he
drew her immediately in 1810. Yet the
symbolic content of the background depicting
a cathedral and the sea – recurring Romantic
metaphors for faith and freedom in Schinkel's
oeuvre – suggest 1813, the year of liberation
from Napoleon, and of the birth of their son,
though also of the death of Susanne's father.

The signs of new hope in the landscape lead
the eye from the dark shadow on the floor in
front of the woman towards the brightness of
day. Perhaps Schinkel was combining the
major emotional upheavals in his personal life
and the fate of the Fatherland into a single
image commemorating those three years.

Lit.: Berlin 1980, 109.

M.U.R.-R.

20.

Iron and silver, h. 42

SSG Schloss Charlottenburg

On 10 March 1813, seven days before the appeal 'An Mein Volk' ('To my People') to join in the War of Liberation against Napoleon, King Friedrich Wilhelm III instituted the Iron Cross as a military decoration. This Order for services to the Fatherland in the battle against France had a simplicity and lack of material value intended to recall the hard and iron days in which it was instituted.

This, the best known of all Prussian war decorations, consists of a silver-mounted iron cross *pattée*, with slightly curved arms. The outer edge of the silver border is flat and the transition to the black field consists of a grooved beading.

As early as August 1811, August Neidhardt von Gneisenau had proposed the introduction of decorations with Prussian symbols. Notes from the king and early sketches reveal that from the beginning the concept had been that of a decoration comparable to the Cross and Colours of the Teutonic Order.

The final version goes back to a drawing by Schinkel of *c*. 1813, showing the original reverse of the Cross, 2nd Class, with the crowned monogram FW (Friedrich Wilhelm) above an oakleaf trefoil and under this the year, 1813. The front of the cross was originally undecorated. Only later was the reverse worn as the front.

The Iron Cross became the most important military symbol of Prussia and was the first Prussian war decoration which could be awarded to both officers and men. The Grand Cross, worn round the neck, was a special form, twice the size of the original Iron Cross.

Lit.: Berlin 1981, 295.

W.B.

21.

SKETCH DESIGN FOR A CATHEDRAL AS A
MEMORIAL TO THE WARS OF LIBERATION.
1814–15

Pencil, 200 × 160

Nationalgalerie, SMB (SM 20b.25)

The idea of the re-creation of a medieval cathedral in all its various features, which preoccupied Schinkel from 1810 onwards, is one of the most important in his architectural philosophy. A series of preparatory sketches preceded the design of the great cathedral project of 1814–15. The planning of a magnificent cathedral in Berlin was inspired by the victorious end to the Wars of Liberation in 1814.

In June of that year the king gave orders for Schinkel to supply designs for 'a splendid cathedral, a thanksgiving memorial for Prussia, to be erected in Berlin'. By the summer of 1814 the first memorandum had been written, in which (and in a second dated January 1815) he expressed far-ranging ideas about the building as a religious, historical and 'living' monument. By the last he meant that through it 'something is to be established for the people, which by the very nature of its installation, will live on and bear fruit'. From this idea his hope was that 'the erection of this monument must be the supreme point of all the higher art industry of the country, all the outstanding artists must work on it, and throughout this period the highest perfection of execution would become such a beneficent and practical school that the true purpose of artists and their work would be reborn in it'.

In contrast to the site on the Spittelmarkt chosen by the king, Schinkel proposed the Leipziger Platz in its isolated position before the Potsdamer Tor, where Friedrich Gilly had envisaged his project of a memorial to Friedrich II (cat. 5). Early in 1815 Schinkel submitted the design to the king with a second memorandum in the form of a number of large drawings.

The great plan was comparable with the plan for a national Hall of Fame, which arose at the same time, a so-called 'Valhalla' in the old Germanic sense (a favourite idea of that enthusiastic builder, King Ludwig I of Bavaria), but it was never executed. The idea was realised in a greatly reduced form in the Berlin Kreuzberg monument (cat. 23). The nationally conceived plan to complete Cologne Cathedral can also be associated with the ambitions of the king, the Crown Prince and Schinkel to erect a Gothic cathedral in Berlin.

Lit.: Berlin 1980, 156–61a; Hamburg 1980, 4.9–4.13.

G.R.

22.

A MEDIEVAL CITY ON A RIVER.   1815

Oil on canvas, 940 × 1400

Nationalgalerie, SMPK (SM A.2)

In 1814 Schinkel contributed to the decorations celebrating Friedrich Wilhelm III's return from the field. Here, a year later, he depicts a prince returning from a campaign. He rides beneath a canopy towards his castle, in a long procession of warriors. The still uncompleted cathedral, illustrating, in association with the castle, the unity of crown and church, appears under a rainbow, which gives the picture its central image of peace after a storm. Oak trees in the foreground reinforce the landscape's German character, whilst in the background Schinkel depicts a medieval German city, evoking memories of Prague, where he stayed in 1803 and 1811. The positions of the cathedral and the castle on the mountain reinforce this impression. The cathedral itself embodies several ideas. The return to the Middle Ages symbolises hope for future national unity on the pattern of the Holy Roman Empire of the German nation. Accordingly, both a tower towards the middle of the picture on the right and the large white flag waving from the uncompleted cathedral spire display the Imperial eagle. The spire is incomplete for two reasons: first, as a practising architect, Schinkel liked to reflect on the process of building a cathedral, and secondly, the current interest was in finishing projects the Middle Ages had been unable to complete. Later, for instance, Cologne Cathedral was completed in this spirit.

The position of the sun suggests it is evening. A companion picture, destroyed in the Second World War, depicted a Greek city in the morning. Schinkel had Pericles' Athens in mind. He saw both ancient Greek culture and German medieval culture as models pointing towards Prussia's future development.

Lit.: Berlin 1980, 99a, 99b; Berlin 1981, 180; Berlin 1986, pp. 74–6.

H.B.–S.

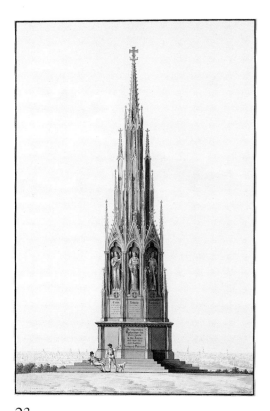

23.

THE MONUMENT TO THE LIBERATION ON THE
    KREUZBERG, BERLIN.   1819

Ludwig Meyer (active 1813–24) and Carl
    Ohmann (active 1817–23)

Lettered below left: *Entworfen von Schinkel*
(Designed by Schinkel); below right: *Unter
Leitung des Major von Reiche, in Stein
geschnitten von Meyer und Ohmann* (Under
the direction of Major von Reiche, drawn
on stone by Meyer and Ohmann)

Hand-coloured lithograph, 665 × 435

Kupferstichkabinett, SMB (KK 619–120)

Crown Prince Friedrich Wilhelm, for whom
Schinkel had designed a series of cast-iron
Gothic war memorials in 1817, suggested that
the National Memorial to the Fallen should be
in patriotic Gothic, not the classical column
first conceived by Schinkel. Even so, the
earliest sketches, of 1818, are a mix of classical
and Gothic. The executed memorial was
placed on the Tempelhofer Berg (which was
immediately renamed the Kreuzberg)
overlooking the Army's exercise grounds. The
massive pinnacled spire, now known as the
Kreuzberg monument, was made in cast iron
at the Royal Foundry between 1818 and 1821,
and is the true descendant of the unexecuted
project for the Cathedral of the Liberation (cat.
21). The whole conception, said by Schinkel to

have borrowed details from Cologne
Cathedral, may have been inspired by an
English Gothic Eleanor Cross.

    The octagonal substructure is carried on a
stepped platform of the same shape, and the
monument seems to be growing out of the soil
of the homeland. On the plinth the dedication
honours the victorious defenders of the
Fatherland; above this, as if crowned by the
spire, stand the geniuses of the great battles (to
be designed and modelled by Tieck, Rauch
and Ludwig Wichmann), on pedestals adorned
with the wreathed Iron Cross, the distinction
for bravery in the Wars of Liberation (cat. 20).
The Cross flowering from the tip of the
monument offers them up to heaven. This
print records an intermediate presentation
drawing; Schinkel was soon dissatisfied with
the hilltop as the natural place for the
monument. He removed it from an
earthbound to an ideal sphere, on a gigantic
platform approached by eleven steps, and
surrounded it with railings commanding
respect, whose corner-posts also pick up the
pinnacle shape. In 1871 the monument was
again raised, and turned.

    This is the first state of the print, without
title (*Das Nationalmonument auf dem Tempelhofer
Berge bey Berlin*). It was apparently published to
commemorate the laying of the foundation
stone in September 1819.

Lit.: Berlin 1980, 177–8a; Berlin 1981, 38;
    Hamburg 1982, 416–19.

                      R.K. and M.S.

24.

DESIGN FOR A MONUMENT TO HERMANN OF THE
    CHERUSCI.   1814–15

Black chalk, watercolour, heightened with
    white, on blue paper, 609 × 899

Nationalgalerie, SMB (SM 36a.1)

This design, arising from the spirit of the Wars
of Liberation and probably parallel to the
1814–15 design for a Berlin Liberation
Fountain, but not linked to any known
commission, is one of Schinkel's most
romantic and idealistic ideas for a monument.
The dimensions of the group of a Germanic
warrior on horseback trying to kill a fallen
Roman, which combines figures from
Raphael's 1512 fresco of the *Expulsion of
Heliodorus* in the Vatican with the idea of St
George vanquishing the dragon, would make
it impossible to execute. On the sides of the
polygonal base, sacrificial fires from projecting
ships' bows create a Romantic atmosphere and
lighting.

    Hermann (Arminius), a prince of the
Cherusci, united the German tribes, inflicting a
traumatic defeat against Quintilius Varus in
AD 9. Inspired by G.F. Klopstock's odes on
Hermann (1769, 1784 and 1787), there had
been renewed interest in the hero as an
inspirational model from the beginning of the
nineteenth century (for example Kleist's
Hermannschlacht and de la Motte-Fouqué's

Hermann of 1808). The idea emerged of a memorial on the supposed site of Hermann's victory over the Roman Legions in the Teutoburg Forest. The originally more anti-Napoleonic tendency, in which Rome is equated with France, has turned into a generally nationalist aim.

Lit.: Berlin 1980, 176d.

G.R.

25.

MEDALLION IN HONOUR OF FIELD MARSHAL
    GEBHARD LEBERECHT BLÜCHER, PRINCE OF
    WAHLSTATT.   1816

Anton Friedrich König the Younger (1756–
    1838) after Schinkel

Inscribed: Obverse: *Schinkel inv: König fec:* Circumscription: *Dem Fürsten von Wahlstatt die Bürger Berlins im Jahr 1816* (To the Prince of Wahlstatt the citizens of Berlin 1816) Reverse: *1813, 1814, 1815*

Cast iron, lacquered, diam. 80

Kunstgewerbemuseum, SMB (M.2941)

The obverse of the medallion shows Blücher in profile, wearing the lion-skin which identifies him as Hercules, as in Schadow's statue of the field marshal for Rostock (1816–19). The reverse depicts St Michael's victory over Satan, a motif often used by Schinkel after the Wars of Liberation (cf. the portal sculpture on the Friedrich-Werder Kirche in Berlin, and cat. 26). It symbolises the victory over Napoleon, as do the three years inscribed on the reverse: 1813 (Battle of the Nations at Leipzig), 1814 (peace concluded in Paris), 1815 (Battle of Waterloo).
    The medallion was originally commissioned by the citizens of Berlin and on 4 June 1817

one gold and two silver copies were presented to Blücher in Karlsbad. Copies were also cast in bronze; this cast-iron copy, made by the Royal Iron Foundry in Berlin, is a rarity.

Lit.: Berlin 1980, 425, 425a; Berlin 1981, 298.

C.M.

26.

SKETCH DESIGN FOR PRESENTATION SWORD.   1817

Pencil, 892 × 198

Nationalgalerie, SMB (SM 37.135)

The hilt of the sword is adorned with a depiction of St Michael, similar to the one on the reverse of the Blücher medallion (cat. 25). A drawing of the archangel (SM 39d.139), erroneously associated by Wolzogen with the medallion, can probably be regarded as another design for the decorative roundel on the hilt. The scabbard shows, above, two figures holding out their hands to each other; a detailed study (SM 37.135d) identifies them as warriors. Then come arabesques and a space for the inscription, which is given in another study (SM 37.135b) as: 'DONNE PAR LES OFFICIERS DE L'ARMEE PRUSSIENNE A HENRI DE LA ROCHE IAQUELEIN FILS DE LOUIS DE LA ROCHE IAQUELEIN NEVEU HENRI DE LA ROCHE IAQUELEIN ET DE LOUIS DE L'ESCURE'. A female robed figure flanked by two shields, the upper one with the three Bourbon lilies, the lower with the Prussian eagle, decorates the lower part of the scabbard.
    In his memoirs Schadow writes: 'A costly sword was made after Schinkel's drawing, on its scabbard, between embellishments, St Michael very successfully executed as the principal emblem. This sword was intended as a gift for the valiant La Roche Jacquelin in France' (Schadow 1849, p. 123). The Fourth Prussian Army Corps Bülow-Dennewitz presented the gilt bronze sword (French private collection) to the son of the Bourbon supporter Louis du Vergier, Marquis de la Rochejacquelein who fell in Prussian service at the storming of Montmartre in 1814. A plaster cast was presented to the Schinkel Museum by the sculptor Wilhelm Wolff (Nationalgalerie, SMB).
    In place of the draped figure we find here Joan of Arc, also shown in detailed study (SM 37.135c). The reverse shows Saint Louis, King of France, and the inscription in German translation. The commemoration of Saint Louis and Joan of Arc is regarded as a Romantic reminder of France's royalist tradition going back to the Middle Ages.

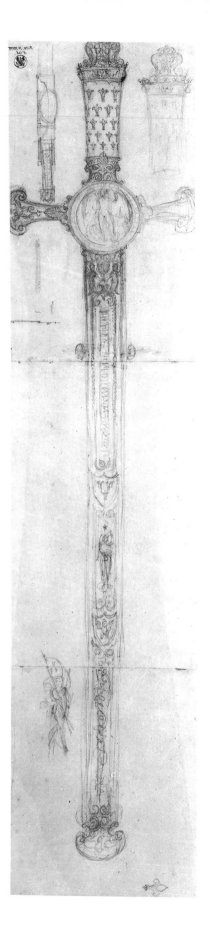

The sword was cast in iron in the second half of the nineteenth century at the Ilsenburg Foundry (SSG Schloss Charlottenburg, Inv. No. KS IV). Schinkel also designed a pair of marble candelabra, carved by Tieck and Rauch, for the La Rochejacquelein mausoleum at St Aubin-de-Baubigné.

Lit.: Berlin 1981, 302; Zick 1980.

C.M.

26a. Detail of the hilt of the gilt bronze sword made after Schinkel's design. French Private Collection. La Roche-sur-Yon, Conservation départementale des Musées de Vendée. Photo reproduced in catalogue, *Traces des Guerres de Vendée dans la Mémoire Collective*, 1983, fig.37.

The Theatre

27.

DESIGN FOR AN OPTICAL PERSPECTIVE PICTURE: THE FIRE OF MOSCOW. 1812

Inscribed bottom right: *gez. von Schinkel* (drawn by Schinkel)

Pen and brown ink and wash, 450 × 640

Nationalgalerie, SMB (SM 1b.32)

Schinkel became interested in theatre at the very beginning of his career. The first piece of work the twenty-one-year-old showed in the Berlin Academy Exhibition of 1802 was his set design for Euripides' tragedy *Iphigenie in Aulis*. Thanks to his outstanding education, strong will, organisational skill and unflagging enthusiasm he was able to master projects which often ran concurrently. Schinkel's genius also enabled him to introduce new and lasting elements into theatre design. Schinkel not only had extraordinary gifts, including a sophisticated musical sense, but he was also able to develop them by meeting and forming friendships with many of the leading intellectuals of his day. His first practical experience as an architect, for instance, introduced him in about 1802 to Prince Anton Heinrich Radziwill, who was highly gifted musically, and stagestruck.

In 1820 Schinkel designed the sets for a second private production: scenes from Goethe's *Faust*, which Prince Radziwill staged in Schloss Monbijou with his own musical score. Only Schinkel's design for Gretchen's

room has survived. Schinkel's place in theatre history is assured not least because this was the first time a room with three walls and a ceiling above was shown on stage.

Schinkel used to read Greek dramas with his childhood friend the philosopher, Karl Wilhelm Ferdinand Solger, and it was traditional for eighteenth-century architects to extend their activities into theatre design. For Schinkel an important step along this road was meeting the entrepreneur Wilhelm Gropius, with his 'Mechanical Theatre'. Schinkel certainly regarded inventing and making pictures for this as serious work, and he started to develop this alongside his oil painting. Accompanied by music and commentaries, these presentations became a fashionable entertainment for Berliners. He constructed scenographic spectacles with perspectives so sophisticated and realistic that they created astounding illusions of space.

Schinkel's magnificent views of distant cities such as Constantinople or Jerusalem (1807), or his enormous panorama of Palermo (1808), which he constructed himself, were on everyone's lips. After pictures of famous Roman buildings and the sights of Italy (1809), when Gropius opened new premises at his theatre in 1812, Schinkel created further sensational spectacles, including the Fire of Moscow. The royal couple's visit to one of Schinkel's presentations helped enhance his growing reputation, and resulted in a civil service appointment in 1810. Now free from acute money worries, Schinkel continued to pursue his theatrical interests.

The skills he acquired working on these spectacles led him straight to set design. In 1813 he approached Iffland, the theatre director about the post of set designer, vacant since the death of Bartolomeo Verona, court and theatre painter. Schinkel was even prepared to work without a salary, immediately putting forward suggestions for innovations in set design. For one reason or another – there was talk of disagreement between Iffland and the court, and at that time Schinkel seemed to be its protégé – Iffland refused his request.

Until 1815, when he was appointed by Count Brühl, the new theatre director, Schinkel concentrated hard on ideas for reforming theatre architecture, especially the stage itself. These studies formed the basis of his so-called 'Memorandum' to Iffland, which looked to the future. When Schinkel was commissioned to rebuild the Schauspielhaus after the fire in 1817, these studies came to fruition.

To inaugurate his fruitful collaboration with Brühl – in just under fifteen years Schinkel designed over a hundred sets for more than thirty plays – Schinkel designed his sensationally successful sets for *The Magic Flute*.

Here, Schinkel's reforming zeal combined with his supreme pictorial ingenuity to create highly convincing effects. He had everything at his disposal: architectonic and technical resources, perspective, artificial lighting, painterly skills. He had studied every style of architecture and his unflagging imagination could exploit them all.

His achievement in reforming the stage lay in replacing Baroque fixed flats by an illusionistic painted background, or backcloth. The actors performed between the proscenium arch and changing flats. A new form of fixed, fairly deep proscenium arch, framed the action; in *The Magic Flute* this represented a dark, rocky grotto in all the outdoor scenes. The flats could be moved downstage or upstage as the drama demanded. The shock effect of these rapid scene changes must have been most impressive. Schinkel's contained stage spaces spelled the end of bulky Baroque three-dimensional sets, with which the actors were often forced to compete, and were a step along the road towards the principle of the proscenium stage which is still effective today.

Instead of a physical illusion Schinkel wanted set designers to foster really 'genuine, ideal illusions' in the audience's mind, as ancient theatre had. A 'simpler' approach to stage design would trigger off the audience's 'creative imagination', allowing the drama to work on them to their spiritual benefit.

Both in form and in content, however, Schinkel's set designs gradually underwent a transformation from an initially idealistic, symbolic approach to one of increasing historical accuracy. In this he was following a general tendency which reached its apotheosis towards the end of the century in the Meiningen company's unimaginative stress on historical fact.

From his base in Berlin Schinkel had brought about a decisive revolution in staging during the Romantic period. Henceforth sets and costumes would blend meaningfully with a play's action and intellectual content giving drama new substance. In his own theatre sets, which harmoniously united archaeological accuracy and artistic imagination, Schinkel provided the most splendid examples of this development.

Only two subjects from the optical perspective pictures relate to specific events: the battle of Leipzig and the Fire of Moscow. The Fire of Moscow spectacle is the only sketch to survive in such finished detail. Like the Battle of Leipzig in 1813 this spectacle was probably completed for Christmas presentation. Three French soldiers which Schinkel cut out of paper (SM 39d.193) also relate to these two projects.

Lit.: Berlin 1980, 80.

M.U.R.-R.

28.

DESIGN FOR THE MAGIC FLUTE: THE HALL OF STARS IN THE PALACE OF THE QUEEN OF THE NIGHT. ACT I, SCENE 2 (SECOND SET DESIGN).
1847–9 (the original 1815)

Karl Friedrich Thiele (1780–1836) after Schinkel

Lettered below: *Schinkel del. Thiele sc.: – Decoration zu der Oper* (Set design for the opera): *Die Zauberflöte* (*The Magic Flute*) *Act I, Scene VI*

Aquatint, hand-coloured, 228 × 349

SSG, Potsdam-Sanssouci

For this scene the librettist Schikaneder suggested a 'magnificent chamber' and a throne embellished with 'transparent stars'. Schinkel shows the queen standing on a crescent moon riding on dark clouds. A vast, dark blue, starry sky arches above her. Surprisingly Schinkel uses here the image of a woman on a crescent moon and crowned by stars which we associate with the madonna (symbolising Mary's Immaculate Conception) – an extremely dramatic way to evoke the dark (female) powers which the Queen of the Night embodies. More significantly, the image of the crescent moon madonna derived from a description in the Book of Revelations of the apocalyptic woman who, clothed in the sun, standing on the moon, and crowned with twelve stars, tramples the serpent underfoot.

Schinkel may well have been influenced by a print of a Baroque set design by Lodovico Ottavio Burnacini. It shows Venus ringed with rays of light, the Milky Way arching behind her, and parellel to this a large arch of flame above and small one below – with the flats stage left and right depicting low rocks and clouds. The set is for Piero Antonio Cesti's 1668 opera, *Il pomo d'oro* (cf. Wolff 1968, pl. 30).

The strictly symmetrical composition of the heavenly vault – a vertical canopy in Schinkel's version – the queen floating on a sickle moon, and Venus radiant in her aureole before arches of flames suggest a common inspiration. In the Baroque design, however, we can also discern the image of 'Majestas Domini' (the Majesty of the Lord): Christ in a fiery ring of light, enthroned on the semicircle of heaven, his feet supported on the smaller semicircle of the earth.

This design for the Queen of the Night was the most impressive of all and is still quite popular for productions. *Das Dramaturgische Wochenblatt*, reviewing all twelve set designs in March 1816, wrote: 'The second set design, the great inner vault of the Palace of the Queen of the Night, is astounding when the Queen herself appears. Even if the décor has little artistic merit – a blue heavenly vault spangled with regular arches of stars – the way the designer conceives the Queen of the Night's appearance could yet prove to be sublime and inspired . . .'

The original design in body colour (Nationalgalerie SMB, SM 22c.121) was published in reduced size as an aquatint in 1823. The present example comes from the reissued plates, published by Ferdinand Riegel in Potsdam, 1847–9.

Lit.: Berlin 1980, 112; Berlin 1981, 210b.

M.U.R.–R.

29.

Body colour over pen and brown ink,
    542 × 625

Nationalgalerie, SMB (SM Th. 13)

Whereas the librettist Schikaneder saw the whole stage transformed into a sun, Schinkel constructed imposing Egyptian architecture. His design shows a mighty gate-like structure downstage, probably intended as wings. Looking further, we see the raised throne bearing the figure of Osiris, with low colonnaded halls on either side surmounted by palm-covered terraces. Two Egyptian pylons reappear, that had previously been used for Sarastro's fortified palace. At the very back the outlines of a vast pyramid glimmer. Within its triangle the sun's halo gleams, encircling Osiris's head and further enhancing the ceremonial quality of the strictly centralised composition.

Schinkel must have carried out extensive research for his Egyptian designs. Among the key works he consulted were the travel journals of Dominique Vivant Denon, who accompanied Napoleon on his 1798–9 campaign: *Voyage dans la Haute et la Basse Egypte*, published in 1802, and *Description de l'Egypte*, of 1809–13. Wolzogen mentions one fascinating drawing by Schinkel among his sketches for scenographic spectacle: *Das ägyptische Labyrinth* (The Egyptian Labyrinth) (1812, SM 22d.92 destroyed in the Second World War), which is inscribed: 'A labyrinth in Crete'. The objects depicted here are very like the architecture in *The Magic Flute*.

The Magic Flute, with a libretto by Emanuel Schinkaneder and music by Wolfgang Amadeus Mozart, was first performed in 1787. Schinkel designed twelve sets for a new production whose first night was on 18 January 1816 (the date of the Coronation and the Celebration of the Peace).

Schinkel's sets became a tremendous success, and with a foreword by Brühl, they were published by Ludwig Wilhelm Wittich from 1819 to 1824 with other Schinkel designs as *Decorationen auf den königlichen Hoftheatern zu Berlin* (Set Designs for Royal Court Theatres in Berlin) in five volumes (32 sheets) of aquatints (volumes 1–3 coloured). Of the twelve original designs for *The Magic Flute* ten are still in the Schinkel Museum (Nationalgalerie, SMB). The first set was destroyed during the Second World War. The sixth was already missing in the nineteenth century.

The simplicity and calm conviction of these compositions have remained unique of their kind. The idea of an exotic Egyptian location for this operatic fairy tale set nowhere in particular and the charm of the unfamiliar, suggested by Schikaneder's libretto, may have contributed to its success. Behind the consistently Egyptian style of architecture, which confirms how thoroughly Schinkel did his research, we can detect the classical architectural principles of his much-admired friend and tutor, Friedrich Gilly. The symmetry of the compositions and the contrast between geometric structural elements and highly mobile organic forms give these designs a monumental quality.

Schinkel is throughout trying to reflect in his décor the symbolism of this magical operatic fairy tale, the struggle between the powers of darkness and light. He also uses chiaroscuro effects and careful colour variation to interpret or clarify the humanitarian ideals of the Enlightenment in the plot. These symbolic backcloths were the first expression of the ideas on the reform of theatre architecture and set design, which had been formulated in Schinkel's 'Memorandum' to the theatre director Iffland of 1813.

Lit.: Berlin 1980, 121; Berlin 1981, 210h.

M.U.R.–R.

30.

DESIGN FOR ARIODANT: THE GARDEN AT EDGAR'S PALACE, ILLUMINATED FOR A SOIRÉE.   1816

Inscribed bottom centre (in red body colour):
Garten bei Edgars Palaste zu einem Nachtfeste erleuchtet

Body colour, 452 × 632

Nationalgalerie, SMB (SM 22c.122)

Ariondant, an *opéra comique* in three acts, with music by Etienne Nicolas Méhul and a libretto by François Benoit Hoffman, opened in Paris in 1799. It was performed at the Königliche Opernhaus, Berlin on 1 June 1816. Méhul, the most famous composer of the revolutionary period, was also popular and not without influence in Germany. The libretto was based on Ariosto's *Orlando furioso*, a source Handel had used in 1735 for his opera *Ariodante*. The action, set in medieval Scotland, is a story of love, jealousy and despair. The noble knight Ariodant's love for Ginevra, a Scottish princess, is severely tested, but finally triumphs after Ariodant wins a 'trial by ordeal' in the form of a duel. Shakespeare used the same psychological situation in *Cymbeline*. In this opera, probably his best, Méhul went beyond the traditional arias and created 'Romantic scenes', a form which reached its zenith with Verdi. The genius of Méhul's music suited perfectly the material's emotional and dramatic content, and Schinkel's set designs underscored the bleakness of the action throughout.

Despite the torchlight laid on for a festive occasion, the scene is forbidding. Even the narrow crescent moon and stars in the slightly cloudy night sky hardly soften the picture's severity. The tall dark firs, towering behind the balustrade to the right and left of the steps which lead directly down to the sea, seem to be responsible for this impression. For Schinkel they symbolise Scotland, as do the cliffs from which the castle rises.

Lit.: Berlin 1980, 125.

M.U.R.-R.

31.

DESIGN FOR FERNANDO CORTEZ: THE PERUVIAN FIRE TEMPLE.   1818

Body colour, 413 × 589

Nationalgalerie, SMB (SM Th.21)

After *The Vestal Virgin* (1807), Gaspare Spontini established his reputation with *Fernando Cortez* in 1809. The opera, with a libretto by J.E. Esménard and V.J. Etienne de Jouy after the tragedy by Alexis Pirow, had already been performed in German in Berlin in 1814, and for the production opening at the Royal Opera House in Berlin on 20 April 1818 it was to have new décor by Schinkel. The king, who had seen Spontini's new version of his opera in Paris in 1817, was fascinated by the beguiling music drama. In the teeth of anti-Italian resentment and nationalism, not least from Theatre Director Brühl, he appointed Spontini Principal Conductor and Director-General of Music in Berlin from 1 September 1819.

In this set design for Act I (one of four designs in three Acts) Schinkel prefers an oblique perspective, giving a sense of depth as the eye travels into the fortified, walled courtyard of a very strange-looking temple. In the centre foreground stands a statue of Telapulcas, the God of Evil, with snakes in his hands and coiling round his feet, supported on a globe flanked by two tigers. The figure of

the god recalls Huitzlipochtili, the God of
War, as depicted, for instance, in an engraving
in Antonio de Solis's *The Conquest of Mexico*.
This work, published in German in 1750–1,
was a source for Cortez's exploits in Mexico
for the opera *Montezuma*, by Frederick the
Great and Carl Heinrich Graun.

Behind the god in Schinkel's picture is a tall,
tower-like edifice with steep walls, and on the
left narrow steps lead up to the top, where fires
are burning on a platform. Doors cut into the
courtyard walls are framed by pointed towers,
studded from top to bottom with skulls which
look like a decorative pattern of dots. Blue
tones make the overall effect at once magical
and sinister.

Lit.: Hamburg 1982, 10.29.

M.U.R.–R.

32.

DESIGN FOR THE MAID OF ORLEANS: AN OPEN
   GOTHIC PORTICO WITH A VIEW OF THE CITY
   OF RHEIMS AND THE CATHEDRAL.   1818

Pen and ink and body colour, 455 × 555

Nationalgalerie, SMB (SM Th.19)

Friedrich Schiller's romantic tragedy in five
acts was performed on 18 January 1818 at the
Royal Opera House in Berlin. Schinkel
designed three sets: the rest were either
designed by other artists or were, in the usual
way, supplemented from stock.

In this set for Act IV, scenes 1–3, Schinkel
was following more closely the trend of the
times, emphasising a scene's historical accuracy
rather than interpreting it in an idealistic or
symbolic way. He turns Schiller's 'festively
decorated hall' into a truly majestic space,
imbued with a particularly appealing charm
which one is tempted to call feminine. A
Gothic portico in the English Perpendicular
style gives on to a balcony with two
ornamental pillars supporting a canopy-like fan
vault. Through them we clearly see the
cathedral, and by this means Schinkel
prefigures the next scene, the coronation.

With all the emphasis on historical accuracy,
Schinkel provides a splendid framework here
for the conversation between the two women
prior to the coronation: St Joan, desperately
sad because her love for an Englishman makes
her feel like a traitor, and Agnes Sorel, elated
because she knows her lover King Charles VII
is about to see all his dreams come true.

Lit.: Berlin 1981, 129, Berlin 1981, 218a.

M.U.R.–R.

Early Interiors

33.

DESIGN FOR AN ARMCHAIR, FOR THE KÖNIGLICHES PALAIS, BERLIN. 1808

Pen and ink, with colour washes, 157 × 136

Nationalgalerie, SMB (SM 37b.113)

In Schinkel's early *oeuvre* hardly any records of his furniture designs have survived. In his perspective Design for a Colonnaded Hall with columns by the Sea of 1802 (cat. 8) the furniture does show clearly that Schinkel borrowed ideas for styles from his mentor, Friedrich Gilly. We first see examples of Schinkel's interior design work in his refurbishing of the Chamois Room in the Königliches Palais (formerly the Kronprinzen Palais, Unter den Linden). In preparation for the royal couple's return to Berlin from Memel, originally expected in 1808, an entry in the inventory dated October of that year tells us the room was refurbished then. Surviving interior designs (Wall and Ceiling Designs, SM 22a.1 and 22a.2) mark this out as the first recorded project Schinkel undertook for the Prussian royal family. Fortunately Schinkel's designs for the upholstered furniture in this room have also survived, including a sofa (SM 37b.125) and a chair (SM 37b.114), as well as the present drawing. Illustrations of the room and inventories indicate that these were made of mahogany with bronze rosettes and silk covers (SSG Potsdam-Sanssouci, Aquarell Sammlung). The design of the walls – and especially the doors – in the Chamois Room shows clear signs of Empire style, whereas the upholstered pieces of furniture are free adaptations of various influences from France, Italy and England.

Lit.: Berlin 1980, 287, 339.

B.G.

34.

SKETCH DESIGN FOR BEDS. 1809

Pencil, 422 × 283

Nationalgalerie, SMB (SM 37c.121)

When the king and queen returned to Berlin in late 1809, Schinkel was given additional commissions. The sketches shown here were his first ideas for the new beds which were then being installed in Potsdam and Schloss Charlottenburg. They illustrate the young architect's search for original forms of expression, and the light touch with which he sketches out various possibilities. A more finished drawing (SM 37c.126) is a design for Queen Luise's bed in the Schloss at Potsdam; a copy of the bed originally built for the Schloss remained there until the furniture was removed in the Second World War.

Lit.: Sievers 1950, p. 12; Berlin 1980, 335.

B.G.

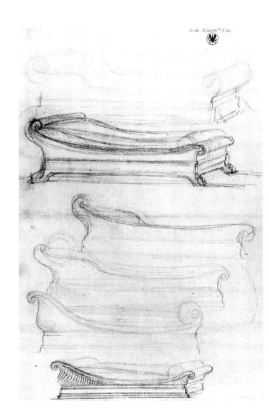

35.

PERSPECTIVE DESIGN FOR THE BEDROOM OF QUEEN
LUISE, FIRST VERSION.   1809

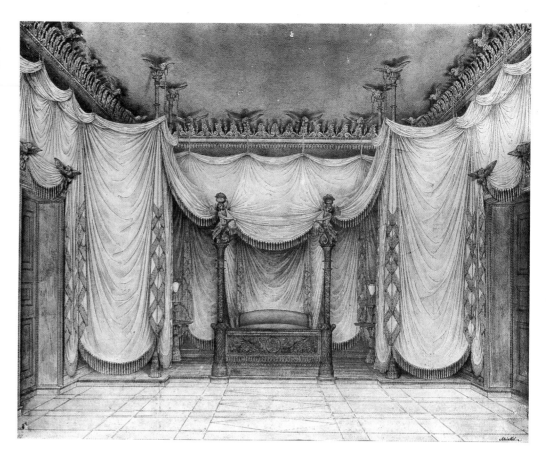

Signed lower right: *Schinkel*

Pen and ink and watercolour, 360 × 510

SSG Schloss Charlottenburg (C. 20a)

The return of the royal couple from
Königsberg on 23 December 1809 was the
impetus for the renovation of their apartments
in the Königliches Palais on Unter den Linden
(cat. 33) and in Schloss Charlottenburg. In the
winter apartment of Friedrich Wilhelm II in
the new wing at Charlottenburg Schinkel
designed a bedroom for the queen. In this first
draft a strictly symmetrical arrangement was
planned: the bed with its foot towards the
window in the middle, between stands that
were to be draped with hangings in a white
material and of which the left was meant to
hide the stove standing before the hearth. On
either side of the bed was to be a 'table for
various conveniences with an alabaster lamp'.
Schinkel also notes on a sketch: 'The pillars . . .
supporting geniuses, over whose arms the
hangings are draped, as well as the pillars . . .
and the ornamentation on the front end of the
bed . . . are carved in wood, as are both
bedside tables . . . the cornice is executed in
stucco but painted the colour of wood,
together with all the walls, so that the entire
room appears to be made of wood. The ceiling
is painted in oil, dark blue in the centre, fading
to a softer violet towards the edges and thus .
giving the effect of the sky.' Schinkel intended
to arouse landscape associations in the
Romantic sense, to transcend the boundaries of
the interior and admit a cosmic resonance.
Legendary motifs of nature are introduced in
the owls which decorate the doors, cornices
and pillars, as birds of the night and attributes
of Minerva. The hangings are intended to
recall clouds or evening mists. This somewhat
eerie world is given a friendlier note, directed
towards morning, by the geniuses with their
flower pots.

In the end a less ceremonial design was
executed, with white mousseline stretched over
rose-pink wallpaper, hinting at morning mist
and sunrise (see cat. 36).

Lit.: Berlin 1980, 334; Berlin 1981, 20.

H.B.-S.

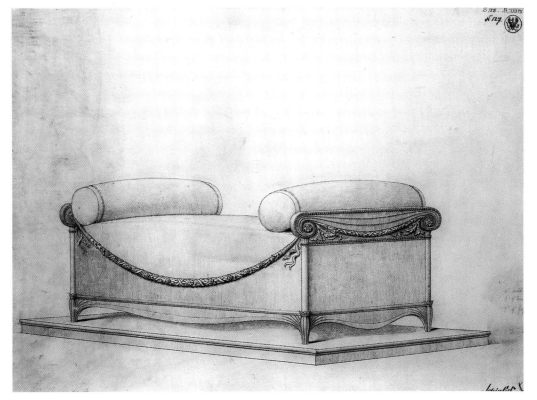

Between 1810 and 1811 Heinrich Gentz and Schinkel drew up a series of designs for the refurbishment and extension of the Königliches Palais on Unter den Linden, but only two projects were completed. The first was a modest extension of the former palace of the Margrave of Brandenburg-Schwedt with the so-called Kopfbau, known together as the Prinzessinnenpalais because the royal couple's daughters then occupied this building. A bridge connecting it with the Königliches Palais was also built. Schinkel helped supervise the construction, and installed a new library for the king, the one shown in this design, in the bridge structure. Along with the Chamois Room (see cat. 33) it is one of the earliest of Schinkel's known designs for interiors, and his first attempt at finding a formal language for library design. The Library was quite a large room, occupying the whole of the bridge structure. This made the bookcases especially monumental, an effect counteracted by the slender design elements and austere ornament.

Lit.: Sievers 1950, p. 14; Berlin 1980, 288.

B.G.

36.

DESIGN FOR A BED FOR QUEEN LUISE.   1809–10

Signed bottom right: *Schinkel*

Pen and ink and pencil, 285 × 390

Nationalgalerie, SMB (SM 37c.127)

This meticulous drawing was the working design for the pearwood bed for the refurbished Queen's bedroom in the New Wing of Schloss Charlottenburg, 1810. Also for this room, Schinkel designed a pair of bedside 'flower' tables in the same material. Schinkel's original scheme for this interior was very ambitious and strongly influenced by the Empire style (cat. 35). It was not executed and the design was scaled down to more modest proportions, including this design for a bed. In spite of its fundamentally 'lit-bâteau' form, the carved garlands and the rounded corner supports of the bed are a subdued and modified recollection of Empire-style models, echoes of which occur principally in the bedside tables. The bed and tables survive in Schloss Charlottenburg, in a recreated setting (fig. 36a).

Lit.: Sievers 1950, p. 12, pl. 14; Berlin 1980, 336; Berlin 1981, 230.

B.G.

36a. Bed and flower tables made for Queen Luise. Pearwood. SSG Schloss Charlottenburg.

37.

DESIGN FOR THE WALLS AND CEILING OF THE LIBRARY OF THE KÖNIGLICHES PALAIS, BERLIN.
1810

Inscribed: *Wand der Bibliothek mit den Bücherschränken* (Wall of bookcases in the Library) and with notes.

Pen and black ink and watercolour, 365 × 265

SSG Potsdam-Sanssouci (Plankammer)

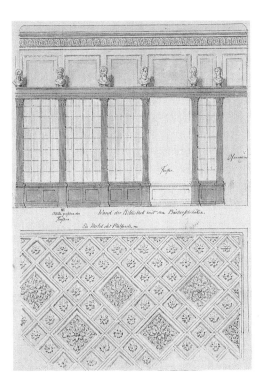

38.

THE RED OR STATEROOM IN THE PALAIS OF PRINCE
AUGUST, BERLIN.   1816

Attributed to Wilhelm Berger

Signed and inscribed bottom right *Genehmigt.
August* (Approved. August)

Pen and black ink and watercolour, heightened
with white, 260 × 371

Nationalgalerie, SMB (SM B.7)

In 1815 Prince August (1779–1843), a son of
Frederick the Great's brother, Prince
Ferdinand, commissioned Schinkel to redesign
the interior of his eighteenth-century Palais at
65, Wilhelmstrasse. With this commission
Schinkel began his series of decorative and
furniture designs for the Prussian princes.
Unfortunately the destruction of the Second
World War spared only a few of the princely
interiors, furnishings and other decorations
which had survived until then. Schinkel's work
for Prince August was completed by 1817. The
wealthy owner's desire for imposing elegance
gave Schinkel what might have been his first
opportunity to refurbish a whole interior in an
interrelated way free of serious financial
constraints. A series of individual designs and
views of entire rooms testify to this.

   This presentation drawing of the Red room

is probably the work of Wilhelm Berger,
Schinkel's brother-in-law and collaborator on
the project. It is an attempt at a kind of
grandeur which suggests the Empire style in
the individual ornaments – the door-frames
flanked by Ludwig Wichmann's caryatid
sculptures, the door-leaves, the stove and the
chairs.

Lit.: Sievers 1954, pp. 6–59; Berlin 1980, 291.

B.G.

39.

UPHOLSTERED CHAIR.   *c.* 1815

Anonymous maker, after Schinkel.

Alderwood, with black lacquer, the seat and
    back covers renewed, 880 × 420 × 430

Nationalgalerie, SMB (Id. 69)

Schinkel himself owned this simple
upholstered chair, as well as three others of the
same type, which were given to the Schinkel
Museum by his son-in-law and biographer,
Alfred von Wolzogen. The clarity of its
austere lines suggests the influence of late-
eighteenth century English chair design.
Among Schinkel's projects for the palaces of
Prussian Princes, we find more highly wrought
and elaborate examples of this type of chair,
such as those made in 1817 for the Palais of
Prince Friedrich of Prussia (1794–1863) in
Wilhelmstrasse. From these examples we can
date Schinkel's conception of this form of chair
to around 1815.

Lit.: Sievers 1950, pp. 15, 19, illus. 21, 23–4;
    Berlin 1980, 341, 346.

                                        B.G.

40.

MAP OF BERLIN.   1843

Unknown engraver after J.C. Selter

Inscribed: *Grundriss/von/Berlin/Aufgenommen
    und gezeichnet mit Genehmigung/der Königl.
    Academie der Wissenschaften/von/J.C. Selter./
    Im Verlage bei Simon Schropp et C^{omp}. 1843.*
    (Ground plan/of/Berlin/Recorded and
    drawn up with the approval of the Royal
    Academy of Sciences/by/J.C. Selter./
    Published by Simon Schropp & Co. 1843.)

Hand coloured engraving, laid down on linen,
    726 × 984

SSG Potsdam-Sanssouci (Plankammer, B
    10,897)

The historic centre of the city is shown by the
irregular streets clustered around and on the
island in the bend of the river Spree, formed
from the old towns of Kölln (on the island),
Berlin (on the east bank) and Friedrichs-
Werder (on the west bank). Running west,
and linked to the island by the Schlossbrücke,
is the avenue of Unter den Linden terminating
in the Brandenburger Tor (gate). North and
south of the avenue are the regular grid
patterns of Dorotheenstadt and the triangular
Friedrichstadt, developed in the seventeenth
and eighteenth centuries. The whole city is
generously surrounded by a wall with gates. In
1786 the population was 145,000, of whom
33,000 were in the garrison.
    The map shows the stage of development
Berlin had reached by the time Schinkel died.
In the north-west, by the Neues Tor and
Oranienburger Tor, iron foundries and
engineering works had been established, which
is why the district was known as Feuerland
(Fireland). By the Hamburger Tor and
Rosenthaler Tor to the north lies the densely
populated Voigtland. The suburb of Köpenick,
on the other hand, had only just started to
expand. The Luisenstadt Canal with its two
pools, Engel- and Torbecken, is marked on the
map but only as a project, like
Michaelkirchplatz and Mariannenplatz. Four
railway lines start from Berlin. Only the
Frankfurt Line station lies within the city
walls; the other stations are outside the gates.
    Schinkel's contribution to the cityscape of
Berlin is well documented on this map: the
integrated network of streets from the
Brandenburger Tor to the Schlossbrücke, the
formal design of the Lustgarten and the
reorganisation of the Packhof (Customs
House).
    The map pinpoints the positions of all
Schinkel's buildings – the cathedral, Altes
Museum and the Packhof in Kölln; the Neue

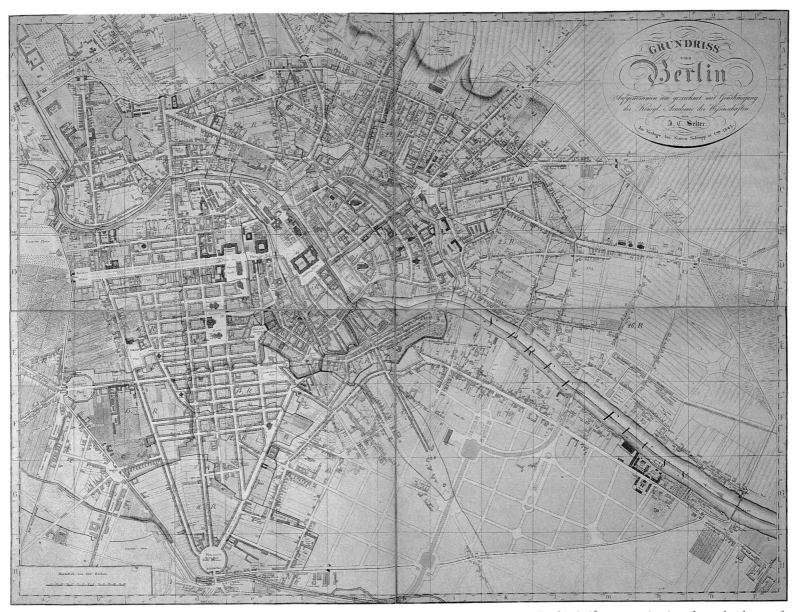

Wache House (New Guard House), Friedrich-
Werder Kirche and Bauakademie in
Friedrichswerder; the Schauspielhaus in
Friedrichstadt; the Palais Redern at 1, Pariser
Platz by the Brandenburger Tor, and the
Feilner House, Hasenhegerstrasse in
Luisenstadt.

   The city is divided into police districts,
which are indicated by different colours.

R.K. and M.S.

41.

PANORAMA OF BERLIN, VIEWED FROM THE
CATHEDRAL.   *c.* 1835

Johann Hürlimann (1793–1850) after J.H.
   Hintze (1800–before 1862)

Aquatint and etching, hand coloured,
   326 × 1110 (the lettering cut)

SSG Schloss Charlottenburg

In this 360° panoramic view from the dome of
Schinkel's Cathedral, the eye starts in the east
crossing the Spree to reach the city quarter.
Here, skirting the river, we see first the
Burgstrasse with the Joachimsthal Gymnasium
on the left of the picture, and the Military
Academy on the far side of the Kleine
Burgstrasse. The sea of houses is overshadowed
by church towers: to the left, that of the
Marienkirche whose neo-Gothic upper
structure was built by C.G. Langhans (1789–
90); behind this, further back on the left, are
the windmills on the Prenzlauer Berg, with the
Georgenkirche in the suburb of König to the
right. South-west of this is the tower of the
Klosterkirche and nearby, the parish church. Its
tower was built from Jean de Bodt's design to
house the carillon originally intended for the
tower of the Mint. The eye travels on to the
tower of the Waisenhauskirche and the

medieval Nikolaikirche, the oldest parish church in Berlin.

The central section is taken up by the Lustgarten at whose eastern edge, between the Königliches Schloss and the Stock Exchange, the cathedral is situated. Along the bottom of the picture we can see the tips of the poplars which conceal all of it except the entrance façade. Between the hospital wing of the Schloss and the cathedral the Kavalierbrücke, which a commercial company commissioned Master Carpenter Steinmeyer to build in 1831–2, leads to the Kleine Burgstrasse. In front of the north face of the Schloss was left an open square the length of the Court Hospital whose Renaissance gables rise above the trees on the left. Outside the Museum the large granite basin, cut by Cantian, stands on the pedestal designed by Schinkel and completed in 1834. Behind the Museum is the former Orangerie, used to store the royal collection of porcelain. The western edge of the Lustgarten is bordered by the Zeughaus (Arsenal), situated on the far bank of the Spree Canal which separates the district of Kölln from Friedrichswerder and across which the Schlossbrücke connects the square in front of the Zeughaus with the Lustgarten.

Above the front of the Stadtschloss rises the tip of the spire of the Jerusalemer Kirche designed by Schinkel and completed in 1836. Looking west, from the Königliches Schloss the eye moves from the houses along Schlossfreiheit and the district of Friedrichswerder, with the Bauakademie and the Friedrich-Werder Kirche, to the Victory Monument on the Kreuzberg. On the far bank of the Spree Canal we can clearly make out the Hotel de Russie on the square by the Bauakademie (Academy of Architecture) and, in front of the Zeughaus, the Military Headquarters and the Königliches Palais, at that time called the Kronprinzen Palais.

Further west, behind the Zeughaus, is the Brandenburger Tor. Between this and the Optical Telegraph on Dorotheenstrasse towers the Church of Neustadt.

The right-hand section is devoted to the area north of the cathedral, with the roof of the Royal Laundry in the foreground, and the Stock Exchange further back. Behind this the Friedrichsbrücke leads to Neue Friedrichsstrasse, with its Garnisonkirche, whose high roof appears on the right of the picture. Further downstream, beyond the Fruit Market, is the imposing block of rented apartments built by the Speicher Company at the confluence of the Zwirngraben and the Spree, then the Kleine Präsidentenstrasse. J.F. Grael's tower for the Sophienkirche rises above the rooftops of the suburb of Spandau. Further left of this in the Voigtland is the Elisabethkirche, one of Schinkel's suburban churches.

The print was published in Berlin by L. Sachse & Co., and in Paris by Rittner & Groupil. The example reproduced is from the Kupferstichkabinett, SMB (846–110).

R.K.

42.

THE NEUE WACHE (NEW GUARDHOUSE): DESIGN FOR THE SECOND SCHEME. 1816

Inscribed bottom right: *erfunden und gezeichnet von Schinkel 1816* (Invented and drawn by Schinkel 1816)

Pen and dark grey ink, 450 × 654

Nationalgalerie, SMB (SM 23b.48)

43.

PERSPECTIVE VIEW OF THE NEW GUARDHOUSE IN
BERLIN.   1819

Johan Conrad Susemihl (about 1767–after
    1847) after Schinkel

Lettered: *Perspectivische Ansicht des Neuen
    Wacht: Gebäudes in Berlin. Entworfen und
    gezeichnet von Schinkel. J.C. Susemihl in
    Darmstadt gestochen.* (Title as shown, then:
    designed and drawn by Schinkel. Engraved
    by J.C. Susemihl in Darmstadt)

Engraving, 204 × 395

Nationalgalerie, SMB

With the return of King Friedrich Wilhelm III
to Berlin in October 1815, the rebuilding of
the Guardhouse on the Platz am Zeughaus,
facing the Königliches Palais was put in train.
In the same year came Schinkel's first design,
showing a round-arched hall, set far back in
the chestnut grove between defensive ditches
and the Zeughaus at the end of an avenue. The
preparatory sketch shows figures planned to
stand in front of the pillars, with an inscription
above them and a cornice adorned with eagles.
Probably under the influence of the Crown
Prince, Schinkel changed this design, even
though the king had approved it.

The second scheme is fronted with a portico
of six piers beneath a pediment (cat. 42). On
the corner towers of the building stand
trophies surrounded by eagles. On the
entablature of the portico is a row of warriors'
heads inspired by Schlüter's masks in the
courtyard of the neighbouring Zeughaus. The
Neue Wache is no longer hidden away in the
depths of the chestnut grove but brought
forward on to the square. The importance that
Schinkel must have attached to this unexecuted
design is shown by the fact that in 1819 it was
engraved as the first plate in the *Sammlung
architektonischer Entwürfe*, which he was then
initiating. Cat. 43 was plate 2.

The definitive plan intended for execution
alters the hall with piers into a Doric
colonnaded hall. From the first sketch to the
ultimate design, Schinkel's idea of a small
cubic building remained the same, although it
is impressive enough to hold its own between
the large eighteenth-century buildings – the
Zeughaus, the Opera and the University – in
its special position in the urban setting. Because
Schinkel does not place it on the building line
of the Zeughaus but allows it to stand further
back, a special area of significance arises in
front of it, flanked by the statues of generals.

The contrasting 'Castrum' block ('. . .
designed more or less in accordance with a
Roman castrum' – Schinkel's own formulation
in the accompanying text to the *Sammlung
architektonischer Entwürfe*) and Doric portico
have become one. The cubic tendency of the
designs of his master Friedrich Gilly and the
massive quality of his early plans have become
enhanced in Schinkel's first mature work.

This, the earliest of his great Berlin
buildings, already displays the characteristics of
his architectural outlook: the perfected unity
and harmony of main buildings and
ornamental elements. The closed exterior walls
of the block stand in contrast to the integrated
and at the same time forward-thrusting hall of
columns, and the sandstone of the front and
the portico contrasts with the use of brick on
the sides and back, and yet the whole
represents a perfect unity, which also includes
the three-dimensional programme of the
portico decoration.

By the time the building was dedicated, on 18 August 1818 (work having begun in 1816) there were only the ten Victories on the frieze after J.G. Schadow's models, produced in cast zinc. A first, plaster model had been made by Henri François Brandt for the pediment. The idea of executing it in a more permanent material was revived in 1822, but postponed until 1842, when it was made, again in cast zinc – and modelled by August Kiss and put up in 1846. In 1822 came a new design by Schinkel for two Victory emblems on the corner pylons, as they had appeared in the plan from the beginning, but in more opulent form, with two female figures on each side of the trophies. No such crowning features were ever made.

By 1816 the plan to put two marble statues of the Prussian Generals Gerhard David von Scharnhorst (d. 1813) and Friedrich Wilhelm Graf Bülow von Dennewitz (d. 1816) in front of the Neue Wache had already been conceived; this was carried out by Rauch from 1816 onwards. Schinkel designed the pedestals and iron railings, which were put in place in 1822.

Lit.: Rave 1962, 142–71; Berlin 1980, 142, 145; Berlin 1981, 33.

G.R.

44.

TSAR NICHOLAS I OF RUSSIA AND PRINCE WILHELM OF PRUSSIA BEFORE THE NEUE WACHE.   1835

August von Rentzell (1810–91)

Signed and dated bottom right: *A. von Rentzell. | pinx. 1835.*

Oil on canvas, 710 × 890

SSG Potsdam-Sanssouci (GK 1 4818)

In front of Schinkel's Neue Wache, adorned with Rauch's marble statues of Generals Bülow von Dennewitz and Scharnhorst, Tsar Nicholas I of Russia and, on his right, Prince Wilhelm I of Prussia (later King Wilhelm I and Kaiser), a brother-in-law of the Tsar, appear in an open carriage and pair. In the next carriage are Prince Albrecht of Prussia and the heir to the Russian throne, Grand Duke Alexander. The alliance forged between Russia and Prussia against Napoleon was sealed dynastically in 1817 by the Tsar's marriage (while a Grand Duke) to the Prussian Princess Charlotte (called Alexandra Feodorovna). We can take it that Rentzell is alluding to the alliance's political background when he depicts the two leading characters in this canvas right in front of the Neue Wache.

G.B.

45.

THE SCHAUSPIELHAUS: PERSPECTIVE VIEW OF THE EXTERIOR.   1818–20

Pen and ink and wash, heightened with white, 474 × 745

Nationalgalerie, SMB (SM 50.11)

An aquatint by Friedrich Jügel (1820) was based on this illustration, which was also engraved as Plate 7 of the *Sammlung architektonischer Entwürfe*, Part 2, published in 1821.

46.

THE SCHAUSPIELHAUS: PERSPECTIVE DESIGN FOR THE AUDITORIUM.   1818

Signed and dated lower right: *Schinkel 1818* and inscribed below: *Perspectivische Ansicht des Theater-Saals* (Perspective view of the auditorium)

Pen and ink and watercolour, 617 × 802

Nationalgalerie, SMB (SM 50.5)

47.

THE SCHAUSPIELHAUS: PERSPECTIVE VIEW OF THE CONCERT HALL.   1821–6

Pen and ink and pencil, 488 × 427

Nationalgalerie, SMB (SM 21b.73)

Preliminary drawing for Plate 16 of the *Sammlung architektonischer Entwürfe*, Part 2, published in 1826.

On 29 July 1817 the National Theatre on the Gendarmenmarkt, built by Karl Gotthard Langhans the Elder, was gutted by fire. Karl Graf von Brühl, who succeeded A.W. Iffland from 1815 as General Director of the Royal Theatre, reported to Friedrich Wilhelm III on the suspected causes of the fire. Von Brühl requested 'to be permitted to invite plans and proposals for a new building from a number of important artists, perhaps including foreign artists, but in particular from Geheimer Oberbaurat Schinkel'. Brühl had been associated with Schinkel from the beginning of his time in office, having commissioned designs from him for stage sets for both the royal theatres, the Opera and the National Theatre. On 10 August 1817 Karl Ferdinand Langhans, the son of K.G. Langhans, applied to the king with designs for the rebuilding of the theatre.

The decision on these designs was postponed, but was not subsequently taken up.

Brühl's proposal to reuse the walls and six portico columns of the old building in the reconstruction of the theatre was entirely to the king's taste, since in the period following the Wars of Liberation the slow progress of Prussian building works could take place only with the strictest economy. On 19 November Brühl received the royal decree for the reconstruction, with instructions to equip the stage for use for comedy and small dramas and to restrict the size of the auditorium and stage in order to fit in a concert and festival hall. The size of the theatre was to be between that of the Opera House and a smaller, third Berlin theatre planned by the king.

On 13 January 1818 Brühl wrote to Schinkel, passing on the precise data, with the note that the king was expecting a 'harmonious exterior'. In his reply, Schinkel asked for much more precise details and also requested an express commission to undertake the project and to take over its direction. Architect and theatre director were thus opposed in their claims to authority.

On 28 April Schinkel submitted his design, which the King accepted on 30 April, and approved for execution. He wanted to leave it to Schinkel and Brühl to carry out the building, and expected 'costs to be moderated as much as possible'. After a theatre building committee had been formed, with Brühl as chairman, Schinkel representing the architectural side and Councillor Triest the technical, the work began on 4 July 1818.

In Schinkel's explanatory paper to the king, he comments on the exterior of the building: 'Since the Theatre, as the most essential part, occupied the middle of the building, there was a heightening here, which interrupted the long, uniform mass of the old building and rendered the whole pyramidal. By means of flat roofs with the main façades towards the entrances, the [new] building will be able to present a noble style on the lines of Greek edifices.

'The podium, so essential to the scenery store, actually contributes a great deal to the beauty of the whole, in that it raises the architecture above the usual level of urban construction. The six remaining usable columns of the original building which are to be used in the new one will be set more worthily upon this podium, with a fine flight of steps, and will thus have a greater effect, as befits a public building . . . .

'The architecture of the future façade is to be executed as strictly as possible in the Greek manner, in order to be in harmony with the portico, already present . . .'.

In the *Sammlung architektonischer Entwürfe* Schinkel wrote in 1821 on the method of

construction: 'On the style of architecture I have given to the building I would make only the general comment that, to the extent permitted by a work assembled through such varied means, I have been concerned to abide by the Greek forms and methods. Consequently all curved roof vaults are avoided both in the exterior and in the main interior rooms and horizontal architraves are used throughout. The construction of pilasters, as seen in the Greek monuments, e.g. the Thrasyllos monument in Athens, seemed to me to accord better with the character of a public building and to be more in harmony with the peristyle of the main façade than ordinary windows, to which is added the advantage of gaining more light for the building which, thanks to its great depth, was otherwise very difficult to light within . . . .

'The auditorium is so planned that for the most part the boxes have the theatre almost directly before them and the poorest seat has a full view of the front of the stage and more than half of the background. As in many French theatres, a gallery is positioned in front of the boxes, which offers very pleasant seats and is extremely convenient for persons who wish to visit singly the first and second circles. The boxes behind them can then in some cases be fully closed off.

'This outer gallery, together with the iron balustrade of the boxes, forms a semicircle highly advantageous to both seeing and hearing and at the same time allowing a fine apportionment of the ceiling decoration. The boxes which, thanks to the galleries, project for some distance, are supported by slender iron columns which do not impede the view,

as used in a number of English theatres . . .'

On 26 May 1821 the theatre opened with Goethe's *Iphigénie auf Tauris*. Brühl had asked the poet, who was a friend, to provide a dedicatory prologue and also to attend the performance, which proved impossible on health grounds. The ceremonial dedicatory prologue was spoken in front of a stage set painted by Karl Gropius after Schinkel's design, which surprised and delighted the public with a view of Berlin showing the Gendarmenmarkt and the very building in which they sat. After the performance the king was cheered and there were calls for Schinkel, who had modestly already left the building. Accordingly Brühl, the artists, Professors of the Academy, students, colleagues and audience serenaded him enthusiastically in front of his house on Unter den Linden.

In the building of the Schauspielhaus, Schinkel did not fully succeed in realising his plans for the ideal theatre. There is evidence for this in the limiting conditions, such as the use of the foundations of the former building, the co-ordination of a very extensive programme of rooms and Brühl's technical conditions – a mutually stimulating collaboration having apparently developed between them. The moderately large stage offered an opportunity for the desired traditional deep flats, but was also equipped for the shallower stage with backdrop. Both were made possible by the development of the fly tower, with the technical scenery system above, top lighting, machinery underneath, orchestra pit, and the semicircular auditorium with its new scheme of tiers, consisting of boxes and a balcony projecting in front of them optically and acoustically directed towards the stage. Schinkel wanted to reform theatre design, yet here he had to find an architecturally comprehensive solution to the problem under limiting conditions. He succeeded in harmonising ideal forms with functional and economic requirements.

The Schauspielhaus was restored after war damage, with extensive internal alterations, forming a large concert hall.

Lit.: Rave 1941, pp. 88–138; Berlin 1980, pp. 115–30, Berlin 1981, 36.

C. H.

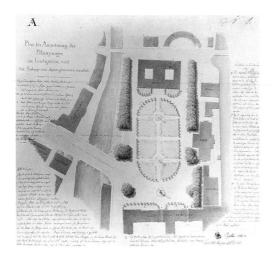

48.

PROPOSAL FOR THE REDESIGN OF THE LUSTGARTEN.
1828

Inscribed at the top: *Plan für Anordnung der Pflanzungen im Lustgarten und für Anlage von Springbrunnen daselbst* (Plan for the planting of the Lustgarten and for the location of fountains in the same) and with notes. Signed and dated lower right: *Schinkel. 1828*

Pen and black ink, watercolour and pencil, 438 × 490

Nationalgalerie, SMB (SM 21c.161)

By combining the squares at the Opernhaus and the Zeughaus (Arsenal) and making them a continuation of the avenue Unter den Linden, linked to the Lustgarten by the impressive Schlossbrücke, Schinkel enabled this area, which originally lay outside the fortifications of Kölln, one of the component parts of Berlin, to develop into the real centre of the city. From 1573 the Elector Prince Johann Georg of Brandenburg had a pleasure and kitchen garden laid out north of the Schloss, and from 1645 it was redesigned by the gardener, Michael Hanf, and the architect, Gregor Memhardt. King Friedrich Wilhelm I had the garden levelled in 1715 to make a parade ground. Only on the Spree and the Pomeranzengraben were trees left standing, and it was not until 1803 that the part north of the palace bridge was replanted with poplars and chestnuts, and the area directly beside the

Schloss paved.

Schinkel's exterior for the Altes Museum gave the Lustgarten its architectural distinction as a public place. In 1828, when this was nearly finished, he also designed new gardens, intended to relate the main buildings to each other. Planting began in 1830 with the co-operation of the director of the Royal Gardens, Peter Joseph Lenné.

Lit.: Hamburg 1982, 5.12.

R.K.

49.

THE SCHLOSSBRÜCKE WITH THE ALTES MUSEUM
AND THE ZEUGHAUS. *c.* 1838

Carl Daniel Freydanck (1811–87)

Inscribed on the stretcher: *Die Schlossbrücke*

Oil on canvas, 270 × 375

KPM-Archiv, Schloss Charlottenburg (Nr. 32)

With Schinkel's Bauakademie behind him the viewer looks over the Kupfergraben, alive with boats, and sees the Schlossbrücke. It was Schinkel's intention that the bridge should not only form a continuation of the great tree-lined avenue, Unter den Linden (to the left), which contained the monarchy's most impressive and important buildings, but also be a fitting link to the main objective and chief structure in the area, the royal residence (to the right).

Designed in 1819 and executed between 1821 and 1824, the new broad stone bridge was a masterpiece of bridge engineering. A cast-iron railing of seahorses, tritons and dolphins links the pedestals, which are shown empty. It was only in 1853–7 that the groups of sculptures, which Schinkel had designed in 1823 and which were executed, with some changes, by sculptors of the Rauch School, were set in place.

When designing the bridge Schinkel had already planned the redesign of the entire surrounding area, and Freydanck's view shows that these ideas had been realised. Behind the bridge rises the massive block of the 'New Museum' (1825–30) with its colonnaded front, and to the centre left behind the Museum the head office building of the Neue Packhof (new Customs House, 1829–32). This is now the 'Museumsinsel'. Between the Museum and the Stock Exchange, on the right of the picture, the obelisk shape of the chimney of the engine house towers up; its steam-engine operated the fountains in the Lustgarten, which Schinkel had also redesigned (1828–30).

On the left-hand margin the side façade of Schlüter's Baroque Zeughaus (Arsenal) projects into the picture. This view, like the others by Freydanck in this catalogue, was made as a model for the porcelain painters of the Berlin Royal Porcelain Manufactory (KPM).

Lit.: Berlin 1987 II, 1.

I.B.

50.

THE NEW MUSEUM IN BERLIN. 1838

Carl Daniel Freydanck (1811–87)

Inscribed on the back *Das Neue Museum* (The New Museum) *in Berlin, C.F. fec. 1838*

Oil on canvas, 277 × 357

KPM-Archiv, Schloss Charlottenburg (Nr. 38)

The viewer looks from the south-west corner of the Lustgarten over lawns and groups of figures in Biedermeier dress to the building of the New Museum. Begun in 1825, it was opened by 1830. Although it was founded and built at the express wish of Friedrich Wilhelm III for the royal collections, the building was one of the first real museums in the modern sense in both its purpose and organisation.

Before the colonnade is the bowl which was made by Christian Gottlieb Cantian from a huge block of granite and put in place in 1831; it was intended for the interior rotunda but proved too large.

The redesign of the Lustgarten, which had been used mainly as a military parade ground, became necessary when the museum was finished. Schinkel commented that this inner-city park, the first he had designed, was probably the loveliest spot in Berlin.

Lit.: Berlin 1987 II, 3.

I.B.

PERSPECTIVE DES NEUEN MUSEUMS AM LUSTGARTEN ZU ERBAUEN

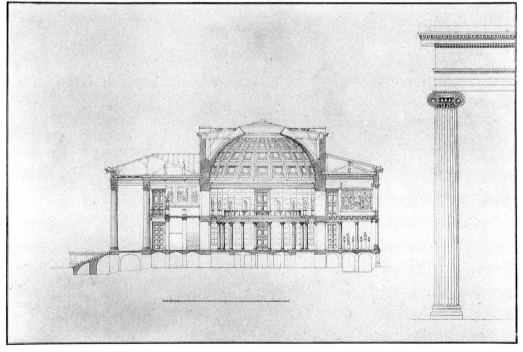

51.

PERSPECTIVE VIEW OF THE ALTES MUSEUM BERLIN.
1823–5

Inscribed below: *Perspectivische Ansicht des Neuen Museums am Lustgarten zu erbauen entworfen und gezeichnet von Schinkel, 1823* (Perspective view of the New Museum to be built at the Lustgarten designed and drawn by Schinkel, 1823)

Pen and black ink, wash and pencil, 407 × 635

Nationalgalerie, SMB (SM 23b.44)

Published in modified form as Plate 37 in the *Sammlung architektonischer Entwürfe*, Part 6, published in 1825.

52.

CROSS-SECTION OF THE MUSEUM FROM NORTH TO
SOUTH, WITH A DETAIL OF THE IONIC ORDER
OF THE FRONT.
1823–5

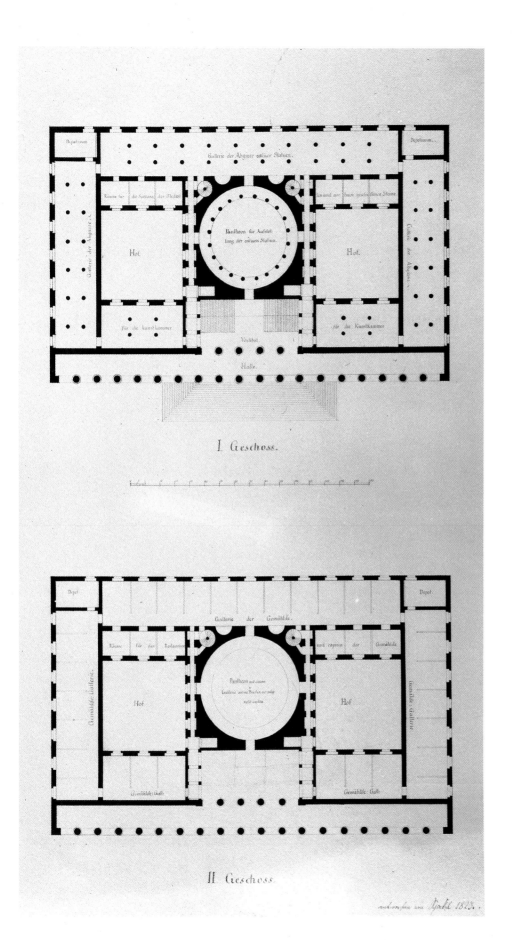

I. Geschoss.

II Geschoss.

Pen and black ink, 366 × 542

Nationalgalerie, SMB (SM 21b.52)

Drawing for Plate 40 in the *Sammlung architektonischer Entwürfe*, Part 6, published in 1825.

53.

PLANS OF FIRST AND SECOND FLOORS OF THE
ALTES MUSEUM.   1823–5

Inscribed lower right: *Entworfen von Schinkel, 1823* (Designed by Schinkel, 1823) and with names of galleries and spaces.

Pen and brush in black ink, 572 × 400

Nationalgalerie, SMB (SM 21b.49)

Published as Plate 38 in the *Sammlung architektonischer Entwürfe*, Part 6, published in 1825.

54.

PERSPECTIVE VIEW OF THE STAIRCASE HALL IN THE
ALTES MUSEUM.   1829

Signed and dated lower right: *Schinkel, 1829*

Pen and black ink and pencil, 391 × 530

Nationalgalerie, SMB (SM 21b.54)

Drawing for Plate 103 in the *Sammlung
architektonischer Entwürfe*, Part 17, published
in 1831.

55.

VIEW FROM THE MAIN STAIRCASE OF THE ALTES
MUSEUM THROUGH THE COLUMNS OF THE
PORTICO TO THE LUSTGARTEN. Before 1843

Carl Daniel Freydanck (1811–87)

Oil on canvas, 276 × 379

KPM-Archiv, Schloss Charlottenburg (Nr.
178)

The standpoint chosen by Freydanck gives a
delightful view through and out of the Altes
Museum, with its open staircase. The viewer
looks through the colonnade of the portico on
to the Lustgarten, with the granite bowl and
fountains, and across to the Königliches
Schloss. Closer at hand, the Bauakademie and
the Friedrich-Werder Kirche are to be seen,
both designed by Schinkel. He had deliberately
planned this view and it was an essential
element in his design. The staircase is a brilliant
combination of internal and external space.

On a pedestal on the double-branched
staircase is a Russian cast-iron copy of the
Warwick Vase (see cat. 134) given by the Tsar
and put in place in 1834.

A painting by M.C. Gregorovius, dated
1843 (SSG Potsdam-Sanssouci) is of an almost
identical view. Previously regarded as
Freydanck's source it is more likely that the
reverse is the case, the Gregorovius being very
much harder in its handling. Freydanck may
well have been inspired by Schinkel's own
version (cat. 54).

The rapid growth of the royal collections
necessitated the erection of another museum in
1841–55. Still known as the 'New Museum', it
was designed by Schinkel's pupil Friedrich
August Stüler; Schinkel's pioneering building
was known from that date as the 'Altes
Museum', the Old Museum.

Lit.: Berlin 1987 II, 4.

I.B.

56.

VIEW OF THE INTERIOR OF THE ROTUNDA OF THE
ALTES MUSEUM

Carl Emanuel Conrad (1810–73)

Watercolour and body colour, 457 × 421

SSG Potsdam-Sanssouci (Aquarell Sammlung
No. 3837a)

The first proposals to set up a museum for the Royal Art Collections had been put forward in Berlin by around 1800. The young Schinkel, still entirely under the formative influence of his master Friedrich Gilly, had designed the ideal plan for a museum. It was his first preoccupation with the new type of building that was to play so great a part throughout the century, and his approach was still utopian. Aloys Hirt, Professor of Fine Arts and member of both academies, had produced a memorandum and drawings in 1798, in which he indicated various possibilities for extending existing buildings, including the Academy Unter den Linden and Prince Heinrich's palace, as well as sites for a new museum.

A new impetus was given in 1815, with the return of the items in the Royal Collection that had been taken to Paris in 1806 and the stimulus which the collections and their accommodation in the great capitals of Paris, Vienna and London had evidently given the king and members of the court. At the same time, the purchase of the great Giustiniani collection of paintings strengthened the resolve to unite the Royal Collections, as Wilhelm von Humboldt had urged. His Majesty first ordered the extension of the older Academy building, Unter den Linden. The plans for this, first by the Hofbauinspektor Friedrich Rabe, and from 1820 by Schinkel, were then enlarged to a design for new buildings for the entire complex, and work on the plans went on until 1822. In the mean time, the quantity of material which was to be housed had grown considerably, especially with the acquisition of the Edward Solly collection of paintings in 1821.

At the end of 1822 Schinkel conceived his decisive idea for a new museum building at the Lustgarten, eclipsing the inadequate and unsatisfactory Academy project. This was no doubt done in consultation with the Crown Prince, who was acting as regent while the king was in Italy from September to December 1822. On 29 December 1822 Schinkel wrote to Sulpiz Boisserée:

A new design, which I have just finished for the project, and which I believe is my best work, also has Rauch's approval, in regard to economy as well. Beauty in itself and for the city, with ensuing benefit to many related objects there; it has a number of very great advantages over all earlier designs and can now take its course.

On 8 January 1823 he presented a memorandum and plans for a museum at the Lustgarten to the king, proposing that a building be erected in the next few years at a major site in the city. 'The beauty of the area will attain its perfection with this building, as the fine Lustgarten will at last have a worthy conclusion on its fourth side'.

Schinkel's memorandum presenting the plans and cost estimates met with the approval of the committee appointed to prepare for the construction of the museum. The only objections came from Hirt, who criticised Schinkel's basic ideas for the building, especially the rotunda and colonnaded front, on the grounds of their lack of utility. But Schinkel's plans won through against requests for modifications, his main argument against these being: 'The design is a completed whole, the parts of which are so related that no essential feature may be changed without detriment to the whole.' With the approval of the king the sum of 700,000 thalers was assigned for the building on 24 April 1823, and while the designs and estimates were being worked out the preparatory work also started on regulating the Kupfergraben branch of Spree river; this was followed by the complicated foundation work. The structure was not started until 1825 and the foundation stone was laid on 9 July of that year; the roofing ceremony was held on 10 November 1826.

Schinkel intended that his visit to Paris and Britain from April to August 1826 should provide stimulus and new ideas for the interior of his building, and it did so. He came back with proposals for changes, especially to the rotunda and exhibition rooms, mainly involving the use of more costly materials like marble and granite, instead of stucco and sandstone, or at least scagliola instead of plaster. But few of these ideas could be realised in the interior, built in 1827, as the king refused the requests for reasons of cost. In 1828 discussions began on the display of the works of art, and in 1829 a few rooms were shown to visitors. For the opening on 3 August 1830, Friedrich Wilhelm III's sixtieth birthday, only the rotunda, painting gallery and the north room of the sculpture gallery were accessible. The other rooms were handed over on 1 June 1831.

Schinkel commented on his design and its intended effect in his memorandum of January 1823:

The front facing the Lustgarten has so excellent a situation, one could say the finest in Berlin, that it requires something of a very special kind. A simple columned hall in a grand style, and proportionate to the importance of the location, will most certainly give the building character and ensure a fine effect. In time the rear wall of the hall can be decorated with a number of murals, perhaps a cycle from the history of the culture of the human race; it will be a task on which major talents, which His Majesty holds to be worthy of this, could display all their skill.

The strong effect of the Lustgarten front is determined by the arrangement of eighteen Ionic columns before the space of the portico, rising to the full height of the two storey building. They stand on a base before which is placed a flight of steps, in a calculated proportion of one third of the width of the front. This is the only architectural element to have changed from the original plan: the steps are open on three sides and have flat areas on the sides to take groups of statues, which were later carried out.

The portico was designed with a function: 'In order to give the museum building an exterior befitting its site, which is the finest in the capital, a public portico has been devised, in which monuments can be placed to worthy individuals of recent times and protected from the weather.' The rear walls, like those of the staircase, were to be decorated with murals 'on subjects related to the purpose of the building.'

Beside the majestic colonnaded front the side and rear façades are less imposing. Arranged on two storeys and broken by rows of large windows, they are dominated by the triple arrangement of the horizontals: the base zone, the cornice and the broad attic. A complete harmonious balance of horizontals and verticals, of breadth and height, has been achieved on the exterior. The effect of breadth is contrasted by the corner pilaster strips, which accentuate and delimit the front, and the encasing of the rotunda, which rises above this.

After the initial uplifting experience of the columned front and the portico, the visitor was to proceed through a second row of four columns when entering the interior, and have a choice of two routes. He could walk straight ahead into the rotunda, or use the stairway that ascended on both sides, and from which the rooms of both the collection storeys were immediately accessible. First narrow and dark, the way then broadened and culminated in the open space of the second storey, with the double row of columns linking the interior and the exterior. It remains one of the most impressive staircases in modern architecture and one of Schinkel's most brilliant ideas.

The ground plan is a clearly divided

organism of inspired simplicity. It is a rectangular building (86 × 53 m), with the decisive spatial complexes clearly differentiated in the same way in each of the two storeys: the square middle section with the rotunda, the relatively narrow portico, the staircase leading from this to the rotunda, and the rooms for the collections, which go round all four sides and enclose two inner courts with the rotunda in the centre. They form one long north room, two shorter rooms on the sides and two other small rooms behind the walls of the portico. The rooms on the first floor intended for the collection of antique sculptures are distinguished by double columns, a structural feature which also divides the space. In contrast, the rooms of the upper storey, where the paintings were to be shown, have no supports and are subdivided by a new means, rows of partition walls. These start at the window walls and create thirty-one compartments which both articulate the rooms and enable the collection to be presented in an easily accessible way.

The rotunda dominates the centre of the Museum, receiving the visitor and heightening his experience as soon as he enters. Schinkel explained his intention in making this the spatial and conceptual centre of his museum building in his answer to the criticism expressed by Aloys Hirt while the building was still in the planning stage: (*Comment on the Report by Hofrat Hirt* of 5 February 1823): 'Finally, so mighty a building as the Museum will certainly be must have a worthy centre. This must be the sanctuary, where the most precious objects are located. One first enters this place coming from the outer hall, and the sight of a beautiful and sublime room must make the visitor receptive and create the proper mood for the enjoyment and acknowledgement of what the building contains.'

The round space was intended to symbolise the conjunction of the two great fields of art of the collections, and create a higher unity. Apart from its practical function, a rotunda was to Schinkel both the inherent concept of and the ideal shape for such a space. His model was the Roman Pantheon, the proportions of which he adopted – half height and half width (height 24 m, diameter 21 m) – as he did its handling of light from the top of the dome.

The gallery which runs round the space, supported by twenty Corinthian columns, both divides it and articulates the division into two storeys. The areas between the columns and the corresponding niches in the upper gallery also provide space and subdivisions to display the sculptures. The space has a special function as starting-point for the visitor: each storey has four doors, leading not only to the staircase and the two long north rooms but also to the narrow connecting corridors which are direct links between the staircase and the north rooms between the rotunda and the inner courts. The fact that these latter doors were never executed suggests that during the building work the endeavour to isolate the 'Pantheon' more from the rest of the building became of great importance to Schinkel. Four rows of cofferwork subdivide the great dome. Initially designed to be simple and uniform, they were executed in a richer manner with figurative ornament.

Schinkel expresses his own views about the domed room in his *Sammlung architektonisher Entwürfe*: 'The picture is composed so that we can look out through the entrance doors of both the lower room and the gallery past the portico into the Lustgarten, where we see the outlines of the fountain and the Royal Castle. As regards the antique sculptures displayed here between the columns and in the gallery recesses, a different selection was later made. The walls of the Rotunda give the impression of pale grey marble, the shafts of the columns are modelled in bright yellow *giallo*, the cornices and capitals are white, with the cornice ornamentation painted bright red and golden yellow. The friezes around the dome are light, reddish yellow, intensifying progressively through the sections of coffering to a dark fiery red – the colour of the panel backgrounds, against which the figures are painted in bright golden yellow. Illuminated from the dome's apex, this warm colouring creates a very agreeable impression for the whole room and the works of art displayed within it.'

Double columns and architraves placed crossways divide the rooms of the antique storey into smaller sections. Schinkel comments on the ceilings of the sculpture rooms in his *Sammlung architektonisher Entwürfe*:

The timber-beamed ceiling extends through all the sculpture rooms. In order to create meaningful variety in the uniform appearance of this ceiling, which was necessitated by it's construction, each ceiling compartment has in its centre a scene resembling an antique gem, so enabling a large number of interesting ideas to be conveyed throughout the suite of the five rooms of this storey. The beams have raised decorations and mouldings, cast in metal, and are all the colour of bronze. The areas between the beams are light in colour and defined by coloured lines, and in each room these harmonise with the colour of the columns, artificial granite, green and red porphyry, *giallo* and pink marble.

The rooms of the upper storey where the paintings were to be displayed were divided by 'screen walls' placed on the window sides.

These formed closed cabinets, but as they only rose up to two-thirds of the height of the room the overall effect of the great rooms was not diminished. The idea of using top lighting was not implemented for reasons of economy.

Lit.: Rave 1941, pp. 25–78; Berlin 1980, 135–57; Berlin 1981, 47.

G.R.

57.

SCHLOSS GLIENICKE; PERSPECTIVE VIEW WITH
SURROUNDING LANDSCAPE, GROUND PLAN,
ELEVATIONS AND VIEWS OF THE EARLIER
BUILDING.   1837

Signed and dated lower right: *Schinkel 1837.*
Inscribed: *Ansicht der ganzen Schlosses von
Glinike nach der Herstellung und Ergänzung*
(View of the entire Palace of Glienicke
after restoration and extension) and with
notes.

Pen and black ink and pencil, 401 × 505

Nationalgalerie, SMB (SM 34.2)

Drawing for Plate 137 of the *Sammlung
architektonischer Entwürfe*, Part 28, published
in 1840.

58.

SCHLOSS GLIENICKE; VIEW OF THE GARDEN
COURT.   1854

August C. Haun (1815–94) after A.W.F.
Schirmer (1802–66)

Lettered: *Gem. v. Schirmer – Lith. v. Haun*
(Drawn by Schirmer – Lith. by Haun) and
with the publication line of the Royal
Lithographic Institute, Berlin

Hand-coloured lithograph, 596 × 434

SSG Potsdam-Sanssouci (Plankammer
Portfolio 125, P8566)

Plate 3 from *Glienicke – Sommer-Residenz
Seiner Königlichen Höheit des Prinzen Carl
von Preussen erbaut von Schinkel und Persius,*
Berlin and Potsdam, 1854.

The estate of Klein-Glienicke, about three
kilometres from Potsdam, on the far side of
the Havel, came into the possession of the
Chancellor, von Hardenberg, in 1814. He had
the inside of the house renovated in 1816 and
the façade painted 'three times in oil paint in a
greenish-grey'. The exterior of the house was
retained. The building was erected in the
middle of the eighteenth century and
presumably had been converted in the 1790s
for the previous owner, Count Lindenau, in
the Berlin early neo-classical style. In 1824,
two years after the death of Hardenberg,
Prince Karl of Prussia bought the property
from Hardenberg's son. In the next three years
the Schloss was redesigned to plans by
Schinkel, with Ludwig Persius in charge of
their execution. The impressive change is
evident from the contrast between the old and
the new on the drawing. Although the Lion
Fountain, also designed by Schinkel, was
placed before the Schloss in 1840, the architect
clearly preferred to publish the first design,
with its fine terrace before the south front,
feeling this was more successful. He had
already made a drawing of this in 1825 for his
client.

Unlike the severe main front, Schinkel gave
the garden court behind, which is bordered by
the Kavalier wing, a serene and southern
character. The covered walk beside the court
front softens the effect of the façade and, like
the buildings adjoining the pergola, acts as link
between the architecture and the open space.
The tower added to the Kavalier wing in 1832
to a design by Schinkel greatly enriched the
court and added an architectural accent to the
whole group of buildings that was visible from
afar. Further elements that enlivened the court
were the fountain bowl and particularly the
well with the group of Castor and Pollux
copied from a group now in the Prado; the

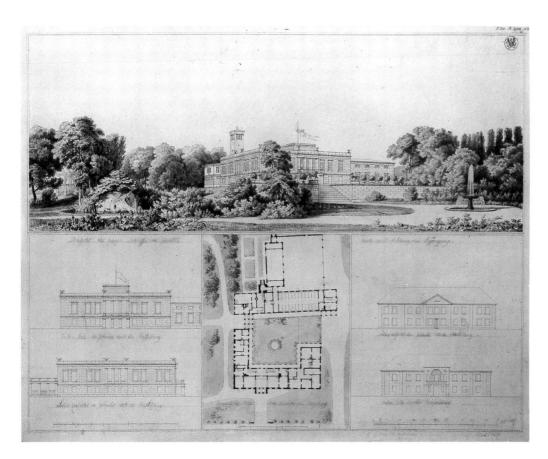

figures were then very popular (particularly in Germany) and known as the 'Dioscuri'.

Schloss Glienicke and its subsidiary buildings formed the core of a great park, in which Peter Joseph Lenné was able to continue the work he had begun in 1816 under Prince Hardenberg for Prince Karl of Prussia, after the property had changed hands. Beside Schinkel's palace, casino and hunting lodge, a number of other no less remarkable smaller buildings by Schinkel, Ludwig Persius and Ferdinand von Arnim made Glienicke an ensemble of special artistic quality and individuality, not least on account of the costly architectural details and antique sculptures collected by the owner.

Lit.: Sievers 1942; Berlin 1980, 312–16; Berlin 1981, 62; Berlin 1987 I.

A.S.

59.

VIEW OF SCHLOSS GLIENICKE FROM SCHLOSS BABELSBERG.   *c.* 1838

Carl Daniel Freydanck (1811–87)

Inscribed on the back: *Ansicht des Schlosses Glinicke vom Babertsberge aufgenomen* (View of Schloss Glienicke from the Babertsberge)

Oil on canvas, 280 × 360

KPM-Archiv, Schloss Charlottenburg (No. 60)

The staffage figures before the neo-Gothic balustrade of the terrace of Schloss Babelsberg near Potsdam, the summer residence of Prince Wilhelm of Prussia (later King and Kaiser Wilhelm I), appear to be looking from the south-west directly on to the Palace of Glienicke, which lies like a flat block on a gentle slope on the far bank of the Havel.

Although Freydanck here exaggerates the proximity of the two buildings, Schinkel always intended them to form part of the same composition.

The square tower that linked the Kavalier wing with the coach-house and dominated the whole is shown on this view in the simpler form planned by Schinkel with the triforium in the upper storey. Both the tower and the flat roof of the house afforded a view far across the Havel landscape and the city of Potsdam.

To the right of the palace is the Orangery, which was demolished in 1840 for safety reasons. In its place Persius set the stibadium

(semicircular seat) (cat. 60). The building with the two windows and the triangular gable in front, on the road linking Berlin with Potsdam, offered the chance to observe the traffic and was thus known as the Kleine Neugierde (Little Curiosity). Its place was later taken by the 'Grosse (great) Neugierde', built 1835–7 (see fig. 48).

Lit.: Berlin 1987 II, 64.

I.B.

60.

VIEW FROM THE STIBADIUM AT KLEIN-GLIENICKE
TO POTSDAM.   1844–7

Carl Daniel Freydanck (1811–87)

Oil on paper, 280 × 408

KPM-Archiv, Schloss Charlottenburg
(Portfolio 41, No. 13)

This oil sketch, set down lightly but surely, is full of sunlight and colour. It served Freydanck as the basis for his carefully finished oil painting, *View from the Park of Prince Carl at Klein Glienicke to Potsdam* (KPM-Archiv, No. 200). The painter's standpoint is what was known as the stibadium on the left next to the drive up to the Schloss. The designs for this (1840) are by Ludwig Persius, a pupil of Schinkel. The form was partly derived from a structure on the grave of Mamia, the priestess

of Venus, at Pompeii, which was very well known at the end of the eighteenth century, being mentioned by Goethe on his journey to Italy in 1787. Schinkel was extremely fond of these seats, as was his royal client, Friedrich Wilhelm IV, and they were not only placed in the Potsdam parks but in many of his interiors (cat. 62, 64, 69).

From this raised seat, which also serves as a viewing platform, the gaze passes over Schinkel's Lion Fountain and the Pleasure Ground to Potsdam on the other side of the Havel. This can be linked to a letter from Pliny the Younger, in which he describes one of his country seats, Tuscum, and makes particular mention of a stibadium there. As in Glienicke, it is placed opposite a fountain, so that here we have in effect, 'a free translation of literary testimony into architecture'.

Before the central support is a granite bowl by Christian Gottlieb Cantian, erected here in 1840. Unlike Freydanck's finished painting, this sketch does not include the cupola of

Schinkel's Nikolaikirche in Potsdam, which was built between 1843 and 1848.

Lit.: Berlin 1987 I, 251–2; Berlin 1987 II, 66a.

I.B.

61.

THE NEUE PAVILLON IN THE PARK AT CHARLOTTENBURG.   *c. 1825–30*

Wilhelm Barth (1779–1852)

Signed lower left: *W. Barth* and inscribed lower centre *Zu Charlottenburg*

Body colour; 425 × 600

Kupferstichkabinett, SMB (KK 256–1980)

In 1824 Friedrich Wilhelm III conceived the plan for a summer house in the park at Charlottenburg for himself and his second wife in a morganatic marriage, Auguste, Princess von Liegnitz, and Schinkel drew up the designs before he left for Italy in the same year. By the autumn of 1825 the building and its interior were finished.

The king wanted a building as similar as possible to the Villa Reale Chiatamone in Naples, where he had stayed in 1822. Schinkel followed the model for the arrangement of his ground plan and in details, but characteristically made it his own with a typical contrast between smooth surfaces and the sharply contoured lines of the individual mouldings. The interior follows the simple clarity of the external divisions, and is of the same high quality, its effect created by the contrast of white and strong colours.

The relatively small building stands, thanks to its proportions, as an organism independent of the Schloss. The long five-bay sides have three French windows in the centre, above them a loggia framed by pillars with two engaged columns. The shorter sides of the building have only three bays, of which the outer are blind windows in both storeys. The loggia above the central French window is narrow and without columns. The symmetrical exterior reflects the division of the interior. The square rooms in the corners of

A. Camin   Niche mit dem halbrunden Sopha   Camin   Pilaster   Thür nach dem Vestibule   B   Spiegelwand dem Cabinet gegenüber mit der Ansicht der beiden Pilaster

AB Hauptwand des Sallons den Fenstern gegenüber.

Seite 232. Mappe XXII. N° 151.

Schinkel . 1825.

the building are linked by passages in the upper storey between the loggias and the staircase. The loggias open out in all four directions, creating a free space that can be enjoyed from the balcony which runs round the outside of the house. This linking of built space and open space, residential rooms and park, related to the contemporary feeling for nature. Barth's gouache was made soon after the building was completed, before agaves and aloes were planted on the eastern front to underline the Italian character of the building.

Lit.: Berlin 1980, 307–9; Berlin 1981, 60.

G.R. and R.K.

62.

NEUE PAVILLON: SECTION THROUGH THE GARDEN ROOM AND CABINET. 1825

Signed and dated, *Schinkel 1825*. Inscribed *AB Hauptwand des Sallons den Fenstern gegenüber* (main wall of the salon opposite the windows), *Camin* (fireplace), *Niche mit dem halbrunden Sopha* (alcove with the semicircular sofa), *Camin* (fireplace), *Thür nach dem Vestibul* (door from the vestibule), *Spiegelwand dem Cabinet gegenüber mit der Ansicht der beiden Pilaster* (mirrored wall opposite the cabinet with an elevation of both pilasters)

Pen and ink, pencil and wash, 250 × 525

Nationalgalerie, SMB (SM 22.151)

The largest room in the Pavillon, the garden room, was divided into two. The left-hand side shown here contained a large semicircular seat based on the so-called Tomb of Mamia at Pompeii; Schinkel provided a richer example at the same date for the Teesalon in the Königliches Schloss (cat. 64). The bench was carefully positioned to take in the long view across the garden front of Schloss Charlottenburg. The walls of the room were covered with scagliola, with a curtain draped behind the bench. The Neue Pavillon was gutted in the Second World War; now known as the Schinkel-Pavillon, its interiors (including the garden room) have been restored.

Lit.: Berlin 1980, 309; Berlin 1981, 60.

M.S.

62a. The restored Garden Room at the Neue Pavillon (now the Schinkel-Pavillon).

63.

VIEW OF THE TEA SALON IN THE KÖNIGLICHES
SCHLOSS.   *c.* 1830

Anonymous artist

Watercolour, 155 × 225

SSG Potsdam-Sanssouci (Aquarell Sammlung,
No. 2906a)

64.

KÖNIGLICHES SCHLOSS, BERLIN: ELEVATION OF A
WALL IN THE TEA SALON   *c.* 1825

Pen and black ink, watercolour and pencil,
241 × 457

Nationalgalerie, SMB (SM 34.51)

Crown Prince Friedrich Wilhelm, the future
King Friedrich Wilhelm IV, had in 1815 taken
up residence in part of Frederick the Great's
former apartment in the Königliches Schloss.
After marrying Princess Elisabeth of Bavaria
he commissioned Schinkel to redesign these
rooms, which he did in 1824–6. This was his
first major commission from the Prince and
celebrated Berlin artists were engaged. The

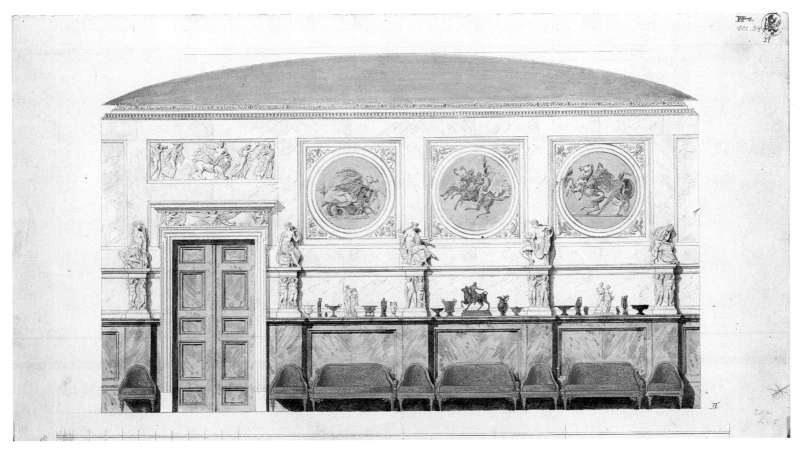

apartments of Friedrich II lay on the first floor, in the north-east corner, overlooking the Spree and the courtyard, and six rooms were refitted as private apartments and reception rooms. They included the former Erasmus Kapelle, a relic of the Renaissance palace that was redesigned from 1538 by Kaspar Theiss under Joachim II (see cat. 4). Only the circular writing cabinet used by Friedrich II, an outstanding example of rococo created in 1745 to designs by Johann August Nahl and Johann Michael Hoppenhaupt the Elder, was retained in its original form.

The Tea Salon beneath Frederick the Great's concert room was designed by Schinkel in the antique manner from a sketch by the Crown Prince; it was also to be used as a large drawing-room for smaller gatherings. The walls were subdivided by panelling, with cabinets for collections and rich sculptural groups of figures by Christian Friedrich Tieck; circular paintings by Carl Wilhelm Kolbe, Julius Schoppe and Hermann Stilke were set into the walls. The sculptures and paintings represented mythological figures and legends of the Greek gods. The ceiling was painted in the style of an antique velarium spanning the whole room. Against the wall opposite the windows stood a semicircular seat, like an exedra, with antique-style small sculptures and *objets d'art*, collected by Friedrich Wilhelm IV on his journeys to Italy, along its back and on the wall cabinets. Schinkel was among the guests the Crown Prince and Princess regularly received in this room, as were Alexander von Humboldt, Ranke, Schelling and Niebuhr. Cat. 65 shows a preliminary design for the furniture. The Königliches (or Berliner) Schloss was demolished following war damage.

H.D.

65.

DINING CHAIR. 1824

Anonymous maker, after Schinkel

Birch wood, with cane seat, 850 × 450 × 395

SSG Potsdam-Sanssouci

Several examples of this type of dining chair are to be found in residences occupied by King Friedrich Wilhelm III. Schinkel used them in his refurbishing work from 1824 to 1826, and so this example probably dates from then. The inventory of the Königliches Palais lists under the dining-room: '3 dozen birch wood and cane dining chairs newly completed in December 1824'. A watercolour confirms that the chairs were of the same kind, and proves that this is their earliest recorded location. More examples were made for the Chapel. In 1825 they were also supplied to the Neue Pavillon in addition to versions made of mahogany and upholstered. The design of chair recalls those made for the Royal Palaces in the first decade of the century, which were based on the ancient Greek *klismos* type.

Lit.: Sievers 1950, p. 23, pl. 122; Berlin 1980, 348; Berlin 1981, 237.

B.G.

66.

DESIGN FOR AN ARMCHAIR AND A SOFA FOR THE KÖNIGLICHES SCHLOSS, BERLIN. 1825

Pen and black ink and watercolour, 231 × 343

Nationalgalerie, SMB (SM 43a.33)

67.

ARMCHAIR FOR THE KÖNIGLICHES SCHLOSS, BERLIN. *c.* 1825

Anonymous maker, after Schinkel.

Gilt wood, the upholstery renewed, 925 × 855 × 510

SSG Schloss Charlottenburg

Schinkel's series of heavy, grand gilt seat-furniture begins with the furnishing of the rooms of Crown Prince Friedrich Wilhelm's apartment in the Königliches Schloss, the highlights of which were the Star Hall (Sternsaal) and the Tea Salon.

Although this type of armchair can be found only in the Star Hall, there were similar chairs but without arms in both rooms, and also, in the same suite, backless sofas in the Tea Salon, as shown in Schinkel's design.

In this grand furniture Schinkel intended to evoke the extreme pomp and stiff elegance of French Empire furniture. Borrowing from antiquity, he reached back, in the spirit of the Empire, to elements found in Pompeian murals, such as the front legs turned in conical sections and gadroons, backward-sweeping sabre legs, the turned rail ending in rosettes, and the arms resting on sphinxes. In addition, Plates 21 and 29 of C. Percier's and F.L. Fontaine's *Recueil de décorations intérieurs . . .* (Paris, 1812) have clearly played a role in the design.

As with French and English antique-style furniture, Schinkel bounds his flat surfaces with moulded profiles ending in acanthus leaves. His fondness for scrollwork, which can also be seen as in his ornate table ends, is evident in the arm supports.

Another design for the suite is in the Kunstbibliothek, SMPK (Hdz 5843).

Lit.: Sievers 1950, p. 29, pl. 32; Berlin 1980, 358; Berlin 1981, 239.

W.B. and B.G.

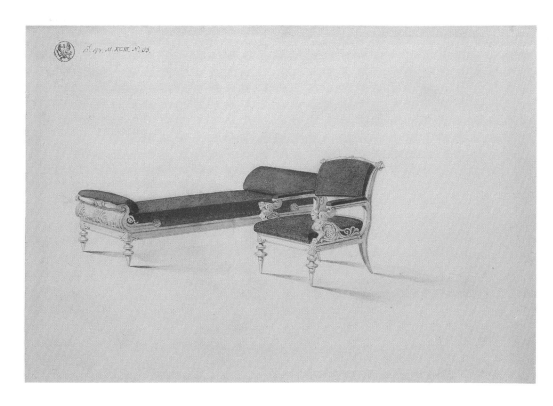

68.

VIEW OF CROWN PRINCESS ELISABETH'S PRIVATE
DRAWING-ROOM IN THE KÖNIGLICHES
SCHLOSS, BERLIN.   1828

Eduard Biermann (1803–92)

Signed and dated bottom right: *Biermann 1828*

Watercolour, 280 × 349

SSG Potsdam-Sanssouci (Aquarell Sammlung,
    No. A–S 215)

In his work in the Königliches Schloss Schinkel
completely transformed all the rococo rooms
except Frederick the Great's circular study. In
redesigning the corner space, which had one
window overlooking the River Spree and
another the Schlossplatz, Schinkel combined
the circular study in the bay window with the
room. The smooth, green-coloured walls
formed the backdrop for a great variety of oil
paintings. Mirrors attached to pillars and
lightweight muslin curtains – both
undoubtedly designed by Schinkel – give the
room a greater sense of space. The grand piano
came from the older Schloss furniture, and
even the suite of furniture, based on Schinkel's
designs, was completed before the room's
conversion, possibly shortly before 1820. It had
furnished the rooms the Crown Prince

occupied whilst the building works were in progress. In later watercolour views of the room a new, bulky suite of furniture has taken its place. These pictures also show a contemporary grand piano and heavy *portière* curtains. Another striking feature of the original arrangement is the number of sculptures, three marble busts and two bronzes.

B.G.

69.

SCHLOSS CHARLOTTENHOF: TWO PERSPECTIVE VIEWS, INCLUDING THE OLD MANOR HOUSE.

1829

Signed and dated bottom right: *Schinkel. 1829*

Ink over pencil, 550 × 439

Nationalgalerie, SMB (SM 21c.118)

Drawing for the *Sammlung architektonischer Entwürfe*, Part 18, 1831, Plate 111.

In 1746, Johann Boumann, the future Oberbaudirektor (Supervisor of Public Works), had bought a piece of land between the Rehgarten (Deer Park) the western part of Sanssouci Park, and the path leading from the

suburb of Brandenburg in Potsdam to Werder. Here he built a house, which was subsequently purchased and further extended by Johann Büring, a landscape architect, and Carl von Gontard, also an architect, among others. In 1825 the last owner, after repairing the manor house in 1822, offered to sell the estate 'now known as Charlottenhof' to Friedrich Wilhelm III. As an alternative to spoiling the view from the Deer Park by 'gardens full of cabbages and weeds', an opportunity arose to increase the narrow east–west expanse of Sanssouci Park by landscaping further terrain towards the south. The king listened to his advisers, especially Peter Joseph Lenné, purchased the house and land and told the Crown Prince he would receive the estate as a Christmas present. By the time the Crown Prince was given this present in March 1826 a plan Lenné had drawn

up the previous year could serve as a basis for landscaping the grounds. It opened up the new park area of nearly 100 hectares by creating an almost semicircular broad path connecting it with Sanssouci Park, as did several linking sightlines. The remaining surroundings, however, were hidden behind densely planted trees, with the old manor house forming the focal point of the whole area.

The Crown Prince accepted Lenné's idea: 'I shall connect the park with Sans Souci and put plants in it, replace the house's pitched roof with a flat one and thus give it the loveliest possible form.'

Schinkel was commissioned to convert the house and carry out the architectural works in the park. Here he could draw on the experiences of his collaboration with Lenné at Glienicke. For his part, the Crown Prince had studied Percier and Fontaine's *Choix des plus célèbres maisons de plaisance de Rome et de ses environs* (1809), and had visited Fontaine in Paris in 1815. Schinkel countered the notions the prince had thus formed of antique estates and Italian villas with a selection of his own sketches from Italy. Schinkel began making plans for Charlottenhof after 1824, an extremely creative year for him, and after his second journey to Italy which took him to Pompeii. The building work began in 1826 whilst Schinkel was travelling to France and Britain and was completed in 1829, under the supervision of Ludwig Persius.

'My task was to landscape the area which had hitherto been only a kitchen garden and meadow in as beautiful a manner as the flat terrain would allow. My first priority was radically to alter the house which was built on a very small scale in an unattractive style.

'In view of its small size, the cost of converting this property was to be moderate, and so the building plan had to utilise as much of the original structure as possible . . .; accordingly, a projection was added to the vestibule . . . a new portico was constructed, and a semicircular extension built on to the bedroom. The staircase in the vestibule was rebuilt . . .

'With the extremely low-lying, meadow-like terrain, it was essential to install a terrace providing an area permanently dry underfoot, where one could enjoy the fresh air near the house. The portico stands on this terrace, but to prevent the terrace from making the basement level with its essential servants' quarters, kitchens, cellars, etc., damp and dark by overshadowing it, courtyards were built at ground level between the terrace and the house, which were connected beneath the portico.

'[To the south] the terrace is bordered by a colonnaded passage with vines growing over it, [to the north] by a gentle lawn-covered slope, with broad stone steps to either side of it, leading down to the pool. [To the east] the terrace is bordered by a large semicircular seat above which a tent roof can be spread. The pool, with a raised basin from which a powerful fountain gushes, lies in the middle of the terrace; small streams trickle between flowers and lawns and from both sides of this pool, where one sees small fountains; other fountains gush from the pool below; in the vestibule between the flights of steps yet another fairly small fountain leaps from the pool, and a larger one between the lime trees. All these aquatic effects are produced by a steam-pumping engine situated on a hill further back on the bank of an artificial lake, with a chimney like a large candelabrum which embellishes the landscape.

'Plate 111 [cat. 69] consists of two views of the whole area: the upper one principally depicts one of the courtyards between the terrace and the house, the gently sloping terrace and the pool below with its two small fountains, the large fountain, the arbour, the semicircular seat, the candelabrum and a tower in the town of Potsdam in the distance; the lower one reveals the projected greenhouses as well as these other features.' (*Sammlung architektonischer Entwürfe*, part 18, 1831)

The 'lovely lime tree' from the old estate garden, supported by posts on the western end of the terrace, prefigures the pergola which was erected there in 1840. The Elisabeth Column (a marble bust by Tieck, 1828) was not placed in the lower pool until 1835. The orangery and fence west of the Schloss were not completed.

The lower section of cat. 69 depicts the west front of the manor house as it looked in 1825 before conversion. It shows the bays, the central projection and the sloping base which were retained and the heavy roof which was removed.

Lit.: Berlin 1980, 261; Berlin 1981, 68.

H.S.

70.

SCHLOSS CHARLOTTENHOF. 1841

Wilhelm Barth (1779–1852)

Signed and dated: *W. Barth 1841*

Oil on canvas, 1030 × 1410

SSG Potsdam-Sanssouci (GK I 16668)

As well as using the official name of Charlottenhof the Crown Prince almost always called his property 'Siam'. This was not merely playful: at this time Siam was regarded as the 'land of the free'. Friedrich Wilhelm's tutor Delbrück had introduced him to the intellectual world of German philanthropy whose followers based their belief in the world's perfectibility on examples drawn not only from the Golden Age but also accounts of the Antipodes, 'where Europe's veneer of

politeness' was not applicable. Because these distant lands had few archaeological remains of the kind that fuelled nostalgia for ancient civilisation and medieval fantasies they offered greater scope for speculation about social behaviour.

Delbrück taught the Crown Prince the principles of Rousseau's philosophy, recreating his idyllic universe among the 'Romantic environs' in and around Potsdam. The Crown Prince therefore envisaged the plans for an idealised landscape around Charlottenhof as a utopian domain of peaceful human existence.

Lit.: Berlin 1980, 284.

H.S.

71.

A VIEW OF CHARLOTTENHOF NEAR POTSDAM. 1841

Carl Daniel Freydanck (1811–87)

Inscribed on the back: *Ansicht von Charlottenhof bei Potsdam*. Signed and dated *C.F. fec. 1841*.

Oil on canvas, 281 × 354

KPM-Archiv, Schloss Charlottenburg (No. 69)

In converting the old house of Charlottenhof the tall windows and window bays of the upper storeys were retained, as was the emphasis observable in the old building of the axial central projection. Schinkel drew it forward from the restricted west façade and balanced it architecturally with the pedimented, Doric portico on the east façade shown here. The vestibule of this portico was painted in 1833 'in accordance with Pompeian models'. While the pitched roof connects the two gables, the side wings are flat-roofed and completed with an attic.

This view shows the terrace added on the east side in 1828 up to the level of the residential storey, and geometrically designed with a pergola on the pattern of the Renaissance layout at the Villa Albani in Rome. Facing the house is a semicircular seat (exedra) designed by Schinkel, with a winged lion finishing off the end, which can be seen at the right-hand side of the picture. It was embellished with a running frieze of Pompeian motifs and crowned by two bronze statues: Paris and Mercury, copies of works by Canova and Thorvaldsen (in this view only Mercury is visible). In summer the semicircular seat was covered with a tent roof, as in Schinkel's drawing (cat. 69).

A rose garden extends from the terrace towards the east. To the south it is bordered by an arbour, and a pool was installed to the north. A pergola leads from the steps to the park – with a restored classical statue of Caesar (by Rauch, 1831) embellishing the end of the wall.

A basin-fountain graces the centre of the lawn. Schinkel's original design was later altered: in 1838 the original sandstone rim was replaced by the marble one shown in Freydanck's view. In the 1840s the cast-iron basin much admired by contemporaries was replaced by a marble copy.

A marble conduit, framed by hydrangeas, ferns and irises, connects the basin fountain to two bell-shaped fountains made of Carrara marble on the eastern and western borders of the lawn.

Lit.: Berlin 1987 II, 35.

I.B. and M.H.

72.

SCHLOSS CHARLOTTENHOF: THE VESTIBULE.

After 1829

Anonymous

Watercolour over pen and black ink, 174 × 220

SSG Potsdam-Sanssouci (Aquarell-Sammlung, No. 3862)

In addition to Schinkel's sketches for the interior decoration of Schloss Charlottenhof, a few anonymous watercolours from about 1830 provide detailed information on the design of individual rooms. On 12 April 1827 Schinkel wrote to Hofmarshall von Massow: 'I have thus completed the enclosed design for decorating the staircase vestibule and installing a small fountain which will issue from a square pool set into the ground.'

Instead of 'the previously agreed wrought-iron railings' the Crown Prince had a pair of large sliding doors built for the portal which, when open, lead the eye obliquely into the

vestibule. This room extends through both floors and with the hall behind it dominates the centre of the Schloss. Two flights of stairs set against the side walls lead to a landing on the first floor. From here one can enter the hall through a double door framed in white, or the rooms at the side through doors glazed in three rectangular panels.

The wooden staircase is painted in imitation of light grey marble. The simple three-sided balustrade consists of straight brass rod banisters, moulded wooden rails and green marbled newel posts. Up to landing level the walls are marbled: the base and upper border like the stairs, alternating with areas of *verde antico* green. Blue and green stripes divide the white surfaces of the upper wall into rectangular sections, with a sinuous yellow frieze at the dado level. Above this on the hall wall hang framed coloured engravings after Raphael, like those in the hall. They conceal paintings of genii and gods on a blue ground, set into the walls as tondi or panels, which are shown in a drawing by Schinkel signed and dated 1829 (SM 21c.119).

The top of the wall carries a frieze of winged demi-figures linked by garlands (cf. Percier and Fontaine, *Recueil des décorations intérieures*, Paris 1812, Plate 52: Frise de la chambre à coucher de Malmaison). All the painting was carried out in gouache on paper by the Berlin artists Müller and Eyrich.

The double door to the steward's quarters on the ground floor is golden bronze in colour. In 1828 the sculptor Kleemeyer attached decorative pewter scrollwork to the panels. Brownish-beige tiles cover the floor, in the middle of which a square pool has been installed, with a small fountain in the form of a baluster, which echoes the water candelabrum on the Pfaueninsel (Peacock Island), to which the candelabrum-shaped chimney of Schinkel's steam pumping engine by the Maschinenteich ('engine pond') at Charlottenhof is also related. In 1843 Schinkel's Gewerbe-Institut fountain (cat. 146) was placed in the vestibule (fig. 75).

Lit.: Hamburg 1982, 15.11.

R.M. and H.S.

73.

SCHLOSS CHARLOTTENHOF: THE CROWN PRINCESS'S WRITING ROOM.

1833–4

Anonymous

Watercolour over pen and black ink, 172 × 220

SSG Potsdam-Sanssouci (Aquarell Sammlung, No. 3867)

The walls and ceiling of this room – like eight other rooms on the first floor – were papered in 1827 and painted in 1828: the ceiling white, the curved cornice grey, the walls pink, the cornice moulding, skirting and door-frame green. The walls, windows and doors have silver mouldings. The green cornice mouldings are decorated with silvered strings of beads and pewter palmettes. The scrollwork on the panels of the silvered doors were also meant to be painted, but in 1828 they were modelled in relief using a wax technique.

The writing-desk is the only item of the furniture Schinkel designed for this room that is visible in the watercolour. The back legs are shaped like columns, the front ones have lion's-paw feet and bulky scrolls at the top. The writing surface is covered with green

material, secured with silver nails, and has a double gallery of pierced pewter on three sides: scroll tendrils below, wave tendrils above. There are two shelves of pigeon-holes. The folding metal chair, made in Tula in 1744, was substituted for a semicircular armchair which was not made.

Looking through the open doors gives an impression of the colour and decoration of several rooms in the small Schloss. Next door, in the Crown Princess's living-room, the walls are coloured blue and a chair from Schinkel's suite can be seen.

The hall adjoining this room, with some of its doors highlighted in red paint, was the largest room in the building. On its white walls hung coloured engravings after Raphael's frescoes in the Vatican loggias, taken

73a. Anonymous. The Tent Room, Schloss Charlottenhof. After 1830. Pen and ink and watercolour (SSG Potsdam-Sanssouci 38b6). This room, recalling a military tent, was set up in this form about 1830 for the use of the ladies-in-waiting. The beds and folding chairs are made of iron. It was also used by guests, including Alexander von Humboldt and Schinkel.

73b. Anonymous. The Red Corner Room, Schloss Charlottenhof. After 1834. Pen and ink and watercolour (SSG Potsdam-Sanssouci 38b8). This room concluded the enfilade from the writing room (cat. 73) and opens on to the pergola in the garden. It is hung with gouache landscapes of *c.*1820. The caned side chair is after a design by Schinkel. It had arrived in the room by 1834, possibly from the Königliches Schloss.

for the most part from Giovanni Volpato's collection of engravings: *Le Loggie di Raffaele nel Vaticano* (Rome, 1772–7). Beyond it is the red corner room. The writing room, like the other rooms at Charlottenhof, has survived with its furnishings and decorations substantially intact.

Lit.: Hamburg 1982, 15.14.

R.M.

74.

SCHLOSS CHARLOTTENHOF: THE PORTICO.   *c.* 1834

Anonymous

Watercolour over pen and black ink, 155 × 202

SSG Potsdam-Sanssouci (Aquarell Sammlung, No. 3864)

Three steps lead from the gravelled terrace by the eastern façade of the Schloss to the Doric portico, creating a direct link between the garden and the building. The floor is covered with light sandstone and black marble slabs. The ceiling and rafters are wooden, with an external cladding of zinc.

Three open doors in the rear wall of the portico allow a clear view through the hall to the painted window over the portal in the vestibule, where blue panes of glass with yellow glass stars bathe the whole room in a cool light. The motif of yellow stars on a blue ground is repeated in the canted semicircular niches of the hall. Both niches have red fabric curtains, secured at the top by decorative gilded palmettes, and with hems of scroll tendrils and gold braid. Small gilded stars decorate the semi-domes, which are painted blue. White marble sculptures stand in front of the curtains: Ganymede by Wredow and David by Imhof.

A sketch by Schinkel (SM 51.1) which can be dated to 1831 shows the plan and elevation of the right-hand niche with the statue of Ganymede, but undecorated. Schinkel's note on the sheet gives precise instructions: 'The walls to be painted the colour of the scarlet curtain, with a matt finish like the fresco colours in pictures from Pompeii.' The more opulent decoration of the niches was undoubtedly the Crown Prince's idea. Since designing the set: 'Hall of Stars in the Palace of the Queen of the Night' for Mozart's *The Magic Flute* (cat. 28), Schinkel had repeatedly used the decorative motif of rhythmically orbiting stars in palaces in Berlin.

For the gallery in the Palais of Prince Karl, which Schinkel designed in 1827–8, he decorated part of the wall with statue recesses

to give 'the illusion of three dimensions'; once completed, these were broadly similar to the hall recesses at Charlottenhof. Schinkel made two further drawings in 1830 showing very similar recesses for the banqueting hall in the Palais Redern (see Berlin 1981, 71c).

The remaining decoration of the portico was associated with the construction of the small entrance hall connected to the pergola. On 18 April 1833 the Crown Prince's instructions on building this entrance hall, complete with measurements and a drawing, reached Persius, who was supposed to confer with Schinkel about it.

In the same year Bernhard Wilhelm Rosendahl began transferring Schinkel's decorative designs for the portico to the walls with encaustic colours. Pompeian motifs are arranged in five sections one above the other. At the base are fabulous sea-creatures and genii painted green on black grounds. Above these, on a blue ground are human figures, animals and tendrils in a grotesque. A black frieze runs above the doors, divided into regular sections by garlands of fruit. Each section contains a figure from the Herculaneum Dancers. Acanthus tendrils trail along the architrave. The upper area is only partially visible – here light sections alternate with black ones, with a design of figures among foliage. These are similar to the murals in Neustrelitz Orangery; after 1842 Schinkel's pupil Buttel commissioned Rosendahl to complete these.

In subsequent years (until 1841) twenty-eight porcelain medallions showing portraits of the royal family, their relatives and well-known personages were inserted into the blue sections of wall. These were made from original designs by August von Kloeber at the Königliches Porzellanmanufaktur, Berlin.

Lit.: Hamburg 1982, 15.13.

R.M.

75.

SCHLOSS CHARLOTTENHOF: VIEW FROM THE SMALL
PORTICO TO THE RÖMISCHE BÄDER (ROMAN
BATHS). After 1835.

Anonymous

Watercolour over pen and ink, 184 × 232

SSG Potsdam-Sanssouci (Aquarell Sammlung,
No. 3869)

The small portico was not built until 1833 and,
like the large entrance hall, it was painted by
Bernhard Wilhelm Rosendahl from a sketch
by Schinkel (SM 34.38). The watercolour very
clearly illustrates the location of the small
Schloss in its generously proportioned
surroundings. Schinkel, collaborating with
Lenné, landscaped spacious sightlines which
closely connect the building to the original
area of Sanssouci, allowing us to look through
the portico beyond the buildings of the
Römische Bäder to the park's northern
boundary, where we can make out the
Historische Mühle (Historic Windmill) and
further away, the Ruinenberg (Hill of Ruins).
The artist gives us the only proof that a
sculpture – identified by Kuhlow as a

monument with a recumbent female figure
from the Villa Borghese – was indeed placed
on the edge of the large pool. The sculpture
was envisaged on the very earliest of Schinkel's
and the Crown Prince's designs (SM 34.37) as
a fountain.

R.M.

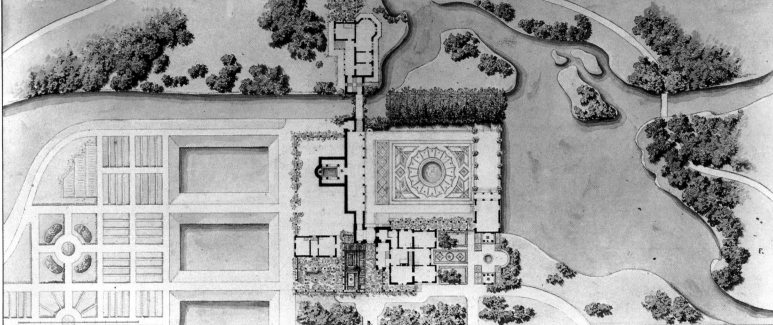

76.

THE GARDENER'S HOUSE, CHARLOTTENHOF:
PERSPECTIVE VIEW FROM THE WEST, AND A
PLAN OF THE WHOLE SITE.   1834

Signed on the left: *Schinkel inv.* and signed and
dated bottom left: *Schinkel inv. 1834*

Pen and ink, 423 × 540

Nationalgalerie, SMB (SM 21c.122)

Drawing for the *Sammlung architektonischer
Entwürfe*, part 24, 1835, pl. 145.

77.

THE GARDENER'S HOUSE, CHARLOTTENHOF: VIEW
FROM THE SOUTH.   Before 1835

Signed bottom left: *Schinkel inv.* and inscribed
underneath: *Perspective vom Gärtnerhause in
Charlottenhof bei Potsdam von Punkte E, im
Grundrisse, aufgenommen* (view of the
gardener's house in Charlottenhof near
Potsdam drawn from point E on the
groundplan) and inscribed bottom right: *F.
Berger*

Pen and ink, 323 × 519

Nationalgalerie, SMB (SM 21c.123)

Preliminary drawing for the *Sammlung
architektonischer Entwürfe*, part 24, 1835, pl.
148.

'Another principal building on this property
. . . is the gardener's house, which is not a
conversion of an older building on the same
site . . . but an entirely new construction. . .
. Conceived in a picturesque style, the
property was intended to reveal a succession
of idyllic ideas . . . and form a varied
ensemble of architectural features which
could blend agreeably with the surrounding
landscape.

'The gardener's house itself, the most
substantial piece of architecture in this
group, was conceived in the style of Italian
country houses; above half of the main

structure there is an additional floor, containing several pleasant loggia rooms. Beside it a moderately tall tower rises still higher from the main building; this contains an attractive bathroom, which one climbs up to by means of narrow stone steps attached to the outside wall but which appear to float. . . . At the front and back, vines, supported by stone pillars, surround the entrance to the gardener's residence. Along the rear façade [of the house] these are more extensive and connect the main building with an ornamental salon . . . which forms a self-contained temple-like structure. . . .

'One walks out of this salon through a peristyle of Attic pillars to an open space, decorated with mosaics and enclosed by low parapet walls on which flower-vases stand, just above a small lake. At one end of this a flight of steps leads down to the water, which at this point runs from the lake as a canal beneath a long arched pergola parallel to the vines along the rear façade of the gardener's house; this arbour forms the boundary of a sizeable plot of garden in the centre of which a pool with a high-leaping fountain adds grace to the whole area . . . . Beside the tower [of the gardener's house] an open arch leads into this inner garden; in front of this arch and to the side of the gardener's house spreads a canopy of leaves, supported by short columns, a herm of Bacchus and vine-bearing piers.

'A large flight of steps leads from beneath this broad arbour up to the terrace above the arch and arcaded hall, which offers pleasing views of the whole area. In one of the corners beneath the arbour is a stibadium [stone seat] in the antique manner, approached by a short flight of steps, where

a large table-top rests upon a Corinthian capital, surrounded by benches and with a cavity in the centre where water bubbles gently from a bell-shaped fountain. The walls around this table are decorated with bas-reliefs and ivy; from the walls rise antique sculptures, as do the short columns supporting the canopy of leaves on this side. On the small flight of steps leading up to the stibadium an antique sarcophagus catches the water issuing from the mouth of a fish positioned on a bracket attached to the base of the herm of Bacchus, thus enhancing the charming freshness of this area.

'Behind the wall crowned with columns is a separate small building with a few rooms and a courtyard, roofed with luxuriant vines, for the livestock of the small dairy farm. In the courtyard behind the arcaded hall a small atrium was planned, to be entered from the arcaded hall . . . . The appealing layout of this small villa allows one to enlarge or add to the various buildings in the same style as one desires, and the atrium was accordingly later designed on a more spacious scale, then completed with yet further extensions to the basic building plan . . . .

'There is another important area on the far side of the gardener's house near the gable-end of the small salon, namely a small flower garden by the lake. A semicircular seat juts out towards the water and there is a pool in the centre of this small garden . . . . On both sides of the garden are ornamental Doric tabernacles . . . beneath which the bronze busts of King Friedrich Wilhelm III and Queen Luise, both of blessed memory, stand on marble pedestals . . . . Around this small villa there is an Italian kitchen garden, well stocked with produce, where artichokes

and other tall plants flourish among grapevines densely twining round trees. The whole site forms a picturesque ensemble, offering varied and agreeable views, secluded places to rest, comfortable rooms and open spaces in which to enjoy country life. By its nature it is capable of infinite extension and enrichment, thus giving continuous creative satisfaction.'
(*Sammlung architektonischer Entwürfe*, commentary to part 24, 1835)

Cat. 73 shows the chief view from the west, with, from left to right, the courtyard, the assistant gardener's house, the great arbour (and stibadium), the head gardener's house and the temple-like salon (now called the Teesalon) with the two tabernacles. The plan, which is aligned with the west at the bottom, shows the arcaded hall running east with at its centre the atrium which ultimately developed into the Römische Bäder (Roman Baths). Across the channel is the dwelling (never built) for the engineer who looked after the steam pumping engines for the fountains. The water was drawn from the lake called the Maschinenteich (engine pond).

Lit.: Berlin 1980, 277, 278; Berlin 1981, 79.

M.S.

78.

THE COURT GARDENER'S HOUSE AT
   CHARLOTTENHOF.   1847

Carl Daniel Freydanck (1811–87)

Inscribed on the back: *Ansicht der Hof-Gärtner
   Wohnung in Charlottenhof.* (View of the
   Court Gardener's residence in
   Charlottenhof.). Signed and dated *C.F. fec.
   1847.*

Oil on canvas, 290 × 365

KPM-Archiv, Schloss Charlottenburg (inv.
   Nr. 206)

In his very first working ground plan (SM
34.37) Schinkel had envisaged extending
Charlottenhof with a gardener's house, though
in a different position. In the south-east corner
of the grounds a narrow rectangle
accommodated an elongated building whose
elevation (SM 51.57) already reveals the
characteristics of the future court gardener's
villa. A tower, together with a long narrow
building and a short tall one, are aligned on a
longitudinal axis, with a pergola attached at an
angle to the latter building. A wagon-shed
occupies the position *vis-à-vis* the house taken
up by the pavilion near the lake in the built
scheme. In the end, the buildings were placed
nearer to the present old gardener's house
(known as the dairy farm), on a site in the

north-east corner of the estate. Known today
as the Römische Bäder (Roman Baths) they
were built – with continuous modifications –
between 1829 and 1840. The interiors were
finished in 1845.

Their design was a collaborative effort
between Schinkel, Ludwig Persius, who
prepared the plans and supervised their
execution, and the Crown Prince. The group
of buildings is composed of the house of the
court gardener Hermann Sello (1829–30), the
gardener's assistant's house (1831–2), the baths
themselves (1834–40) behind that, and the
temple-like pavilion (1830) by the so-called
Maschinenteich (engine pond).

Freydanck's view, taken from the garden of
the main front, shows the first building, the

gardener's house, with accommodation on the ground floor for the court gardener, and rooms used for guests such as Alexander von Humboldt on the upper floor.

In 1832 it became necessary to build the assistant's house to the left of the court gardener's residence. The 'great arbour', covered with vines and linking the two houses, with a raised stibadium flanked by two Bacchic herms, allows just a glimpse of the house, once again completely in the Italian style, and hidden deep in greenery and shadow. The archway in the background leads across to the arcaded hall from which the Roman Baths themselves are reached.

Marohn's view, taken from further away and from a different angle, shows the Italian vegetable and flower garden which surrounded the house.

In design and detail the court gardener's house follows the pattern of a detached Italian farmhouse composed of well-defined horizontal and vertical units with low-pitched roofs on open roof-frames, surrounded by the leafy pergolas which fascinated all northern travellers to Italy.

The external flight of steps, which Schinkel recorded seeing on a farm on Capri and which forms a dynamic bridge between the main buildings, became the dominating theme of Friedrich Wilhelm's ideas for the structural design of the court gardener's house, the liberating effect of Schinkel's Italian sketches becoming even more marked than in the Schloss.

The Crown Prince was responsible for the idea of the leafy pergola over the channel on the east. It was directly inspired by an etching of 1806 by C.W. Kolbe after Salomon Gessner, which hung from 1829 onwards in the Crown Prince's study in Schloss Charlottenhof. In his work on the Gärtnerhaus complex Schinkel applied a grid system to blend the different elements into a painterly outline. In this way, he developed a masterly architectural composition around the pivot of the tower, organising buildings and spaces, both closed and open and all placed at different levels, into a complete three-dimensional design. Openly visible, and set at an angle to each other, the court gardener's complex and Schloss Charlottenhof in one sense play the game, familiar since the Renaissance, of the tension between the imposing main house and the picturesque annexe. In this case, however, juxtaposing unequal buildings on equal terms gives the once light-hearted game of palace and cottage a profoundly serious social significance.

The contrast between the Schloss and the gardener's house is not concealed; instead the differences arising from their different purposes are emphasised and brought into play. By

being part of an overall plan Schinkel and Peter Joseph Lenné's creative powers transformed the Crown Prince's dreams of 'Siam'. The system they created out of elements of landscaping, spatial organisation, architecture and horticulture, including the way these communicate visually and functionally, emerged as a blueprint for social harmony and a vision of a world of reason.

Lit.: Berlin 1980, 286; Berlin 1987 II, 40.

I.B. and H.S.

79.

VIEW OF THE RÖMISCHE BÄDER (ROMAN BATHS)
1848

Ferdinand Marohn (active 1839–59)

Signed and dated: *Ferdinand Marohn 1848*

Watercolour, 198 × 300

SSG Potsdam-Sanssouci (Aquarell Sammlung No. 2110)

80.

VIEW OF THE BATHS AT CHARLOTTENHOF. 1844

Carl Daniel Freydanck (1811–87)

Inscribed on the back: *Blick in die Thermen zu Charlottenhof.* (View into the Baths at Charlottenhof.) Signed and dated *CF fec. 1844.*

Oil on canvas, 283 × 364

KPM-Archiv, Schloss Charlottenburg (Inv. Nr 186)

Through the archway between the court gardener's house and the assistant's house is the inner garden of the private grounds of the complex, invisible from the outside.

To the north the garden is bordered by the arcaded hall, used as an orangery (1833), which further stresses the southern character of the group of buildings. This serves as a vestibule to the free-flowing series of antique-style rooms, the Römische Bäder (Roman Baths) built immediately behind it between 1834 and 1840. Despite the names from antiquity, the rooms of the Roman Baths have little in common with Roman thermal baths, being more closely related to antique villas.

Once again the designs came into being – although in a manner which is unclear – through the joint efforts of the Crown Prince, Schinkel and Persius, 'making use of examples of antique Roman houses from Herculaneum'.

The Roman Baths were a step-by-step development from the projection added on to the north side of the arcaded hall, originally envisaged as the exterior wall with one central extension (cf. cat. 76). Today the rooms behind the hall are the atrium, followed by the impluvium and apodyterium to the north, then the vestibule leading to the viridarium (courtyard with a fountain) and a billiard-room. To the east is an arcade along the channel from the Maschinenteich. Up to this point we can assume Schinkel had a direct influence on the building. To the east of the channel he had envisaged another picturesque wooden or half-timbered building as the residence of the Director of Machinery (Maschinenmeister); neither this nor the bridge on the upper floor leading across the channel was completed (see cat. 76). On the west, the building connects with the calidarium built by Persius.

Freydanck's view into the baths from the arcaded hall in the garden was painted just after the decoration of the hall was completed in 1844. Black-and-white marble slabs cover the floor, and the wall between the arcade and the atrium is hung with wallpaper in coloured stripes, finished with a border. Two black (in reality, grey) marble Ionic columns with marbled cast zinc capitals and Carrara marble bases support the openings into the atrium, both to the outside and into the interior of the impluvium behind. Schinkel was responsible for the painted decoration of the atrium in dark red and black. The walls of the impluvium were painted by Rosendahl with Pompeian motifs.

In the middle of the atrium, effectively and softly lit by muted side lighting, stands a gift from Tsar Nicholas I, a precious bath made of green jasper in the form of an antique sarcophagus, while two restored Pompeian marble statues of Bacchus (left) and Apollo stand beside the passages to the open impluvium behind, which is lit from above. Between the two front columns is a scaled-down bronze copy after the antique sculpture of the 'Spinario'. Today a copy of the Dying Gaul occupies this position – the Spinario is at the entrance to the calidarium.

The real *point de vue*, however, is the marble

group of *Hebe and Ganymede* by Emil Wolf, a pupil of Rauch. This is situated in front of the blue-painted semicircular niche of the rectangular apodyterium lying behind the impluvium. In the late 1840s this group was replaced by one of a youth and girl by a well, carved by Werner Henschel.

Lit.: Berlin 1987 II, 43.

I.B. and H.S.

81.

THE GÄRTNERHAUS: PERSPECTIVE VIEW OF THE INTERIOR OF THE BATH.   *c.*1835

Pen and ink, pencil and watercolour, 314 × 284

Nationalgalerie, SMB (SM 34.39)

In this early scheme by Schinkel the atrium is fitted with a bath. Instead of the open compluvium there is a skylight, arranged as an aquarium, which would have given the bather the illusion of being under water.

Lit.: Hamburg 1982, 15.25.

H.S.

82.

SIDE CHAIR. *c. 1837*

Berlin Royal Iron Foundry after (?) a design
by Schinkel

Cast iron, lacquered

SSG Potsdam-Sanssouci

For a country like Prussia, which was short of
raw materials, home-produced iron was
especially important in the dawning industrial
age. Two new royal iron foundries were built,
at Gleiwitz (in 1796) and Berlin (in 1804). The
Royal Iron Foundry in Berlin, which had
developed a very successful method of casting,
also achieved great things artistically, by
collaborating with leading artists in Berlin.
Schinkel created many works from this
material. Examples include garden gates,
monuments, tombs, candelabra and works
connected with architecture, such as the
splendid staircases for the Berlin residences of
Princes Karl and Albrecht, portals, and
handrails for structures such as bridges,
balconies and platforms. Schinkel also designed
cast-iron fountains for Charlottenhof and
Glienicke. From the 1820s, probably while
working in Charlottenburg (on the Neue
Pavillon) and at Glienicke, Schinkel designed
his first garden furniture (c.f. Sievers 1950, pp.
40, 41). He also used iron furniture when
designing the garden for the Römische Bäder
in the grounds at Charlottenhof. Among the
pieces supplied were tables, benches, and this
chair, which, like the garden benches, was
supposedly based on a design by Schinkel.

B.G.

83.

THE PALAIS OF PRINCE KARL IN BERLIN. 1838

Carl Daniel Freydanck (1811–87)

Inscribed on the back: *Das Palais des Prinzen
Carl in Berlin*. (Palace of Prince Carl in
Berlin.) Signed and dated *C.F. fec. 1838*.

Oil on canvas, 275 × 357

KPM-Archiv, Schloss Charlottenburg (No. 42)

In the Palais of Prince Karl of Prussia, formerly
on the north side of Wilhelmplatz in
Friedrichstadt, we have – as so often with
Schinkel – a conversion of an older house. The
building originally begun for Count Truchsess
zu Waldburg in 1738 passed into the possession
of the Order of the Knights of St John in 1742.
In 1796 Prince Ferdinand, Frederick the Great's
youngest brother and Grand Master of the
Order, had the triple flight of steps on the
front replaced by the side ramps seen in this
view. In 1810 the building, also known as the
'Ordens Palais', passed into the possession of
the Crown.

In 1827–8 the poor state of preservation and
the old-fashioned internal arrangement of the
building led to its complete conversion by
Schinkel, since the Palais was to become the
town residence of the new, and newly
married, owners, Prince Friedrich Carl
Alexander, third son of King Friedrich

Wilhelm III, and his wife, Princess Marie-Luise
of Sachsen-Weimar.

Schinkel removed the high, steep Baroque
roof and dormer windows, as well as the
central portion, which carried the emblem of
the Order of St John. He completely
redesigned the facade, while retaining its
division into thirteen bays as well as the
existing triple division of the central portico of
the main entrance, with its three adjacent
doors. The interior was not only almost
completely rebuilt, but was also furnished by
Schinkel. Especially significant was the iron
construction of the staircase, which would not
have been possible without Schinkel's
experience of British buildings in 1826.

On the ground floor of the Palace, in an
armoury reminiscent of the Byzantine style,
Prince Karl assembled what must have been
the best private collection of weapons of the
nineteenth century in the German-speaking
regions. The Prince had been a passionate
collector since childhood, with a special
interest in the Middle Ages as well as in arms
and armour.

In the foreground to the right is the
memorial to General Graf von Schwerin, a
commander under Frederick the Great, which
was erected here on the orders of the king. The
Palais was destroyed in the Second World War.

Lit.: Sievers 1942; Berlin 1987 II, 12.

I.B.

84.

DESIGN FOR A CHAIR, PRINCE KARL'S PALAIS, BERLIN. 1827

Inscribed bottom right: *Die hellste schwarze Platte und die Schatten im Golde u. polster größer (?)* (the plain surfaces in brightest black and the shadows in gold and upholstery fatter (?)) and with notes.

Pencil and grey body colour, heightened with white and yellow, 262 × 421

Nationalgalerie, SMB (SM 49.8)

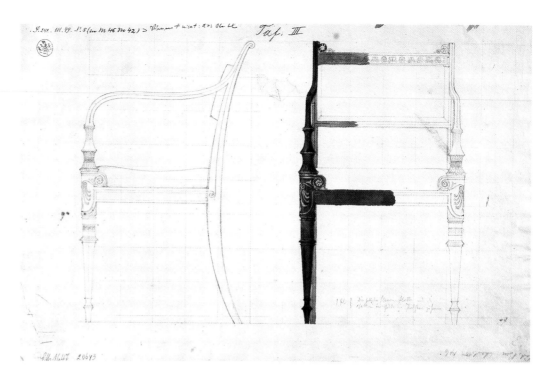

85.

ARMCHAIR IN PRINCE KARL'S PALAIS. 1828

Johann Christian Sewening or Karl Wanschaff after Schinkel

Hornbeam (?), lacquered black, with lead ornaments and gilding, the upholstery renewed, 880 × 550 × 500

Kunstgewerbemuseum, SMB (Inv. No. 1879, 2928)

In 1827–8, for Prince Karl of Prussia (1801–83), Schinkel completely remodelled, inside and out, a Baroque palace constructed on the Wilhelmplatz between 1736 and 1740 – his hitherto biggest and most far-reaching residential conversion. Schinkel made the drawing, which he has squared up as for a working drawing, as a design for the suite of furniture in the private drawing-room of Princess Marie (1808–77), Prince Karl's wife. In this design Schinkel makes wholesale use of English prototypes from the late eighteenth and first third of the nineteenth centuries. On his visit to England in 1826 he saw similar chairs with arm-rests in Lansdowne House, among other places; but we know from comments he made that he searched widely, in furniture shops and elsewhere, for ideas on how to furnish Prince Karl's new Palais. Surviving working drawings for a couch (SM 46.46), a sofa (SM 46.50), and a chair (SM 46.42) give us an idea of the appearance of the entire suite. This drawing was copied as a colour lithograph by Carl Boetticher for Ludwig Lohde's *Schinkel's Möbelentwürfe*, Part I (1835), Plate 3.

Lit.: Sievers 1950, p. 32, pl. 107; Berlin 1980, 379, 380; Berlin 1981, 244, 258.

B.G.

86.

DESIGN FOR A SOFA FOR PRINCE KARL'S PALAIS, BERLIN. 1827

Inscribed at the top: *Sopha im Marmorsallon 9 Fuß lang* (Sofa in the Marble Salon 9 feet long . . .) and with notes.

Pencil, 905 × 701

Nationalgalerie, SMB (SM 46.41)

This is a full-size working drawing for two ornate nine-foot (*c.* 275 cm.) long sofas designed as day-beds, with detachable back cushions and arm-rest rolls. The left-hand detail is an elevation of the end, which was symmetrical, and the right-hand detail the front. The material indicated on the drawing is silvered wood and gold, and the ornaments were obviously gilded. Towards the top of the sheet Schinkel has made a lightning sketch of the whole sofa. Two examples of this sofa were made for the Marble Salon in the apartment of Princess Marie. Schinkel also used the rich tassels on the ornate armchairs for the room. This drawing formed the basis of Plate 9 in Lohde 1835–7, part III, (1836).

Lit.: Sievers 1942, p. 214, pl. 204, 205; Berlin 1980; Berlin 1981, 264.

B.G.

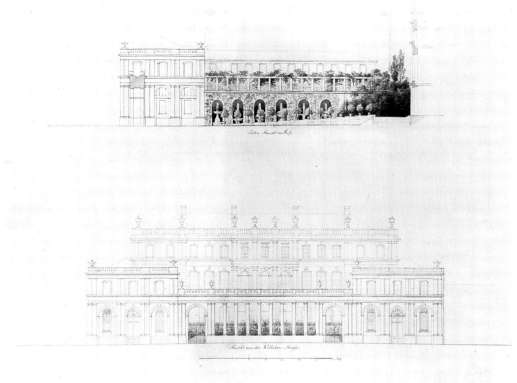

87.

PRINCE ALBRECHT'S PALAIS, BERLIN: FRONT
ELEVATION AND SIDE ELEVATION OF THE
COURTYARD. 1830

Inscribed below: *Ansicht von der Wilhelmstrasse.*
(View from Wilhelmstrasse.) and above
Seiten-Ansicht im Hofe (side view of the
courtyard)

Pen and ink, pencil and watercolour (with a
movable flap), 577 × 580

Nationalgalerie, SMB (SM 46.2)

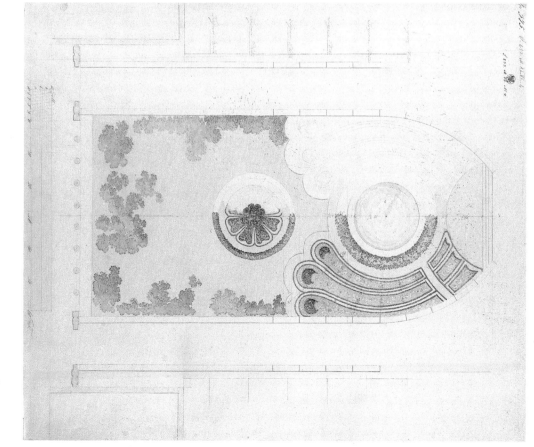

88.

PRINCE ALBRECHT'S PALAIS: PLAN OF THE
COURTYARD GARDEN. 1830

Watercolour and pencil

Nationalgalerie, SMB (SM 46.4)

89.

PRINCE ALBRECHT'S PALAIS: DESIGN FOR THE WALL
    DECORATION IN THE OVAL SALON
    (DINING-ROOM).   1830

Watercolour and body colour over pencil,
    273 × 390

Nationalgalerie, SMB (SM 22a.36)

90.

PRINCE ALBRECHT'S PALAIS: ELEVATION DESIGN
    FOR THE LONG WALL OF THE BALLROOM.   1830

Pen and ink and watercolour, heightened with
    white and gold, 162 × 381

Nationalgalerie, SMB (SM 22a.27)

The conversion of the Baroque Palais
Vernezobre in Wilhelmstrasse, Berlin for
Prince Albrecht (1809–72), who had married
Princess Marianne of the Netherlands in 1830,
was the last commission Schinkel carried out
for the Prussian princes. The work was carried
out between 1830 and 1832.

   Externally this conversion consisted of
modifying the street façade by inserting a
colonnade in front of the *cour d'honneur* and
restructuring the side wing. The courtyard was
redesigned as a highly original combination of
architectural and natural elements: the niches
with their fountains and semicircular arches
and a pergola arranged above are skilfully
enlivened by plants and trees. On the ground
plan Schinkel laid the courtyard out as a
garden with classical motifs set out in bedding
plants. In the interior Schinkel devised a cast-
iron staircase, based on ideas he had gathered
in Britain in 1826, for the imposing stairwell
(see figs 77, 78).

   The unexecuted wall decoration in the
Pompeian style for the oval salon or dining-
room is immensely rich and beautifully
coloured, making it exceptional among
Schinkel's interior designs. The illusionistic
effect of the architecture is particularly
remarkable. In both the dining-room and the
ballroom (cat. 90, fig. 79) Schinkel was
inspired by ideas from late-18th century
English interior design, especially those of
Robert Adam, examples of whose work he
had seen on his visit to Britain in 1826. Prince
Albrecht's Palais was damaged in the Second
World War and subsequently demolished.

Lit.: Gropius 1869–72 (coloured lithograph
    after cat. 89); Sievers 1954, p. 159; Berlin
    1980, 318, 320; Berlin 1981, 81, 275.

                            G.R.

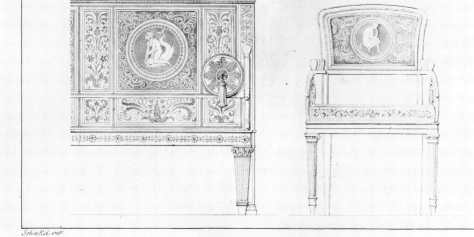

91.

DRAWING OF A SUITE OF FURNITURE.   *c. 1830*

Signed bottom left: *Schinkel inv.*

Pen, brush and ink, 515 × 322

Nationalgalerie, SMB (SM 43a.12)

This is a drawing for an engraving by Ferdinand Wilhelm Schwechten in the *Vorbilder für Fabrikanten und Handwerker* (Part 2, illus. II, sheet 14). Schinkel drew the original designs in 1830 for the conversion of the reception rooms in Prince Albrecht of Prussia's Palais at 102, Wilhelmstrasse. As part of this work, he made a large number of very opulent furniture designs. These examples of a sofa and a chair with arm-rests have austere frames, which nevertheless look very light because the arm-rests are of gilt cast iron. Schinkel expresses his delight in decorative effect by using sumptuous covering material with figured, richly ornamental medallions and by giving the frames ornamental touches. When completed the front legs were square, not turned as in this design. The original items of furniture disappeared in 1945.

Lit.: Sievers 1950, pp. 60, 106, pls. 43, 53; Sievers 1954 pl. 158; Berlin 1980, 394; Berlin 1981, 322a.

B.G.

92.

DRAWING OF A SUITE OF FURNITURE.   *c.* 1825–30

Signed bottom left: *Schinkel inv.*

Pen, brush and ink, 515 × 324

Nationalgalerie, SMB (SM 43a.13)

This is a drawing for the engraving by F.W.
Schwechten in *Vorbilder für Fabrikanten und
Handwerker* (Part 2, Section II, sheet 16). To
date these drawings of a sofa and chair have
not been related to any item of furniture
designed or made for palaces owned by the
Prussian princes or the king. The austerity of
the wooden frames and the upholstery's muted
pattern suggest that the items were made in the
1820s. Some details show structural similarities
with items of furniture in the Crown Prince
and Princess's apartments in the Königliches
Schloss (1824–8) and Prince Karl's Palais
(1827–8).

Lit.: Sievers 1950, pp. 60, 106, pl. 40; Berlin
     1981, 322c.

B.G.

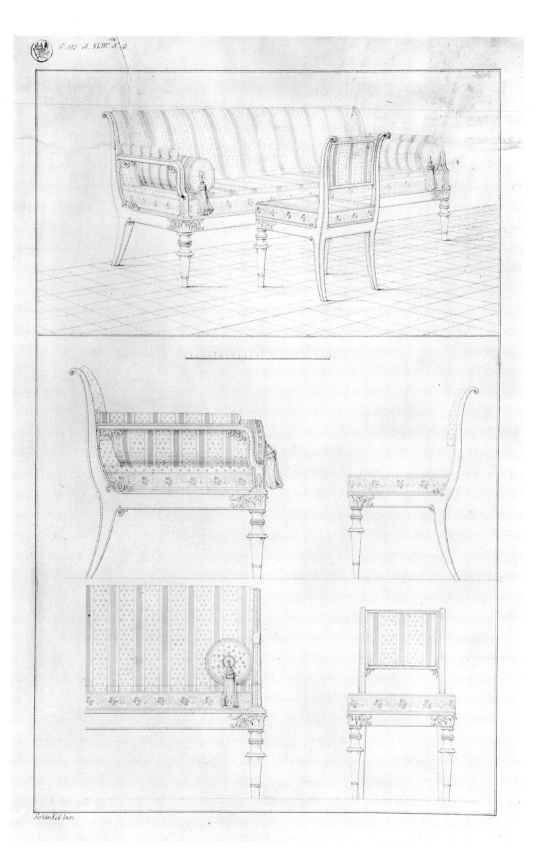

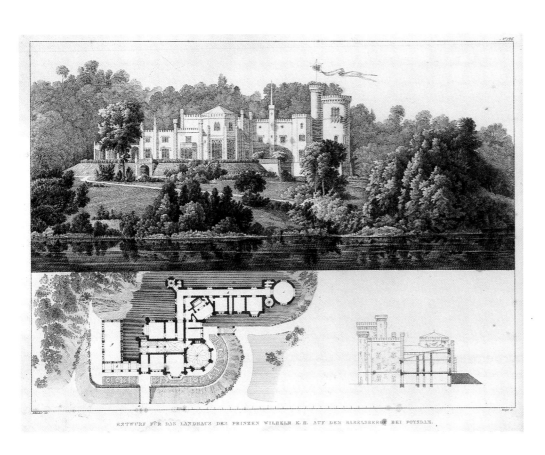

93.

Anonymous maker after a design by Schinkel

Wood, lead ornamentation, gilded, granite
   top, 780 × 550 × 1000

Kunstgewerbemuseum, SMB (Id.71)

This ornamental table, with its harmonious
proportions and austere decoration, is among
the best examples of Schinkel's small furniture.
It was owned by Alfred von Wolzogen, and so
had probably once belonged to Schinkel
himself. It is closely related to an ornamental
table made in 1831 for the Palais of Prince
Albrecht of Prussia (cf. Sievers 1950, p. 58, pl.
59), which had richly decorated claw feet,
rather than straight bases.

Lit.: Sievers 1950, p. 58, pl. 58.

B.G.

94.

DESIGN FOR THE COUNTRY RESIDENCE OF H.R.H.
   PRINCE WILHELM ON THE BABELSBERG NEAR
   POTSDAM. ELEVATION, SECTION AND PLAN. 1838

Ferdinand Berger (active 1830–44) after
   Schinkel

Lettered lower left and right: *Schinkel inv.*
   Berger sc. and with title in German.

Engraving, 345 × 475

Nationalgalerie, SMB (SM 21c.126)

Published as Plate 162 of the *Sammlung*
   architektonischer Entwürfe, 1838, Part 26.

ENTWURF FÜR DAS LANDHAUS DES PRINZEN WILHELM K.H. AUF DEM BABELSBERG BEI POTSDAM.

Entrée. ~   Wohnzimmer. ~   Salon. ~

95.

SCHLOSS BABELSBERG: DESIGN FOR THE WALLS IN THE ENTRANCE HALL, DRAWING ROOM AND SALON.   1834

Signed and dated lower right: *Schinkel, 1834, Mai*. Inscribed at the top: *Fensterwände dieser Zimmer* (Window walls in these rooms). Inscribed at the bottom *Entrée – Wohnzimmer – Salon. –* (Entrance hall – drawing room – salon)

Watercolour and pencil, 288 × 287

Nationalgalerie, SMB (SM 51.33)

96.

VIEW OF SCHLOSS BABELSBERG.   1838

Carl Daniel Freydanck (1811–87)

Inscribed on the back: *Palais des Prz. Wilhelm auf den Babertsberge*. (Palace of HRH Prince Wilhelm on the Babertsberge.) Signed and dated *CF 1838*.

Oil on canvas, 278 × 355

KPM-Archiv, Schloss Charlottenburg (No. 56)

The Babertsberg, later known as the Babelsberg, has a view of the waters of the Havel, the city of Potsdam and the Neue Garten, making it one of the most appealing spots in the surroundings of the city. So it is not surprising that Prince Wilhelm of Prussia expressed the wish to build a small residence here. His brother, Crown Prince Friedrich Wilhelm, marked out a site for him on the slope of the hill in 1827, which was to be crowned by a castle tower. For the residence itself he proposed an arrangement in the classical style of which he loved to sketch ever new variations. Schinkel then made a drawing,

working out the Crown Prince's idea in more detail.

Augusta, *née* Princess von Sachsen-Weimar and the wife of Prince Wilhelm, had other ideas for what was to be her personal residence. Goethe had designed Gothic houses with the Princess when she was small, and this may have been the root of her preference for the Gothic style. Naturally pro-English, she wanted a Gothic cottage, like those in the latest English books which were sent to her from Weimar, which included Robert Lugar's *Architectural Sketches for Cottages, Rural Dwellings and Villas in the Grecian, Gothic and Fancy Styles*, (London, 1815), and J.B. Papworth's *Rural Residences . . .* (London, 1818). Whether Schinkel had suggested the study of this literature to the Princess we do not know. She made a number of drawings reworking these English ideas, but for the present the scheme got no further, as the King had not given permission.

Ludwig Persius had made a design in the style of a Norman castle in 1831, but this unusually severe building was probably never seriously considered. Meanwhile Princess Augusta had obtained Humphry Repton's *Fragments on the Theory and Practice of Landscape*

Gardening, including Some Remarks on Grecian and Gothic Architecture (London, 1816), which confirmed her ideas for a building in the Gothic style. Certainly, Repton's ideal sketch for a Gothic castle integrated into a hilly landscape was a major influence on the development of the Babelsberg plans.

When the building was finally approved in 1833 Schinkel was commissioned to make the designs. Persius was in charge of building, but we cannot assess how great a part he may have played in the design of this first phase. The wishes of the Princess are evident in the overall Reptonian approach and the cottage-like eastern section. At first only the eastern part (on the left of cat. 94, including the octagon) was built, no doubt in deference to Friedrich Wilhelm III's desire for economy. Now, however, the Prince and Princess were no longer thinking of a modest cottage and the project was for a much more extensive palace building.

In his design Schinkel was tied not only by the wishes of the Prince and Princess but also by the site itself. The residence was to lie half-way up the slope of the hill, parallel to the Havel river. It was not a natural building site, and it would not have been possible to erect a palace proper here, such as he had designed for Kamenz, with its echoes of the architecture of the Teutonic Order of Knights. If his clients persisted in their wish for Gothic, a structure based on that of medieval castles, following Repton's ideas, would indeed be more appropriate, and Schinkel proposed an elongated building, rising from the pergola in the east through the octagonal tower to the flag tower in a gently ascending line. Behind the octagon the front recedes, to give spatial effect to the façade. This also creates a terrace. On the ground floor only the octagon has large, broad windows, otherwise the whole design is characterised by the severity of its walls. The flag tower was to have round arched windows, to recall older architecture. Gothic could hardly have been conceived more classically than by Schinkel in his Babelsberg designs. This is an austere building, utterly different from the Romantic Gothic fantasies of Schinkel's paintings.

Following Schinkel's death in 1841, first Persius and then (from 1845) Heinrich Strack continued to supervise the building, deviating more and more from Schinkel's original plans. Between 1844 and 1849 the modest country house shown in cat. 96 was expanded westwards into an ornamental palace in an eclectical medieval style.

Simultaneously with Schinkel, Peter Joseph Lenné was commissioned by the Prince to redesign the forest area of Babelsberg on the lines of English landscaped parks.

Lit.: Sievers 1955, pp. 157–218; Berlin 1980, 325; Berlin 1981, 88; Hamburg 1982, 15.28; Berlin 1987 II, 61.

S.H. and I.B.

97

UPHOLSTERED CHAIR FROM SCHLOSS BABELSBERG. 1835

Johann Christian Sewening (?) after a design by Schinkel

Rosewood, the upholstery renewed, 1000 × 455 × 430

SSG Potsdam-Sanssouci

Schinkel clearly did not work out a unified design scheme for the furnishing of Schloss Babelsberg. Only a few individual items match his designs. The royal couple was probably more inclined to create an ambience that suited them in their summer residence, so the original furnishing of Schinkel's rooms, some of which is depicted in watercolours, was made up of many separate purchases, genuine and reproduction antiques, and gifts and souvenirs.

Schinkel designed this type of neo-Gothic upholstered chair, used in the study and reception room, during the first stage of building work.

Lit.: Sievers 1950, p. 63, pls. 198–9; Sievers 1955, p. 199, pl. 188; Berlin 1980, 413.

B.G.

98.

Signed and dated bottom right: *Schinkel 1834*

Pen and ink, pencil and wash, 487 × 318

Nationalgalerie, SMB (SM 37c.179)

Crown Prince Friedrich Wilhelm sketched a design for this oil-lamp combining antique and Gothic motifs as a fitting for the Castle Chapel at Burg Rheinstein, which belonged to his nephew, Prince Friedrich of Prussia (1794–1863); it was probably meant to be used as a hanging lamp (cf. the Crown Prince's sketch in Sievers 1950, p. 99, pl. 255). Schinkel was obviously commissioned to complete the working drawing from which the sculptor August Kiss would produce the finished article.

Lit.: Sievers 1950, p. 99, pl. 256; Berlin 1980, 444.

B.G.

99.

A SCHEME FOR THE RESTORATION OF STOLZENFELS ON THE RHINE (ELEVATION, PLAN AND SECTION). 1836

Signed and dated lower right: *Schinkel 1836*.
    Inscribed with title and notes.

Pen and black ink, watercolour and pencil,
    644 × 1020

Nationalgalerie, SMB (SM 30.20)

The archbishops of Trier built Burg Stolzenfels between 1242 and 1259 on the left bank of the Rhine, opposite the junction with the river Lahn. In the fourteenth century they extended it as a residence. Until it was destroyed by Louis XIV's army, the dominant features were the keep, the residential quarters in the centre of the eastern wing over the Rhine, and the adjutants' tower at the top of the northern section. The ruins served as a stone quarry until 1823, when they were donated to the Prussian Crown Prince by the City of Koblenz. The renovation of the castle needs to be seen against the background of the 'Rhine Romanticism' that had been flourishing since the beginning of the nineteenth century (motivated by nationalism since the establishment of the Confederation of the Rhine) and the efforts by the Hohenzollerns to integrate the Rhine Provinces ceded to Prussia in 1815.

After the Bauinspektor in Koblenz, J.C. von Lassaulx, had made a survey and the first drawings, Schinkel was commissioned to handle the rest of the work, in which the

Crown Prince may also have played a part. Schinkel had been filled with enthusiasm by the scenic effect of the castles on the Rhine on his first visit to the area in 1816, when he made his drawings of Ehrenfels, Ehrenbreitstein, Kaub and Rheinstein. However, he had reservations about renovating castles in a way that gave them new appeal but did not restore them to their true medieval state, for he felt that their 'picturesque appearance' was often lost through modern restoration. Curiously, high medieval roofs did not fit his ideal of a castle, and on occasions he proposed that surviving roofs should be removed, not least because of the difficulties of maintenance. For Stolzenfels the Crown Prince had ordered that the old parts of the building should be left as undisturbed as possible. In 1823, in the first planning phase, Schinkel had only envisaged renovating the core of the castle with its crenellated, flat-roofed buildings, but when the Crown Prince decided that building could begin in 1834, he also approved the project to renovate the entire complex. It became his favourite residence when visiting the Rhine as king.

From 1834 Schinkel worked to restore the entire ruin as a medieval castle, leaving no trace of decay and with the disparate parts united. The relationship of the main building to its extensions and the slope of the site appears to have been the essential consideration. By adding some window openings to the gate tower and the adjutants' tower, differing from the original and the first design for the renovation, Schinkel significantly enhanced the effect of the central part. The alteration of the crenellation in order

to gain an attic storey is the most striking
intervention in the old structure. The gate
tower, which was badly damaged, was
necessarily relatively free in its design. The idea
of taking this only to the height of the Great
Hall retains the dominance of the residential
tower with its decorative turrets emphasised by
the terrace wall.

Cat.100 shows the castle after the completion
of the restoration in 1847. After Schinkel's
death the work was continued by Persius,
Strack and Stüler, using·a greater variety of
decorative features.

Lit.: Berlin 1980, 585; Berlin 1987 II, 89.

P.F. and I.B.

100.

VIEW OF SCHLOSS STOLZENFELS ON THE RHINE.
1847–8

Carl Daniel Freydanck (1811–87)

Inscribed on the back: *Ansicht des Schlosses
    Stolzenfels am Rhein*. Signed and dated *C.
    Freydanck 1847/48.*

Oil on canvas, 283 × 363

KPM-Archiv, Schloss Charlottenburg (No.
    213)

Church Architecture

DESIGN FOR THE CONSTRUCTION OF THE CHURCH ON THE SITE OF THE ST GERTRUDE HOSPITAL, BERLIN (SIDE ELEVATION). 1819

Signed and dated lower right: *Schinkel 1819* and inscribed with title in German.

Pen and grey ink, wash and watercolour, 408 × 578

Nationalgalerie, SMB (SM 26b.10)

THE GERTRAUDENKIRCHE: PERSPECTIVE VIEW DOWN THE NAVE. 1819

Signed and dated lower right: *Schinkel, 1819*

Pen and grey ink, wash, 227 × 282

Nationalgalerie, SMB (SM 26b.11)

The desire, which the king approved, to renew the tower on the Baroque Gertraudenkirche (Church of St Gertrude) on Spittelmarkt in Berlin brought this design for a campanile from Schinkel in 1819. In making his designs Schinkel was inspired by the hope of

ENTWURF ZUM BAU DER KIRCHE
AUF DEM PLATZ DES ST. GERTRUDEN HOSPITALS

addition that does not belong to the rest, they often spoil the architectural proportions of the buildings.'

Lit.: Rave 1941, pp. 237–53; Berlin 1980, 162, 163.

G.R.

103.

THE FRIEDRICH–WERDER KIRCHE: INTERIOR
PERSPECTIVE OF EXECUTED DESIGN.   1828–9

Signed and dated lower left: *Schinkel inv. 1828*

Pen and black ink, 496 × 323

Nationalgalerie, SMB (SM 21a.8)

Drawing for Plate 82 of the *Sammlung architektonischer Entwürfe*, Part 13, published in 1829.

extending the project and rebuilding the entire church to replace the unsightly existing building, so taking up again in this context, albeit in modified form, the great plans of 1814–15 for a cathedral as monument to the Wars of Liberation (see cat. 21). Like the cathedral, the scheme was not realised.

Schinkel commented on his proposal: 'The tower is placed in isolation in the middle of Leipziger Strasse, in order to create an effect in the perspective of the street. It is linked to the church by an arch. The style of the tower derives from that of the church, which in turn is determined by the interior. The vault inside rests on very delicate pillars of hard stone, that hardly restrict the view of the pulpit. The high altar space is supported by a single pillar in the centre, to which the crucifix is also attached. The church and the tower will be built entirely in brick, apart from the window and door surrounds and the gallery, which are in sandstone. The masonry needs to be ordered especially from a brickworks and very carefully worked. The design is such that the construction of the tower, the church and the altar area can each be carried out individually, as convenient, and the execution of the entire project spread over any number of years.'

The interior is lofty and spacious. Its star-ribbed vault rests on two rows of tall, slender columns in the nave and a central column in the eleven-sided altar area. Schinkel's approach to Gothic and its structural and decorative elements is evident from his commentary on the scheme in the *Sammlung architektonischer Entwürfe*. He states that his aim in the design was 'to adopt from the style of the Middle Ages only what proved to be of pure advantage for the development of architecture, a true innovation not practised before, and one that could usefully be applied in any age, nor was lacking in aesthetic effect. So the endeavour was to avoid all superfluities in that style, in particular: the decoration of the masses with the imitation of the main forms, in a variety of reduced proportions, resulting in the accumulation and superimposition of tower-like baldachins and many simulated roofings in the form of pointed arches; in addition the decoration of the parts with too much mannered foliage, blurring all the outlines and creating endless repetitions; then the moulding and many intertwinings constructed of segments of the circle. This can no doubt well serve as tracery in windows but used as decoration on the wall surfaces, applied in excess and without proper relations, is often an empty decoration purchased at too high a price; further, the excessively high proportions, particularly in the interior, which cause the spirit to quail; and the high roofs of the buildings. These have a heavy and oppressive effect, and since their great surfaces have no architectural variety and they are a useless

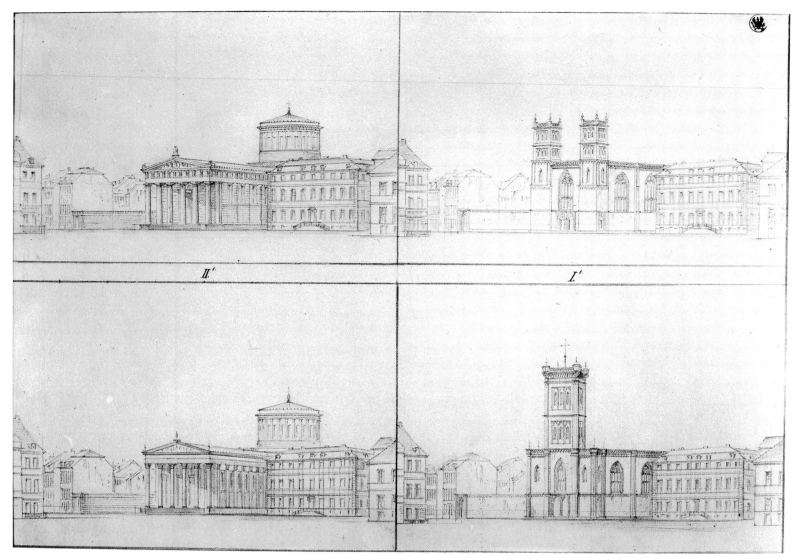

II'

I'

104.

THE FRIEDRICH-WERDER KIRCHE, BERLIN:
    PERSPECTIVE VIEWS OF FOUR DESIGNS.   1824

Numbered respectively above each image: *I*,
I', *II*, *II'*.

Pencil, 421 × 611

Nationalgalerie, SMB (SM 27.11)

105.

THE FRIEDRICH-WERDER KIRCHE: INTERIOR
    PERSPECTIVE IN THE ANTIQUE STYLE.   1821–6

Signed lower left: *Schinkel inv*.

Pen and black ink, 462 × 390

Nationalgalerie, SMB (SM 21a.4)

Drawing for Plate 52 of the *Sammlung
    architektonischer Entwürfe*, Part 8, published
    in 1826.

106.

THE WERDERSCHE KIRCHE IN BERLIN.   1838

Carl Daniel Freydanck (1811–87)

Inscribed on the back with title in German and
    signed and dated C.F. 1838.

Oil on canvas, 274 × 356

KPM-Archiv, Schloss Charlottenburg (No. 33)

The intention to restore the Reithaus that had
been extended in 1700–1 to serve as a church
for both the German and the French parishes
of the suburb of Friedrichswerder was dropped
when Schinkel put forward an ideal plan in
1817 for a new building in the Werdersche
Markt. Aloys Hirt and Gottlieb Schlätzer then
produced a proposal of their own. Both
designs were for a neo-classical structure. In
1821 Schinkel countered with another design
in the form of a Roman temple, a pseudo
peripteros modelled on the 'Maison Carrée' (*c*.

16 BC) at Nîmes. He then made a further design, probably in 1822, a variant on the project 'in the antique style'. The reason for choosing this style was that the Werdersche Markt was then dominated by the large neo-classical structure of the Neue Münze (New Mint) on the right of cat. 106, built between 1798 and 1800 to designs by Heinrich Gentz.

Following suggestions by the Crown Prince, Schinkel also made designs 'in the medieval style' in 1823–4 which was in the Crown Prince's view the most appropriate to the restricted site and the irregular street pattern of the area. His medieval designs, partly derived from English Gothic chapels which he knew from engravings, show two variants in unplastered brick. In the first sheet, of 1824, the building has four corner towers and a short nave of only three bays.

'For the king to choose' he then made a drawing showing four alternatives (cat. 104): the Gothic version with one and with two towers, and the classical using Doric and Corinthian orders. The decision was taken in March 1824 for the twin-towered Gothic design; work began on construction the same year and was completed in 1830. The church is built entirely of brick, with moulded terracotta details, a return to the techniques of local Gothic buildings. The cast-iron doors were modelled by Friedrich Tieck after Schinkel's design. The terracotta figure of St Michael over the doors was modelled by Ludwig Wichmann and fired by Tobias Feilner.

The interior, far less English in design than the exterior, is characterised by a sequence of five cross-ribbed vaults resting on ribbed piers. Their great arches spring from the capitals of the responds. Between the piers a gallery crosses arcades of pointed arches and the wall above dissolves in huge traceried windows. The division of the nave is continued in the choir, creating a strong sense of depth. The cross-ribbed vault with its painted star ribs recalls the church on Marienburg in East Prussia, the outstanding example of Prussian Gothic. This was discovered by Friedrich Gilly, Schinkel's teacher, and had a formative influence on the neo-Gothic movement in Germany. Schinkel several times considered and made designs for its restoration.

Lit.: Rave 1941, pp. 254–300; Berlin 1980, 166, 168, 169; Berlin 1981, 58.

G.R., R.K. and I.B.

107.

Wilhelm Barth (active about 1800–40)

Signed and dated lower left: *W. Barth 1838*

Oil on canvas, 1020 × 1410

SSG Potsdam-Sanssouci (GK I 6665)

This painting was made a year after the first phase of the building was completed. Schinkel himself had given instructions for the colour of the stucco: 'A fine light sandstone colour in several shades for the various blocks of the wall would certainly be most appropriate.' He also designed the figure decoration in 1833. August Kiss made the stucco reliefs in the pediments: the Sermon on the Mount on the lower and the Ascension on the higher. The upper pediment was taken down in 1844 when the dome was built.

Lit.: Berlin 1980, 253.

H.G.

108.

Signed lower right: *Schinkel inv.* and inscribed
    with title in German

Pen and black ink and pencil, 580 × 430

Nationalgalerie, SMB (SM 21a.42)

Preliminary drawing for Plate 155 of the
    Sammlung architektonischer Entwürfe,
    published in 1834.

On 3 September 1795 the Nikolaikirche in the Alte Markt of Potsdam, built from 1721 to 1724 to designs by Philipp Gerlach, was completely destroyed by fire.

As early as 1796 Friedrich Gilly had drawn up plans for a new building, but they were

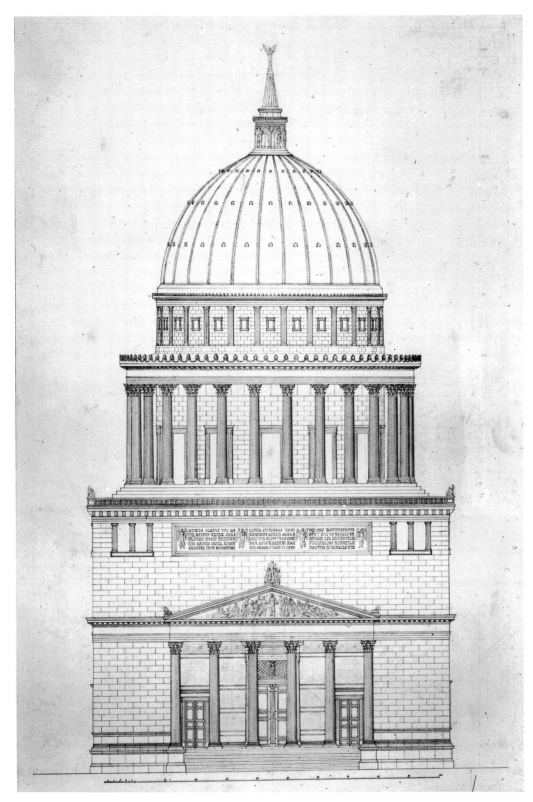

Prince, wanted a centrally planned building with a dome (adopted from Gilly) that would dominate the urban skyline, but the king wanted a basilica with a twin-towered façade. Finally a cuboid body with two low towers on the front was chosen for execution. In the winter of 1832–3, while the building work was proceeding, the king was persuaded to forgo the towers in favour of a pediment, and in this form the church was completed in 1837 (see cat. 107).

Schinkel nevertheless continued to develop his dome project, no doubt in consultation with the Crown Prince, until 1829. While the lower structure has only been changed in its details, the dome itself has become more elongated and more elegant (cat. 108). Five steps lead to the drum, which is encircled by Corinthian columns and has tall slender windows. A pronounced cornice with acroteria crowns the drum, creating the impression that the next section, with small windows and Ionic pilasters, is set far back. The unusually high dome rises above these to culminate in a lantern carrying an angel. The influence of the Panthéon in Paris and St Paul's Cathedral can certainly be traced in this design, which formed the basis for the cupola that was finally built after 1843.

Only after the death of Friedrich Wilhelm III in 1840 was it possible to realise the original plan and install the cupola. Friedrich Wilhelm IV decided to proceed in 1843, and also approved four corner towers which deviated from Schinkel's design. They were needed to stabilise the building and could also serve as bell towers and staircases. The construction work began in the same year under the direction of Persius. 1846 and 1847 saw the drum and the inner and outer domes finished. The interior was completed in 1849 and the church was dedicated in 1850.

Of Schinkel's obsession with domed buildings – the Petrikirche in Berlin in 1810, the cathedral intended as a monument to the Wars of Liberation of 1814–16, the church on the Spittelmarkt in 1819, the Friedrich-Werder Kirche in the antique style in 1824 and the church outside Oranienburger Tor in 1828 – the Nikolaikirche in Potsdam was the only one to be executed, and even that was only built after Schinkel's death and in a somewhat modified form. It occupies a special place not only in Schinkel's work but in the history of great European domed buildings.

Lit.: Kania 1939, pp. 3–60; Berlin 1980, 249; Berlin 1981, 75.

H.G.

never executed, and in the next few years other sites for the church were proposed. The start of the War of Liberation put a stop to any rebuilding plans, but the idea was not forgotten by those close to the king and was passed on to Schinkel. It was not until 1826 that the king approved the building and commissioned Schinkel to design it, and another four years were to pass before the foundation stone could be laid, on 3 September 1830. Right from the start Schinkel, with the approval of the Crown

The British Journey and the Constructional Style

109.

VIEW OF ALL SOULS COLLEGE, OXFORD, FROM THE
RADCLIFFE CAMERA   1826

Inscribed lower right: *Oxford 1826*

Pen and black ink and pencil, 148 × 350

Nationalgalerie, SMB (SM 12.4)

110.

VIEW OF THE POTTERIES NEAR NEWCASTLE UNDER
LYME.   1826

Inscribed lower left: *Potteries bei Newcastel*

Pen and black ink and pencil, 140 × 176

Nationalgalerie, SMB (SM 12.10)

111.

FINGAL'S CAVE   1826

Inscribed bottom centre: *Die Fingalshöhle*

Pen and black ink and pencil, 141 × 354

Nationalgalerie, SMB (SM 12.18)

From May to August 1826 Schinkel travelled
to Paris, London, and through England, Wales
and Scotland, accompanied by Peter Christian
Beuth. The immediate occasion for the
journey was his work on planning and
building the museum on the Lustgarten in
Berlin, which had been in progress since 1823.
Fresh stimulus and ideas, especially for the
details and the interior, may well have seemed
desirable. In Paris sections of the Louvre had
recently been extended or rebuilt for the
collections which Napoleon had enlarged, and
work had started in London in 1824 on
implementing the great plans for the new
British Museum building.

While this was the apparent reason, the
deeper impulses which caused Schinkel to
undertake his journey are to be sought
elsewhere. He was intensely interested in
Britain and its industrial revolution. Beuth had
been to England several times, most recently in
1823, to study industrial development and
manufactories, and the desire to see and assess
the continuing changes that the industrial
revolution had brought about in British cities
and factory districts must have been an added
inducement for Schinkel to travel. More than
anything else, the journey became a study tour
of industrial building, to which Schinkel paid
closer attention than to historical architecture.
If he mentions 'works of superior architecture'
at all in his diary, it is mainly contemporary
buildings by Soane, Nash and others, which
draw his attention. His interest in technical
buildings of every kind predominated. He
admired the engineers and their works, like
Rennie's and Telford's bridges, Brunel's
Thames tunnel, the London docks, the
technical aspects of buildings in Brighton, the
railway tracks and other developments. He was
impressed by machines, and descriptions of
factories and factory products, ironworks,
engineering workshops, spinning mills and
foundries occupy an important part of his
diary. Recognising that industrialisation was
the great challenge of the age, he studied
technical problems like iron frame construction
and the use of glass.

After spending three weeks in Paris,
Schinkel arrived in Dover in 1826. He filled
every day of the two and a half months he
spent in Britain with a tightly packed
programme of inspection. His longest and
most intensive stay was in London, but the
great industrial towns in the Midlands also
drew his close attention. He visited Glasgow
and Edinburgh as well, only permitting
himself brief impressions of the Scottish
landscape on excursions to the Highlands and

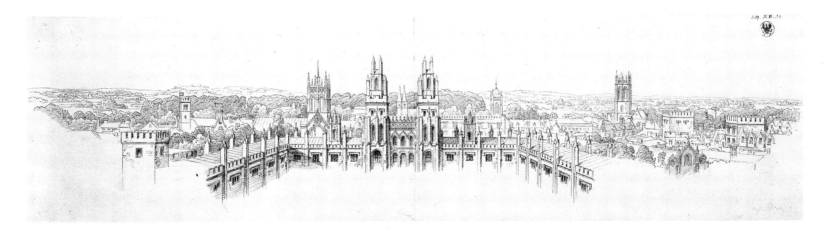

islands.

His objectives were similar in London and the industrial cities: older and new buildings, factories, docks and warehouses. He was stimulated by Beuth's interest, and Beuth's main aim was to see production methods, manufactories and mills, and to acquire ideas for the Prussian Gewerbe-Institut and for Prussian industry. Schinkel himself was also greatly interested in the technical facilities that were still unknown in Prussia. The many sketches in his diary, covering every area of industrial building, canals and road construction, are evidence of this. His sketches show a clear grasp of the comprehensive changes which the years of rapid industrialisation had brought to the structure and appearance of town and countryside. New industrial buildings, mostly erected in great haste and without any plan, form a strong contrast to the park-like countryside.

Schinkel took note of the chaotic and unplanned character which an industrial town like Manchester had assumed as it rapidly mushroomed. His notes and sketches, though quick, are penetrating, and add up to the overall impression: 'It is dreadfully oppressive to see huge masses of buildings put up by a mere foreman with no architectural design, and intended to meet only the barest needs, all in red brick.' His sketch (cat. 112b) shows a typical view of Manchester: a long, unbroken line of factory buildings, mostly spinning mills. They are simple cubes, seven to eight storeys high, with long rows of windows and flat roofs, placed without any relationship to each other along a canal. In the immediate vicinity of factories and shoddy housing lies an

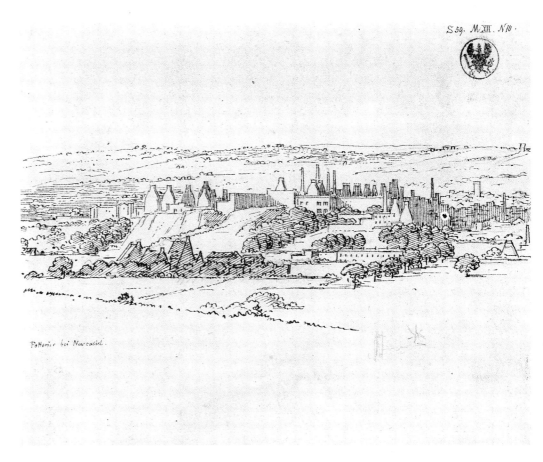

amorphous conglomerate of residential and commercial buildings, the ugliness and density of which did not fail to make their impression on Schinkel.

In Edinburgh he sketched a new gasworks (cat. 112a), a utility building but one whose

clear and symmetrical accentuation was influenced by the Greek Revival. The front elevation shows a raised central part with a towering chimney stack, and its roof is sketched again from the side. A round-roofed gasometer is placed symmetrically at each end,

with the elongated windows running right round these towers forming divisional elements. Schinkel has added detail sketches of the iron roof of the gasworks and 'a railing of wrought iron around it'.

He also devoted close attention to the internal structure of British factory buildings. In the textile centre of Stroud in Gloucestershire he drew the interior of a three-aisled factory shed with iron supports and capping vaults (cat. 112c.). The huge room is divided by two long rows of cast-iron supports running in longitudinal direction, while shallow vaults, running across the room, each rest on two supports. This simple principle created a wide room with little to obscure the view, in a loose, spacious arrangement that was not without aesthetic value. The structural frame was filled in with brick walls and vaulting, a significant idea for Schinkel and one which he later endeavoured to adopt in his designs for the Kaufhaus (cat. 113, 114) Unter den Linden and the Bauakademie (cat. 120–3). He was still mainly concerned with structural solutions when he visited official buildings, such as the Royal Pavilion at Brighton. The Royal Pavilion had been renovated and extended by John Nash in 1815, with spectacular decorations, but in his diary notes and sketches Schinkel, characteristically, first mentions the utility rooms and the kitchen, with their slender iron columns and practical facilities.

In London Schinkel had devoted attention to Southwark Bridge and London Bridge by John Rennie, the latter still under construction. But the greatest achievements of progressive English bridge engineering that he saw were the iron suspension bridges by Thomas Telford. He saw the first as he passed through Wales, at Conway. The bridge, which had just been finished, looks small compared with the town and the imposing ruin of the castle, but for Schinkel it was the most important thing there. He also sketched Telford's much larger bridge over the Menai Straits between Wales and the Isle of Anglesey. He saw this just after it was finished and was impressed by its boldness. Schinkel's drawings make one important aspect of this early bridge construction clear: historical and functional elements are unhesitatingly combined and the structural aspects are partly concealed by picturesque additions. Yet the bridges are perfect examples of the early art of engineering; they spring from an approach that transcends stylistic concepts and this distinguishes them from public buildings that are designed to fit an artistic concept. Schinkel's drawings show that he recognised a pioneering modernity which was possible precisely because there was no ambition to create works of art.

The impressions Schinkel recorded on his journey through Britain show how much the great changes wrought by the industrial revolution were impressed upon him. His detailed studies of towns and factories showed him the extent of the progressive industrialisation and its prospects for the future. This is immediately evident from the descriptions of factories or factory processes in his diary. The way he depicts and comments on these new phenomena, in a tone of growing interest and even open admiration, shows the aspects to which he was most receptive on his journey. But he also notes side-effects of the new industrialisation: the ruthless penetration of the industrial cities into the countryside and their chaotic growth are to Schinkel a new and alien phenomenon, although he endeavours to find its picturesque side. This can be seen in the sketches and drawings as well as the diary, which illustrate the brief and precise text notes with the typical clarity of the architect.

While engineering buildings took precedence over historical architecture, the great variety of historical buildings also aroused Schinkel's interest. He visited Westminster Abbey and the Oxford colleges and chapels. In London he sketched St Paul's Cathedral, choosing the impressive distant view across the Thames. In Bath, he depicted some of the characteristic crescents and the surrounding landscape. Some of the places he visited he recorded only in drawings. He made several panoramic drawings of the impressive urban design of Edinburgh, taken from different standpoints. In the cities it was mainly the contemporary buildings that aroused his interest, especially in London. Here he concentrated on the new terraces by Nash on Regent's Park, and other major buildings of the time, such as Soane's Bank of England, Clarence House by Nash and Nash's own house, Carlton House by Holland, Smirke's Customs House and the Covent Garden Theatre and the Drury Lane Theatre by Wyatt.

Lit.: Berlin 1980, 561, 563, 564, 567, 568, 571; Riemann 1986; Wegner 1990.

G.R.

112.

PAGES FROM SCHINKEL'S TRAVEL DIARY.   1826

(A) GASWORKS IN EDINBURGH, WITH DETAILS

Inscribed: *Gasometer, Construction der Mittelgiebel. Construction der Gasometerhäuser. Gallerie von durchbrochenem Eisen um die Gasometer.* (Gasometer, construction of the central gable, construction of the gasometer buildings. Wrought-iron railings around the gasometer) and with extensive notes.

Pen and black ink and pencil, 210 × 130

(Diary, p. 53)

(B) FACTORY BUILDINGS IN MANCHESTER AND (BELOW) A MARKET HALL IN LIVERPOOL, AND DETAILS

Inscribed with notes

Pen and black ink and pencil, 210 × 130

(Diary, p. 62)

(C) SHED WITH IRON SUPPORTS IN THE TEXTILE FACTORY AT STROUD, A DRYING SHED FOR TEXTILES AND A FURNACE

Inscribed: *fireproof* and with notes

Pen and black ink, pencil, 210 × 130

(Diary, p. 67)

Nationalgalerie, SMB

113.

PERSPECTIVE VIEW OF THE BAZAAR SEEN FROM UNTER DEN LINDEN.   1827

Inscribed below: *Perspectivische Ansicht des Kaufhauses von den Linden geseh.* Signed and dated lower right: *Schinkel 1827*

Watercolour and pencil, 187 × 554

Nationalgalerie, SMB (SM 23b.52)

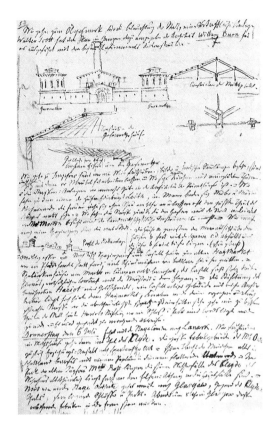

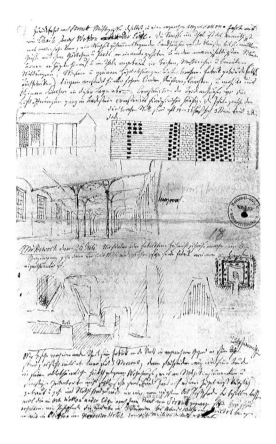

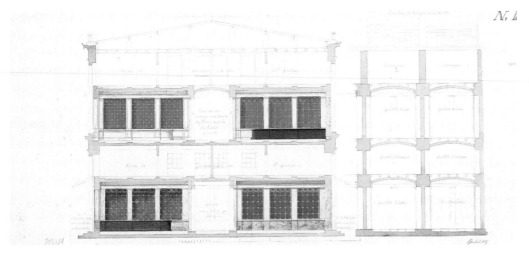

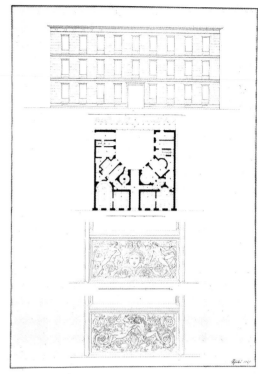

114.

BAZAAR ON UNTER DEN LINDEN: CROSS-SECTION
AND TWO BAYS OF THE LONGITUDINAL
SECTION. 1827

Inscribed: *Querdurchschnitt des Kaufhauses. Ein
Theil des Längendurchschnittes* (Cross-section
of the Bazaar. Part of the longitudinal
section) and with notes. Signed and dated
lower right: *Schinkel 1827*

Pen and black ink, watercolour and body
colour, 263 × 635

Nationalgalerie, SMB (SM 23b.54)

The plans and memorandum on the
construction of a bazaar (Kaufhaus) on the site
of the Academy on Unter den Linden, where
part of the Royal Stables was also located,
were sent by Schinkel to the President of the
State Bank, Christian von Rother, in January
1827. The hope of realising an architectural
idea that was entirely new for Berlin and
Prussia, where the need for a new type of
architecture was recognised, was strengthened
by detailed proposals for the relocation of the
institutions already on the site. But Rother's
memorandum to the king on the establishment
of a joint stock corporation to finance a bazaar,
modelled on the Palais Royal in Paris, was
rejected. Objections to the choice of site, in a
part of Berlin previously without commercial
buildings, and fears that the costs would be too
high for private investors caused one of
Schinkel's most important and most advanced
projects to remain on the drawing board.
Schinkel had obtained his ideas for the project
from his visits to Paris and Britain in 1826 and
his designs would not only have fulfilled their
commercial purpose, but would also have met
a particular need in urban planning and
communication.

Lit.: Rave 1962, pp. 125–9; Berlin 1980, 184,
186.

G.R.

115.

THE FEILNER HAUS, BERLIN: ELEVATION, GROUND
PLAN AND TERRACOTTA DECORATION ON THE
EXTERNAL WINDOW SILLS. 1829–31

Signed and dated below: *Schinkel 1829*

Pen and black ink, 530 × 440

Nationalgalerie, SMB (SM 32.2)

Drawing for Plate 113 of the *Sammlung
architektonischer Entwürfe*, Part 18, published
in 1831.

116.

THE FEILNER HAUS: FACADE, WITH DETAILS OF
DECORATION. 1829–31

Signed and dated lower right: *Schinkel 1829*

Pen and black ink, 530 × 440

Nationalgalerie, SMB (SM 32.3)

Drawing for Plate 114 of the *Sammlung
architektonischer Entwürfe*, Part 18, published
in 1831.

After simple preliminary sketches had been
made by a master bricklayer and a master
carpenter, Schinkel agreed in 1828 to provide
the designs for a house for Tobias Christoph
Feilner, the Berlin manufacturer of stoves and
ceramics with whom he often worked.
Schinkel had provided designs for Feilner's
products and Feilner had made terracotta
decorations to Schinkel's directions,

particularly for the Friedrich-Werder Kirche.
The chosen site, in Hasenhegerstrasse in the
suburb of Köpenick, was not as narrow as the
sites in the city centre, and it enabled a square
ground plan to be used, with a nine-bay front.
To provide adequate lighting for the
residential rooms required on each floor,
Schinkel divided the house into a front section
with two side wings, placing a rectangular
court with canted corners between these. The

residential rooms were located on the canted sides of the court, as in his ideal design for a city apartment house (with an octagonal court), while the reception rooms occupy the street side of the front section and the utility rooms the side wings.

The façade of the house is hard brick with terracotta enrichments. Its arrangement is similar to two of Schinkel's ideal designs for urban dwellings, with moulded bands separating the individual storeys, from which the windows rise. Instead of normal coursing, four rows of red bricks are followed by one of purple fired bricks. Under the narrow windows with their sharply defined contours terracotta slabs serve as sills. They bear reliefs, each showing two genii in plant scrolls. Of the two designs offered, one was modelled by Ludwig Wichmann, Feilner's son-in-law. Similarly decorated terracotta slabs were envisaged for the windows and door casings. The house was built 1828–9 and destroyed in the Second World War. Fragments of the ornament are in the Märkisches Museum, Berlin.

Lit.: Rave 1962, pp. 216–22; Berlin 1981, 70; Hamburg 1982, 8.32, 8.33.

R.K. and G.R.

117.

VIEW OF THE NEUE PACKHOF (NEW CUSTOMS HOUSE), BERLIN.   1834

Signed at the right: *Schinkel inv.*

Pen and black ink, 310 × 560

Nationalgalerie, SMB (SM 21b.80)

Drawing for Plate 28 in the *Sammlung architektonischer Entwürfe*, Part 21, published in 1834.

After initial plans in 1825–6 to build new and larger customs buildings on the River Kupfergraben, Schinkel made his design in 1829, and the complex was built by 1832 under the direction of the Oberbaurat, Carl Ludwig Schmid. The main feature was the great warehouse with its five storeys, on the northern end of the site. It was a brick building, square in plan, its façades divided by rows of round-arched windows, with narrow bands of moulding between the storeys and a stronger, more emphatic cornice on the roof. Between this building and the Altes Museum were two smaller office buildings, for the customs administration and the head tax office. These were stuccoed and with neo-classical details. Only the building for the tax office had decorative elements, in the form of a pediment by August Kiss on the front facing the museum. The overall plan of the Neue Packhof was clearly related to the buildings on the Lustgarten. In their various dimensions the warehouse and office buildings matched the cubic blocks of the Zeughaus (Arsenal), the museum and the Schloss, and the result was a 'Kupfergraben landscape' stretching south to the Werdersche Markt with the Bauakademie and the church, built between 1824 and 1830. It was a new and impressive idea in urban planning for which there were no direct models or contemporary parallels; nor was it ever to be repeated in Schinkel's work. The Packhof was demolished when the Museumsinsel was developed.

Lit.: Rave 1962, pp. 107–24; Berlin 1980, 187; Berlin 1981, 74.

G.R.

118.

PALAIS REDERN, BERLIN. VIEW, ELEVATIONS
BEFORE AND AFTER CONVERSION, GROUND
PLAN, CROSS-SECTION AND INTERIORS OF THE
GREAT HALL AND VESTIBULE AND A
CANDELABRUM.   1835

Inscribed at the top: *Gräflich Redern'sches Palais
in Berlin* (Palais for Count Redern in
Berlin) and with titles. Inscribed below: *Zu
dieser Platte wird der Kupferstecher noch zu
suchen seyn* (The engraver still has to be
found for this plate.) Signed left: *Schinkel
inv.* and below right: *Grützmacher Sc.*

Pen and black ink and pencil, 530 × 410

Nationalgalerie, SMB (SM 21c.113)

Drawing, engraved by Wilhelm Grützmacher
for Plate 143 of the *Sammlung
architektonisher Entwürfe*, Part 23, published
in 1835.

Schinkel designed this scheme in 1828–9 for
Count Wilhelm Friedrich von Redern, who
had succeeded Brühl in 1828 as artistic director
of the Schauspielhaus, for the conversion of the
former Palais Kamecke on Pariser Platz, built
by Johann Friedrich Grael between 1729 and
1736. The conversion of the Baroque building
was undertaken under the direction of Carl
Friedrich Adolph Scheppig, a pupil of Schinkel
and a member of his staff. As in his earlier
unexecuted scheme for Berlin Town Hall, the
exterior recalls a Florentine Renaissance
palazzo.

The Palais interior included several
impressive staterooms, richly adorned with
murals, sculptural decoration and furniture to
Schinkel's designs. Chief among them was a
barrel-vaulted banqueting hall which was also
used for musical performances; it was in the
Pompeian style, mixed with Renaissance
motifs. In this, the design was closely related to
rooms in Schinkel's conversions for the king's
sons such as the great dining hall, known as the
Galerie, in the Palais Prinz Karl (1827–8) and
the dining hall in the Palais Prinz Albrecht
(1831). Schinkel's combination on this drawing
of the different styles of the exterior and
interior is deliberate; he saw them as
testimonies to different epochs in art that were
inherently related. Detailed designs for the
decoration of the banqueting hall are in the
collection of the SSG, Schloss Charlottenburg.
The building was demolished in 1906.

Lit.: Rave 1962, pp. 226–36; Berlin 1980, 194;
Berlin 1981, 71.

G.R.

119.

THE BAUAKADEMIE, BERLIN.   1868

Eduard Gaertner (1801–77)

Signed and dated bottom right: '*E. Gaertner 1868*'

Oil on canvas, 630 × 820

Nationalgalerie, SMPK (NG 1229)

The viewpoint of this – absolutely reliable – painter is the western side of Schlossplatz. The eye moves across the bridge over the lock along the southern façade of the Bauakademie, built by Schinkel (1832–5), the twin-tower frontage of the Friedrich-Werder Kirche, also built by Schinkel (1824–30) into Französische Strasse. In the background we can see the French Cathedral in the Gendarmenmarkt. The red-brick building of the Bauakademie gleams in the morning light. In his later works, Gaertner was particularly fond of this kind of lighting. The brickwork of the church has a slightly lighter tone.

Schinkel's great contribution to Berlin's cityscape was the restoration of unrendered brickwork to its key buildings, re-establishing the tradition of Gothic brick. Acknowledging the scarcity of fine building stone in Prussia, Schinkel attempted to instil charm into the cheaper material by ingenuity of design and quality of craftsmanship – a specifically Prussian approach. The polychromatic effect of the banding in darker violet brick is particularly evident here. An untold number of brick buildings sprang up in the wake of Schinkel's Bauakademie, which was badly damaged during the Second World War and was pulled down in 1961, its artistic and historical value unrecognised. It originally housed the Allgemeine Bauschule (General School of Architecture) and the Oberbaudeputation, of which Schinkel was president, as well as Schinkel's official residence. The ground-floor shops had been envisaged from the outset.

H.B.–S.

120.

VIEW OF THE BAUAKADEMIE FROM SCHLOSS
    BRÜCKE.   1831

Signed and dated lower right: *Schinkel 1831*

Pen and brush and grey ink, and wash,
    511 × 656

Nationalgalerie, SMB (SM 23b.45)

121.

THE BAUAKADEMIE: ELEVATION SHOWING THREE
    BAYS OF THE NORTH FAÇADE.   1831

Signed lower right: *Schinkel*

Pen and black ink and wash, 672 × 540

Nationalgalerie, SMB (SM 31.14)

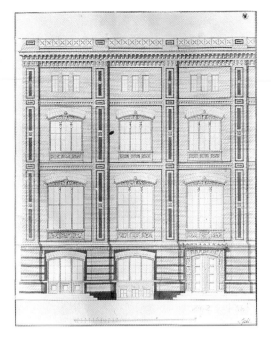

122.

THE BAUAKADEMIE: ELEVATION AND SECTION OF
    THE LEFT-HAND DOORWAY.   1832–3

Inscribed lower centre: *Eine Haupteingangs-
    Thür* (A main entrance door)

Signed and dated lower left: *Schinkel inv. 1832*

Pen and black ink, 518 × 424

Nationalgalerie, SMB (SM 31a.6)

Drawing for Plate 126 of the *Sammlung
    architektonischer Entwürfe*, Part 20, published
    in 1833.

The Bauakademie (Architectural Academy)
was to be a functional building, to house a
school of art and a public body responsible for
art. Hence the design followed Schinkel's 'first
principle of architecture' – utility. He stated
the justification for erecting the building in his
Sammlung architektonischer Entwürfe: 'A
reorganisation of the institute known hitherto
as the Bauakademie, now to be called the
Allgemeine Bauschule, and the very limited
space it has occupied, like the location of the
Oberbaudeputation [Royal Office of Works].
This prevents the great collections of drawings,
maps and models and the library which the
two organisations share from being displayed
and the latter set up to enable the public to
make better use of it; these are the reasons for
the new building.'

A 'General Institution for the Teaching of
Architecture for All the Royal States' had been
set up in 1799, and in 1800 it was located in the
New Mint building on the Werdersche Markt.
In 1806 the institute moved to a residential
building in Zimmerstrasse. After Schinkel had
been appointed head of the Oberbaudeputation
in 1830 and his friend Peter Christian Beuth,
head of the new Gewerbe-Institut (Institute of
Trade), had been made Director of the
Bauschule in 1831, the plan for a new building
for this was drawn up.

Schinkel's letter to Beuth first mentioning
designs and cost estimates for the Bauschule is
dated 9 March 1831. On 12 March Beuth put
the application to the king, requesting
permission to use the site of the old Packhof
(Customs House), and sending designs and a
site plan. The king quickly gave permission for
the site and approved the designs. The rest of
1831 was taken up with the remaining

planning and with preparation of modified designs. Wilhelm Stier, Baukondukteur (Director of Building), did the copying and finished the drawings from Schinkel's designs on 23 September. He sent them to Beuth, who handed them on to the Royal Office of Works, which made alterations to the distribution of the rooms, among other things. On 1 October 1831 Baukondukteur Flaminius was commissioned to direct the building work.

On 8 February 1832 the full computation by Baukondukteur Heinrich Bürde, who was acting as contractor, was finished and the demolition of the old Customs buildings could begin. The new building started on 1 April 1832. The skeleton was finished in 1833, that is, a system of pillars had been built up individually from the cellar to the top cornice, and was held by a network of arches and iron anchors. In 1834 the roofs and arches were vaulted, the infill walls and sills built; the mouldings of the cornices and façade were put on and the violet-coloured clay tiles attached on the buttresses from top to bottom. The exterior was covered with red unglazed bricks between layers of violet-coloured bricks pointed in white. The clay slabs and glazed tiles were fired in the pottery workshop of Cornelius Gormann. Work on the interior continued throughout 1835 and on 1 April 1836 the building was handed over for use. In the same year Friedrich Wilhelm III approved the relandscaping of the square in front of the Bauakademie by Peter Joseph Lenné.

The perspective (cat. 120) shows the intended building with a view of the arm of the Spree that separates the districts of Kölln and Friedrichswerder and the projected street along the bank on the northern side of the building, which is reflected in the water. On its entrance side a triangular area, lined with trees, fills the remaining space between the road along the bank and the houses of Niederlagsstrasse, with the Friedrich-Werder Kirche towering over them. Schinkel did not want the elegant side façade on Niederlagsstrasse to be hidden by trees, and also shortened the area before the Bauakademie optically, creating a clearly definable form in the view from the Zeughaus square.

Schinkel wrote in the *Sammlung architektonisher Entwürfe*: 'The building will be in brick and its exterior will not be plastered or covered in stucco. The material was therefore worked with particular care; all the divisions and mouldings, all the ornamentation and bas-reliefs, the columns in the broad windows and the arches they support were executed in brick with the greatest accuracy, and are only placed in the building when the basic but carefully executed construction work has secured them their place and will protect them from any pressure as the walls settle. Across the entire façade one layer of glazed bricks is arranged at a regular height of five layers of bricks, in a gentle colour that harmonises with the whole, partly in order to break the red of the mass of bricks somewhat and partly in order to create a restful architectural element; horizontal lines characterise the monumental quality of the whole building.'

The construction of the building is in keeping with its material. The square, four-storey building has four equally emphasised fronts, each of eight bays under a flat roof with an inner court. The brick-faced façades are divided by a grid-like scaffold of supporting pilasters and horizontal mouldings between floors, carrying the great tripartite windows. As in English industrial building, the segmental arches of the windows are reflected in the interior by cap vaults linked by iron beams, which were not, however, carried throughout the building. The decoration on windows and doorways consists of modelled terracotta panels, composed according to an iconographical programme.

Lit.: Rave 1962, pp. 38–60; Berlin 1980, 237, 239, 241; Berlin 1981, 82.

R.K. and S.R.

123.

RELIEF OF A GIRL WITH A PLUMB BOB; TRIAL PIECE FOR THE LEFT-HAND DOOR OF THE BAUAKADEMIE.   *c.* 1833

Friedrich Tieck (1776–1851) after K.F. Schinkel

Terracotta, 535 × 330

Nationalgalerie, SMB

The terracotta relief slabs on the two door frames of the Bauakademie have repeated plant ornamentation which is intended to represent Goethe's morphology of plants, and different emblematical figures, illustrating in the right-hand door (leading to the Oberbaudeputation) the concept of architecture as a science and on the left as an art and the outstanding qualities of the architect.

In the left portal, which led to the Bauschule itself, the progression of the figurative decoration begins at the lower left with Hercules, symbolising the Doric style with a Doric column (see cat. 122). A kneeling Egyptian opposite him embodies the Egyptian style. The kneeling figures of girls above him are crowned with ears of corn and baskets of fruit like capitals, symbolising on the left the Corinthian and on the right the Ionic orders. The two slabs above these show the invention

of the Corinthian capital by Callimachus. On the right of the design the boy with a plumb-line was eventually executed as a girl. The figure may represent Architecture. This trial piece was fired by Cornelius Gormann. The top of the arch represents the link between music and architecture.

A number of terracotta decorations survived the destruction of the Bauakademie in 1961, including most of the right-hand portal with its doors.

Lit.: Berlin 1980, 242c; Berlin 1981, 82.

S.B. and M.S.

124.

SKETCHES OF WOODEN AND IRON TRUSSES AND
GIRDERS FOR THE ARCHITEKTONISCHES
LEHRBUCH (TEXTBOOK OF ARCHITECTURE).

Early 1830s

Pen and black ink, 337 × 214

Nationalgalerie, SMB (SM 41a.31)

125.

DESIGNS FOR A PARISH CHURCH FOR THE
ARCHITEKTONISCHES LEHRBUCH (TEXTBOOK
OF ARCHITECTURE): PERSPECTIVE, ELEVATION,
SECTIONS AND DETAILS.

c. 1830

Inscribed with notes

Pen and black ink, 403 × 303 (four sheets
joined together)

Nationalgalerie, SMB (SM 41d.220)

126.

DESIGN FOR THE FAÇADE OF A SUBURBAN HOUSE
FOR THE ARCHITEKTONISCHES LEHRBUCH
(TEXTBOOK OF ARCHITECTURE).

c. 1828–9

Pencil, 186 × 205

Nationalgalerie, SMB (SM 41b.140)

Schinkel's architectural work exercised an
immense influence on the theory as well as the
practice of architecture, through his great
output of buildings, his extensive influence on
official bodies, the illustrations of his work, his
correspondence and finally through his direct
impact on his staff and pupils. A major
contribution to European architectural theory
was lost when he was unable to finish the
work on a large textbook of architecture
which he planned to publish and for which he
made drawings and wrote texts throughout his
life. But even in their fragmentary form
Schinkel's preliminary drawings and texts for
this volume are evidence of a comprehensive
approach to the essential nature of architecture,
both in its theoretical aspects and in its
structural, formal and material qualities. The
preliminary work for the projected volume
illustrates the far-reaching nature of his
developing reflections on and knowledge of
architectural theory.

Schinkel's entire artistic estate was purchased
by the state of Prussia after his death and stored
separately as the Schinkel Museum. Three

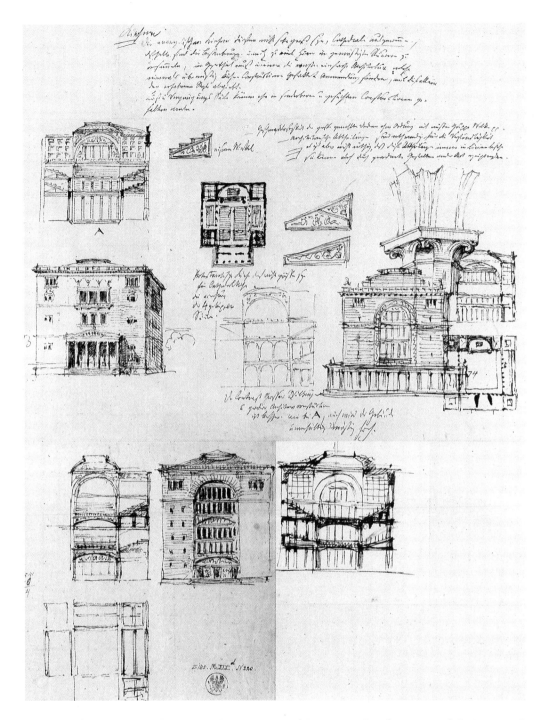

drawings, made after 1830, with ideal sketches (for example for the residence for the Crown Prince) and some sketches on subjects to be included in the textbook. Some of these are in the Crown Prince's hand.

The transition from the neo-classical to what is known as the technological period in Schinkel's output was a continuous development, a process of maturation, as it were, in which the interest in technology that had always been latent in his approach to architecture gradually moved into the foreground. Around and after 1825 he made important series of sketches for his treatise, some of which are related to his practical work. Others, from the late 1820s onwards, are very much more innovative and forward-looking, and Schinkel intended to use these for an enlarged edition of his textbook. If his work on the promotion of trade and industry had in a sense provided some stimulus of this kind before, the trend now evident in the sketches for the textbook and the draft texts is greatly in advance of its time. How far Schinkel had moved in his artistic development was revealed to his contemporaries when the Bauakademie was finished in the mid-1830s. The building was deliberately planned as a demonstration of a new architecture, as the terracotta decoration showed. The extension of the textbook into the technical concept, was a continuation of neo-classicism on a higher level. Schinkel wrote some texts as additions to the earlier introduction or to replace some passages, and his professional concern with construction was now extended to the building material.

'Each work of art, of whatever kind, must always contain a new element, and be a living addition to the world of art. Unless it is that living addition the artist cannot possibly have the true and necessary tension in creating it, nor the public gain an advantage, nor the world indeed a gift, with the work of art . . .

separate portfolios arranged by Schinkel (Nos 40–42) contain the preliminary work for the textbook, in all about 500 sheets of various sizes, consisting of manuscripts, sketches and final drawings.

The earliest sheets are a few manuscripts dating from around 1810, followed by sketches and drawings from the period around 1820. It was only from 1825 that Schinkel collected these more carefully into 'textbook portfolios'. Thirty-five finished drawings, uniform in treatment and prepared for engraving, were evidently intended as an introduction to a

teaching course (on the structural derivation of architectural forms). These are probably connected with the publication of an architectural textbook announced by Schinkel himself in his *Sammlung architektonisher Entwürfe* in 1828: 'I must draw the attention of those who are interested in this subject to a systematic treatise on various subjects in architecture. This is far advanced towards publication and its appearance depends on the leisure which my official business may permit me to spend on it.' The textbook portfolios also contain a small group of carefully finished

The British Journey and the Constructional Style   183

'In architecture the artist needs above all a general education . . . his mind must be so imbued with the essence of the classical period that his activity, which must be directed to new circumstances under new conditions, may freely be conducted in the spirit of that classical period, producing what is true, beautiful and characteristic to a free rhythm under new and changing circumstances . . .

'In architecture all must be true, any masking, concealing of the structure is an error. The real task is to make every part of the construction beautiful. In that word – beautiful – lies the whole story, the whole nature, the whole feeling for conditions . . . . Every perfect construction in a specific material has its decisive character and could not be rationally carried out in the same way in any other material . . . . In an architecture with style therefore every construction in a specific material must be complete in itself and whole. It may exist beside or upon others, but without mingling with them, it should remain independent in itself and display its full character . . . .'

Proceeding as before from the historical tectonic introductory course, Schinkel categorised all the constructions in stone described there as aesthetic styles. Now, however, he abandoned the restriction to stone and gave equal consideration to every material that was technically feasible (brick, wood, iron, cast zinc), if its qualities and properties opened up the way to new and specific forms and proportions. In doing so he drew suggestions from the architecture of all nations and periods.

In the sketches for specimen buildings the country house as an architectural type constitutes the most important addition to the treatise. Then follow sacred buildings, mainly churches, interesting as monumental and challenging architectural tasks for his own age, as well as towers.

Of the drawings shown here, the earliest is probably the set of variant designs for a cubic parish church (cat. 125). It is a development of the early cathedral projects and is also related to the domed schemes for the Nikolaikirche in Potsdam (cat. 107, 108). In the prevailing taste of the period such extreme projects had to remain largely theoretical. Next in date is the astonishingly advanced design for a suburban house (cat. 126), one of a number of drawings in which Schinkel explores the segmental arch in façades and vaulting. Again he is pushing theory well beyond its built expression, which in this case was the Bauakademie. Schinkel's detailed exploration of the techniques of construction is shown in the sketches for roofs (cat. 124). Apart from two details which are

clearly for wood, the members are evidently intended to be made in wrought or cast iron, with decorative elements in zinc. One of the sketches is for the roof of the banqueting hall in the ideal Fürstliche Residenz scheme of 1835.

In the end, all Schinkel succeeded in publishing on the theory of architecture was the odd comment in his largely technical descriptions of executed and projected buildings in the *Sammlung architektonischer Entwürfe* (1819–40). In addition, the *Vorbilder für Fabrikanten und Handwerker* (1821–37 see cat. 133) included plates of basic architectonic structures that are similar to some of the diagrams he devised for his planned textbook on architecture. By contrast with the latter, however, these were not intended to demonstrate theoretical and aesthetic principles, but to provide models to imitate for craftsmen and those going into the building trades.

Alfred von Wolzogen (1862–3) published Schinkel's manuscript notes for his treatise selectively, and divided up somewhat arbitrarily between apparently finished theoretical aphorisms on art, and notes and commentaries specifically concerned with architecture. The editor also made occasional minor changes to Schinkel's wording. It is only in the fine modern edition by Peschken (1979) that the phases of Schinkel's developing theory of architecture can be traced, and the full scope of his project grasped. Peschken corrected the misleading impression given by Wolzogen that the notes towards a systematic architectural treatise were only elaborated in the last few years of the architect's life.

Lit.: Peschken 1979, pp. 125, 131, 141–3, pls. 171, 207, 247; Berlin 1980, 610, 617.

C.H., A.P. and M.S.

127.

DESIGN FOR THE ROYAL LIBRARY, BERLIN: PERSPECTIVE VIEW.   1835

Signed and dated lower right: *Schinkel 1835*. Inscribed beneath the image with topographical notes

Pen and black ink, pencil and watercolour, 318 × 607

Nationalgalerie, SMB (SM 30.10)

Schinkel finished this design for a new building for the Royal Library in Berlin between 21 January and 23 February 1835, but it was never built. The library, designed on the orders of the Prussian Minister of Culture, was to hold about 400–500,000 volumes. In its planning it is transitional, lying between the library in the form of a single large room and the stackroom library with the readers, the book stores and offices separated. The stacks are not accessible to the ordinary reader but the library rooms nevertheless contain the traditional wall shelving, some with a gallery, as in the Bavarian Court and State Library in Munich begun in 1832. In contrast to this Schinkel also uses the space-saving carrel system, which he presumably saw when he inspected various college libraries in Oxford in 1826. The library was to be built in brick.

Lit.: Rave 1962, pp. 24–37; Berlin 1980, 190.

P.P.

Art and Industry

128.

SKETCH DESIGNS FOR SILVER TEAPOTS.   *c.*1810

Pencil, 361 × 215

Nationalgalerie, SMB (SM 37.64)

This sheet of nine lively sketches of teapots can probably be placed among the early designs for furnishings and furniture which Schinkel drew between 1808 and 1811 for the royal couple on their return to Berlin after the Napoleonic occupation (cf. cat. 34). The designs are inspired by French originals. The smooth bulbous bodies have strong profiles, the only ornamentation being on the rims and handles. The exploratory character of sketches, with overlapping forms and inevitable corrections, suggests the early date. Especially striking are the often clumsily attached narrow spouts and the complex handle-designs, the technical execution of which seems questionable. The teapot at the top is reminiscent of Schinkel's design of 1837 for a silver tureen. The finial on the lid is in the form of a perching Prussian eagle with outstretched wings, of a type often found on official gifts and court table-silver.

C.M.

129.

SKETCH DESIGNS FOR FIGURE CANDLESTICK.   *c.* 1815

Pencil, 439 × 285

Nationalgalerie, SMB (SM 37c.86)

The drawing shows two candlesticks. The first, in the form of a caryatid, was executed in cast iron. Two versions of the second are shown: a winged figure of Victory in a wind-blown robe on a ball or a base. Presumably it was to be executed in bronze or iron.

The caryatid motif was used in antiquity both in architecture and in small *objets d'art*, and it is frequently to be found in Schinkel's architectural work (in Schloss Orianda, Palais Prince August, Belriguardo and the Römische Bäder at Sanssouci). A sheet showing four caryatids, designed by Schinkel and reminiscent of the Caryatid Porch of the Erechtheion, with an extensive commentary by Schinkel is also to be found in the *Vorbilder für Fabrikanten und Handwerker* Part I, 6. This drawing illustrates the use of the motif in applied art. The human figure based on antique models plays a major part in Schinkel's designs for candelabra, candlesticks and bases.

Lit.: Berlin 1981, 303; Hamburg 1982, 13.3.

C.M.

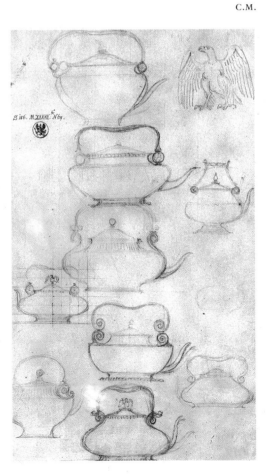

130.

PETER BEUTH IN HIS OFFICIAL FLAT IN THE
GEWERBE-INSTITUT IN KLOSTERSTRASSE,
BERLIN.   1838

Inscribed upper left: *Letzte Lebensphilosophie des
grossen Staatsmannes* (The ultimate
philosophy of the great statesman). Upper
right: *Verschwundene Jugendträume des
emsigen Staatsmannes* (The vanished
youthful dreams of the hard-working
statesman)

Watercolour, 531 × 730

Nationalgalerie, SMB (SM 54.11)

The watercolour is one of the 'souvenirs' that
Schinkel painted to mark public holidays for
his friend, Peter Beuth. Beuth, who donated
the series to the Schinkel Museum in 1844,
dated this work 1838, commenting: 'On the
left my past, on the right my present hover
over my living room.' The past, the 'vanished
youthful dreams', is Italy, here the Bay of
Naples, the time of travelling, collecting and
reflection. The clouds on the left (to the right

of the seated figure) contain the world already
ordered into pictures and framed. This is
shown behind a laden table, a not unimportant
feature of the Sunday gatherings of friends at
Beuth's summer house in Schönhausen. In this
painting Beuth is shown seated in the middle
of his small art collection: on the mantelpiece
small antique sculptures between two copies of
Apostles by Peter Vischer on the grave of St
Sebaldus in Nuremberg (similar copies are in
the Goethe House in Weimar and Schinkel
often used this model). Venetian filigree glasses
are to be seen on shelves, and Beuth, a lover of
horses, holds in his hand a book on that
subject. On the left is the portfolio cupboard
designed by Schinkel for Beuth, now in the
Nationalgalerie, SMB. The art collection
played an important part in Beuth's life; it was,
in effect, the material result of his lifelong
intellectual loves and endeavours. Schinkel's
Christmas painting for Beuth in 1836 (lost
since 1945) also shows 'art objects dear to me
in my study in Berlin' (Wolzogen 1862–3,
Vol. II, p. 337).

Lit.: Berlin 1980, 451a.

A.W.

131.

CENTREPIECE, THE SO-CALLED BEUTHSCHALE
(BEUTH DISH).   *c.*1845

Made at the Gewerbe-Institut Berlin (?) after a
design (1822) by Schinkel

Silver, embossed, electrotype casting, h. 240,
diam. 430

Kunstgewerbemuseum, SMB (Inv. No.
1975.50)

132.

CIRCULAR RELIEF: ATHENA INVENTING THE
COGWHEEL

Anonymous sculptor after a design by Schinkel

Plaster, tinted green, depth 20, diam. 218

Nationalgalerie, SMB

The creation of the Beuthschale has a very long history. A lost drawing by Schinkel, dated 1822, showed it from the side, in particular the base with putti holding a wreath. The relief in the centre is also based on a drawing by Schinkel; Beuth presented it to the Schinkel Museum with the note: 'A birthday present. – An allegory, dedicated to me as Director of the Gewerbe-Institut [Institute of Trade]'. This drawing was also destroyed in the Second World War.

The tinted plaster relief after the drawing (cat. 132) was once in the Beuth-Schinkel Museum. The three figures on the left – Athena, a shepherd and a maenad – are exactly derived from an antique fragment in the Munich Glyptothek. Schinkel was therefore expanding an antique fragment into a modern allegory: Athena, goddess of wisdom, is drawing cogwheels in the sand with her javelin, and a small satyr holds up a sphere which prefigures this technical invention.

The centrepiece based on Schinkel's original drawings must have been completed after his death, since the relief and stem were produced by the electrotyping method, a process known in Prussia only from about 1845. On Beuth's initiative the Gewerbe-Institut offered a prize for the manufacture of three-dimensional objects by an electroplating method. The art historian Gustav Friedrich Waagen, who knew Beuth and Schinkel well, mentioned the dish in his Schinkel address of 1854: 'A worthy testimony both to the members' appreciation of the effectiveness of Beuth's presidency of the Gewerbe-Institut, and to the high artistic level achieved here by Schinkel and by him is provided by the . . . silver dish with an exquisite relief, presented to him by the Gewerbe-Institut . . .'. We can assume that Beuth received the dish as a gift in 1846 on the 25th anniversary of the Trade Association he founded. Rich in associations, it is not only one of the earliest works of electrotyping in Prussia but also symbolizes in both form and technique the harmony Schinkel sought between art and technology, ancient and modern. A separate electrotype of the relief is also recorded.

Lit.: Berlin 1980, 446; Berlin 1981, 209.

A.W.

133.

TITLE PAGE OF VORBILDER FÜR FABRIKANTEN UND HANDWERKER (EXAMPLES FOR MANUFACTURERS AND CRAFTSMEN).

Berlin 1821

Lithograph

Kupferstichkabinett, SMB (KK B 2060)

The *Vorbilder für Fabrikanten und Handwerker* (Examples for Manufacturers and Craftsmen) was published by the Technische Deputation für Gewerbe (State Agency for Trade and Industry), a small body consisting of eight members. Beuth was director, and Schinkel was responsible for all aesthetic questions. The two friends selected the plates together and co-operated on the textual commentaries. The book is divided into three parts: (I) Architectural and other decorations (60 plates); (II) Tools and vessels and other examples of applied art (57 plates); (III) Textile patterns, especially for weaving (33 plates). The examples in the book, which became a standard work, were largely drawn from antiquity and the Renaissance, while some of the textile patterns also come from the Islamic world. The only contemporary designs were by Schinkel, and ran to about forty plates. They fit smoothly into the work, as they are in the same spirit as the older examples he chose.

The first 94 plates, which had been issued separately, were reissued as a single volume in 1830. By 1837 another 56 plates had been made, and these were added to a second reissue volume of 150 plates. In 1830 and 1837 slim volumes of texts were published separately. Beuth wrote the introductions, and he and Schinkel certainly co-operated on the commentaries to the various sections and plates. Within Prussia, individual plates were distributed free of charge to public libraries, appropriate authorities, schools of drawing, artists of merit, and craftsmen. They were not sold through bookshops 'because firstly, something that can be bought cannot also be a mark of distinction, and secondly because many of the copper plates will only yield a few good prints, and the work, as it is executed, will always be a classic and be useful', as Beuth wrote in 1822. In 1859 electrotype copies of the printing plates were made. They were used for an exact reprint, published in 1863.

Lit.: Berlin 1980, pp. 258–9; Berlin 1981, pp. 333–6.

A.W.

134.

TWO VIEWS OF THE WARWICK VASE, WITH DETAILS

Louis Sellier (about 1757–?), after Johann Matthäus Mauch (1792–1856)

Lettered below: *gez. v. Mauch, gest. v. Sellier* (drawn by Mauch, engraved by Sellier)

Engraving, 480 × 330

Kupferstichkabinett, SMB (KK82060 16)

Vorbilder, Part II, Plate 12

The white marble vase was found by Gavin Hamilton in the ruins of Hadrian's villa near Tivoli in 1771, restored by Piranesi, and soon afterwards came into the possession of the Earl of Warwick. It is now in the Burrell Collection, Glasgow.

'For the manufacturers for whom this work was intended, it should be not uninteresting that the manufacturer Thomasson [sic] in Manchester recently executed this vessel in the same size in patinated bronze, but with the handles and decoration in gilded bronze.'

On 19 June 1826 Schinkel noted in his diary of the English tour a visit to the Birmingham factory of Sir Edward Thomason: 'At 10 o'clock we go to Mr Tomason and see his stocks of plated silver work, bronze, glass, etc. and his factory. The great Warwick Vase has been cast in bronze. All the sculpted parts have been plated and the thing has therefore become horrible, but no part is by any means bearably modelled, indeed all is beneath criticism.' (One of Thomason's full-size castings is in front of the Senate House at Cambridge.). Nevertheless in 1826 Bergrat Krigar was taking an example of one of these vases to Berlin, where in 1827 it was modelled in a reduced size by Stilarsky, to be cast in iron (cat. 135). A larger iron copy was displayed on the upper landing of the staircase of the museum on the Lustgarten (see cat. 55).

Lit.: Hamburg 1982, 13.11.

A.W.

135.

THE WARWICK VASE.   *c.* 1830

Royal Iron Foundry, Berlin or Gleiwitz

Iron, finished in black, h. with base 545

Kunstgewerbemuseum, SMB (KGM c.10)

A copy of the famous antique marble vase made in Berlin cast iron was shown for the first time in 1828 at the Berlin Academy exhibition: 'The models were made by the master modeller Stilarsky, and shaped and cast by the foreman of the moulding shop, Grüttner. They were engraved by the engraver Glanz.' The vase is shown on the iron foundry's New Year's plaque as an outstanding casting of 1828. The importance attached to the piece is also evident from the fact that the goldsmith George Hossauer was only given permission to use the model of the Warwick vase for a copy in silver for the wedding of Prince Karl in May 1827 after an extensive correspondence with Schuckmann, the Minister of the Interior. The silver vase, with base and lid to designs by Schinkel, was also shown at the Academy exhibition in 1828. The Academy exhibition of 1836 included two differently sized versions of the vessel from the Royal Iron Foundry in Berlin, and it is also illustrated in the price list of the Prussian foundry in Gleiwitz.

Lit.: Hamburg 1982, 13.12.

A.W.

136.

DESIGNS FOR VESSELS.   1821

Signed and dated at the bottom right: *Schinkel inv. & fec. 1821*

Pen and ink and wash, 561 × 413

Nationalgalerie, SMB (SM 43a.27)

Drawing for *Vorbilder*, Part II, Plate 29.

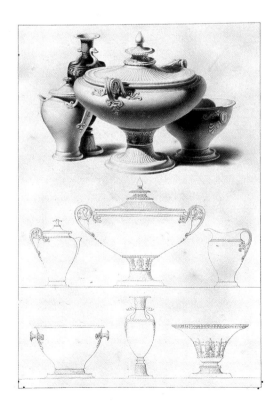

With their antique shapes and applied decoration, most of these vessels convey the impression of English creamware. Schinkel was familiar with this modern material, which had been developed in England from around 1750. From 1797 to about 1800 he had worked for the factory of Freiherr Eckardtstein as a designer of creamware in the English style (Eckardtstein, who acquired a newly built creamware factory in Berlin in 1797 and a faience factory in Potsdam in 1800, concentrated in his Berlin factory on the imitation of English examples). The design for a tureen was modified by Schinkel in 1837 for production in silver.

Lit.: Berlin 1980, 463; Berlin 1981, 309, 325c.

A.W.

137.

DESIGN FOR A CUP TO BE MADE IN SILVER OR GOLD. 1820

Signed and dated lower right: *Schinkel inv. & del. 1820* and inscribed below *Pokal in Silber Oder Gold Auszufuhren*

Pencil, 458 × 297

Nationalgalerie, SMB (SM 43a.23)

This design was engraved for the *Vorbilder* (Vol. I, Part II, Plate 25) with the frieze and the figure group shown on Plate 26 (cat. 140). The group of dancing maenads, bacchantes and the panther derives from the Borghese vase in the Louvre. Variants of the motifs are shown on the frieze on the bowl.

This is a basic pattern, comparable to Schinkel's ideal design for a church, intended for general consumption. The cup for Baurat Redtel (Kunstgewerbemuseum, SMPK), was made from it in 1826, probably in the Gewerbe-Institut as was the cup with lid by George Hossauer in 1828 (cat. 138), which follows the model even more closely. Schinkel himself designed variations on this type in response to specific requests, as in the case of the Winterfeldt cup. Cups of this kind were presented on special occasions, and were the favourite mark of honour in the early nineteenth century. In the *Conversationshandbuch für Berlin und Potsdam* of 1830 Zedlitz mentions that the goldsmith Hossauer, who was then still young, had already made more than 200 presentation cups.

Lit.: Berlin 1980, 510; Berlin 1981, 323, 306–8.

A.W.

POKAL IN SILBER ODER GOLD AUSZUFÜHREN

138.

CUP WITH LID. 1828

Johann George Hossauer (1794–1874) after a design (1820) by Schinkel

Silver, cast, embossed, stamped and engraved, h. 380

Marked: HOSSAUER BERLIN, with master's mark: Beehive

Inscription: *Ihrem Vormunde die dankbaren Mündel* (To their guardian from his grateful wards) MDCCCXXVIII

Kunstgewerbemuseum, SMB (KGM 1980, 166)

Although George Hossauer employed several goldsmiths, the master's mark suggests that this cup was made mainly by the master himself. The bacchante group on the stem is very finely cast and chased, but the bowl and shaft are in thin sheet rolled silver pressed over wooden forms. This new industrial process made the vessels lighter and less expensive than those made entirely by hand, but even so they were not cheap. The simplicity of form and new but carefully handled technical processes are still in a balanced relationship. The positive view taken of mechanised procedures in the crafts during this early phase of industrial development is underlined by a letter from Schinkel. He wrote to the Winterfeldt family that he had handed on their commission for a goblet 'to Goldsmith Hossauer, the most skilful and the only one in Berlin who has command of the latest technical means and uses them. I have already given him several drawings for cups.'

Lit.: Berlin 1980, 509.

A.W.

139.

CUP.   *c.* 1829

Johann George Hossauer (1794–1874) after a design (1820) by Schinkel

Copper mount: stamped, chased and gold-plated. Bohemian glass: colourless, cut and polished, flashed gold and ruby colour within, h. 360 (with lid)

Freunde der Preussischer Schlösser und Gärten, Berlin

Among a number of similar cups made in the Hossauer workshops after an idea from Schinkel, this version is distinctive in its combination of precious materials which enhance each other, with the gilded copper and the deep red of the gold and ruby flashing. Judging by its contours – the gentle wave-like profile of the cup, the strong stem and the S-shape of the foot – it links up with the ideas Schinkel set down in a design in 1820 (cat. 137).

The shape of this lidded vessel lies on the borderline between the secular goblet and sacramental chalice, which is why Hossauer offered this type of vessel, slightly modified, both as a ceremonial cup and as a communion chalice.

The fine cut-glass decoration consists of wavy lines, guilloches, and stylised spirals of leaves with cornucopias and flowers. The illusion of coloured ruby glass is achieved by the flash with which the inner side is treated. The royal court goldsmith Johann George Hossauer had learnt methods of metal spinning and the manufacture of gold and silver-plated goods in Paris and he owned the most important modern industrialised workshop in Berlin.

The cup was once owned by the descendants of George Hossauer. There were other examples in the palace of Kaiser Wilhelm I on Unter den Linden and in the possession of Prince Karl of Prussia. But like the ruby cup acquired by the Berlin Kunstgewerbemuseum in 1918, these have now vanished. The date is based on the information that Prince Wilhelm received his cup in 1829.

W.B.

140.

DESIGNS FOR CANDLESTICKS AND CUPS.   1820

Henry Moses (*c.* 1780–1870) after Schinkel

Engraving, 323 × 460

Lettered lower left: *Erfunden u. gez. v. Schinkel* (Designed and drawn by Schinkel) and in the centre *gedr. v. Prêtre* (Printed by Prêtre) and at lower right: *gest. v. H. Moses* (Engraved by H. Moses)

Kupferstichkabinett, SMB (KK B2060.1b)

Vorbilder, Part II, Plate 26

In the upper part of the sheet Schinkel shows in detail the figurative decoration on the silver cup of 1820 (cat. 137). The three wine goblets were also certainly intended to be made in silver. The left of these shows the twelve apostles and a frieze of angels, and was intended as a chalice. The big relief of the putti harvesting grapes on the central goblet indicates that it was to be used for wine. The right-hand cup is decorated with a frieze of

tritons. The candlestick on the left was made in cast iron (cat. 141). The right-hand candlestick is 'intended for execution in silver or silver-plated copper', with its clear form and simple decoration of intertwining leaves. The fused-plate process, developed in England about 1750, was introduced in Prussia around 1830. The Schinkel Museum has a pencil design for the two candlesticks (SM 37c.91).

Henry Moses was one of a number of celebrated English, French and Italian draughtsmen and engravers who worked on the *Vorbilder* illustrations. It is unclear whether they worked in Berlin or were simply sent the copper plates. The plate of the Medici vase was both drawn and engraved by Moses.

Lit.: Berlin 1980, 466; Berlin 1981, 324.

C.M. and M.S.

141.

PAIR OF TABLE CANDLESTICKS.   *c.* 1825

Probably executed by the Royal Iron Foundry in Berlin, after a design by Schinkel

Iron, finished in black, h. 300, diam. of foot 132

Kunstgewerbemuseum, SMB (KGM C 15 a/b)

The candlesticks derive from Schinkel's design of 1820, made for the *Vorbilder für Fabrikanten und Handwerker* (cat. 140).

The shaft is a slender calyx of acanthus leaves which opens at the top like a bud. Variants of the design are to be seen on a pencil drawing by Schinkel showing three candlesticks (SM 37.89). The decoration on the foot was changed during the casting, and it now culminates in the round profiled disc above the snake knop.

The candlestick was presumably first cast by the Royal Iron Foundry in Berlin, but the Berlin foundry burned down in 1848 and without catalogues or documentary material it has not been possible to substantiate this. The model is known to have been taken up by the Ilsenburg foundry. According to the volume of commentaries to the *Vorbilder* the piece was to have been cast in bronze, and there are examples in iron, not black-finished as here but painted with a bronze-coloured paint.

Lit.: Berlin 1981, 30f; Hamburg 1982, 13.8.

C.M.

142.

Inscribed bottom right: *Nach Angabe des Herrn Geheimen Uber Baurath Schinkel/ ausgeführt in Porzellan im Juli 1824* (made on the orders of Geheimer Oberbaurath Schinkel in July 1824) and *Geschenk des Herrn Geheimer Ober Bergrath Frick 1847* (gift of the Geheimer Oberbergrath Frick 1847)

Pen and ink and watercolour, 938 × 624

KPM-Archiv, Schloss Charlottenburg (Mappe 146, no. 19)

In January 1821 the court in Berlin honoured the Russian Grand Duke Nicholas (the future Tsar) and the Grand Duchess Alexandra Feodorovna, eldest daughter of Friedrich Wilhelm III, with a musical and dramatic performance based on *Lalla Rookh*, Thomas Moore's sequence of Oriental tales (1817). Directed by Count Bruhl, with designs by Schinkel and music by Spontini, the performance involved members of the court (including the Grand Duchess as Lalla Rookh), as well as professional singers.

As in the case of the later Festival of the White Rose (cat. 145), the occasion was marked by royal gifts. This design was for the central vase from a set of three made by the Berlin Royal Porcelain Manufactory (KPM) in 1824. The painting around the centre depicts the festival pageant after a drawing by August von Kloeber. The Oriental form of the vase, which was probably suggested by the sculptor Gottfried Schadow, is apparently based on the so-called Alhambra-vase. Its ornament, using largely classical motifs, conveys an oriental impression. The donor of this drawing, Georg Friedrich Christoph Frick, was joint director of the KPM and in 1832 took sole control, overseeing a great expansion in its production.

Lit.: Pachomova-Göres 1985, pls 8, 9.

M.S. and I.B.

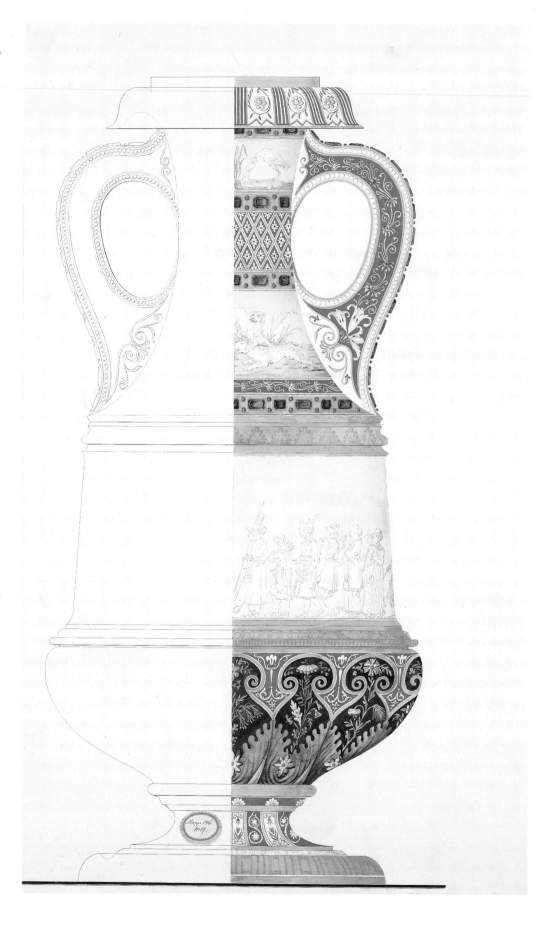

Joseph Caspar (1799–1880) after a design by Schinkel

Copper engraving, 530 × 375

Lettered lower left: *erfunden v. Schinkel* (Designed by Schinkel) and at the centre: *gedr. v. Prêtre* (Printed by Prêtre) and at the lower right: *gez. u. gest. v. Caspar* (Drawn and engraved by Caspar)

Kupferstichkabinett, SMB (KK B 2060)

Vorbilder, Part II, Plate 1

Schinkel designed this candelabrum soon after his return from Italy in 1824 for the Berlin stove factory owned by Tobias Christoph Feilner, where it was made 'to a height of 8 feet in baked clay, a masterly piece of work, at a selling price of 50 thalers. The figures were modelled by the sculptor Ludwig Wichmann [Feilner's son-in-law], the decorations are by a skilful potter in the factory who was trained there, Ferdinand Harnisch.' The structure and shape of the candelabrum are derived from antique Roman models, which Schinkel had seen in the Vatican collections.

   The triangular lower part is supported by sphinxes and rests on a stepped base. The flat sides bear depictions of Nike, the goddess of Victory. For the depiction of Nike sacrificing a bull and that of her leading two horses, as shown in the left detail study, preliminary drawings have been preserved (SM 39c.150). For the right field, Nike decorating a stele, the drawing is missing. The shaft is in four sections, an acanthus leaf bowl followed by a frieze of dancing maidens with wreaths, above them a fluted shaft and finally the bowl supported by swans. Two terracotta examples eight feet tall were shown at the Academy exhibition of 1824, and two more, of terracotta but painted in a bronze colour, formed part of the initial furnishings of the Neue Pavillon at Schloss Charlottenburg in 1826 (see cat. 61–2). A single candelabrum was formerly in the Schinkel Museum. Two others, in cast iron and functioning as street lamps once stood before the Bauakademie in Berlin. A terracotta example is at Schloss Charlottenburg. Schinkel's preliminary drawing is in the Nationalgalerie SMB (SM 39c.150).

   Lit.: Berlin 1981, 290, 317; Hamburg 1982, 13.23.

C.M.

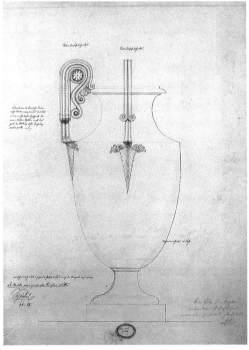

Inscribed by Schinkel bottom left: *wünschenwert würde es seyn des Profil des Fusses nach der Angabe a zu ändern/ Die Modelle würde ich mir zur Revision erbitten./ Schinkel feb: 28* (the profile of the foot should ideally be changed from what is shown here. I request that the model should be given to me for revision. Schinkel 28 Feb.); top *Seiten-Ansicht des Henkels, Vorder-Ansicht des Henkels* (side view of the handle, front view of the handle); to the left *überall wo die Bleistift-Linien/recht dunkel angegeben sind bedeutet/ es einen sehr tiefen Einschnitt der/ einen dunklen Schatten macht und gerade die Wirkung dieser Zeichnung/ wiedergibt* (wherever a dark pencil line is shown it indicates a very deep incision that will make a dark shadow if this design is followed exactly); to the right *Vorhandenes Profil der Vase* (present profile of the vase)

Inscribed by Frick, bottom right: *Dieser Henkel ist in Porzellan/ an dieser Vase nicht auszuführen/ weil es anders schwindet als die gedachte Vase/ Frick* (this handle is in porcelain and will not go on this vase because it will shrink differently to the vase [i.e. in the kiln] Frick)

Pen and ink and pencil, 680 × 440

KPM-Archiv, Schloss Charlottenburg (Mappe 146, Bl. 403)

Seventeen Schinkel designs for the Royal Porcelain Manufactory survive in the KPM-Archiv, dating from about 1812–30, and others have been lost. In this design Schinkel is refining, on the left, a two-handled vase type made in the Nymphenburg factory in 1825, represented by the profile on the right. In production it was known as the Bavarian Pattern and, after 1829, as the Munich Pattern. Interestingly, bearing in mind the comments of the factory director Frick, a variant was made with bronze handles. The design shows the extreme attention to detail devoted by the eminent architect to such relatively humble projects.

Lit.: Pachomova-Göres 1985, 698.

M.S.

145.

DESIGN FOR A PRESENTATION CUP IN SILVER AND
ENAMEL.   1829

Inscribed with a note on the manufacturing
    technique

Pencil, 652 × 504

Nationalgalerie, SMB (SM 37a.26)

In 1829 the goldsmith George Hossauer was
commissioned by Empress Alexandra
Feodorovna of Russia (the Prussian Princess
Charlotte) to make small medals for the
knights for a medieval tournament festival,
'The Magic Spell of the White Rose'. In her
youth the Princess called herself *Fleur Blanche*.
The festival was being arranged by her uncle,
Duke Carl of Mecklenburg-Strelitz to
celebrate the Empress's birthday on 13 July
1829, and it was to be held in the Neue Palais
in Potsdam. The celebrations also included a
ball and theatrical performance, in which the
guests took part and for which Schinkel
designed the scenery. In 1830 Hossauer made
three large cups, to historicist designs by
Schinkel, as mementoes of the celebration. In
the *Neuestes Conversationshandbuch für Berlin und
Potsdam* by Zedlitz (Berlin, 1834), they are
mentioned in the section on Hossauer as 'three
large and magnificent beakers in the Gothic
style with royal and noble coats of arms in
enamel, in the possession of His Majesty the

145a. Presentation cup. 1830. Silver, parcel-gilt and
enamel. Rainer Zietz Ltd.

King, Her Majesty the Empress of Russia and
His Highness Duke Carl of Mecklenburg'.
One of the King's cups was in the
Hohenzollern Museum in Schloss Monbijou
and was lost in 1945. The piece owned by the
Empress Alexandra Feodorovna is still in her
summer residence, the Cottage of Alexandria,
in Peterhof (Petrodvorets) near Leningrad.
145a shows the Mecklenburg example (69cm
high). The cup is parcel-gilt and is placed on a
wide silver stand. The finial is a rose. The
cover bears ten enamelled shields of arms,
including those of principalities, Prussia (twice)
and the Hohenzollerns. On the body, stem and
foot are 63 enamelled shields, presumably of
the participants at the festival, with further
fanciful shields on the stand. Although Gothic
in its ornament, the overall form of the cup
and stand is classical. Another design drawing,
more correct and including the stand, is in the
Plankammer of the SSG Potsdam-Sanssouci
(2906 c).
Lit.: Berlin 1980, 512, 513; Berlin 1981, 206.
                                        A.W. and M.S.

146.

DESIGN FOR A FOUNTAIN FOR THE GEWERBE-
INSTITUT, BERLIN. 1829

Signed lower right: *Schinkel*, and inscribed
with a note

Pen and black ink, 650 × 503

Nationalgalerie, SMB (SM 43a.28)

Engraved for the *Vorbilder*, Part II, Plate 31

In 1826 a third year-long course had been
added to the training given at the Technical
College founded by Beuth in Berlin in 1821.
In 1827 the school was renamed the Kgl.
Preussisches Gewerbe-Institut (Royal Prussian
Institute of Trade) and an adjacent site
acquired to accommodate the growing
number of pupils. The institute rapidly became
a major technical training centre in Prussia.
'To embellish the court Herr Schinkel designed
a fountain to be executed in bronze. The
college workshops set about the task. The
bowl with its beautiful Greek profiles was
modelled with delicacy and feeling by a pupil
at the Institute . . . . The promoters, sponsors
and teachers of the Institute, Professors Tieck,
Rauch and Wichmann, undertook to have the
four groups that crown the bowl executed
under their supervision, the first-named with
two of the four groups and the others with one
each. The bowl and one group will be shaped
and cast by a former pupil of the same, the
teacher Dinger, a pupil of Crozatier in Paris;
the three other, partly finished, groups have
been entrusted to the teacher Frayerabend and
the teacher and academic artist Müller.

The steam engine at the Institute can throw
the jet of water 50 feet into the air if necessary,
and the hydraulic works were made in the
workshop by pupils studying mechanics'
(*Vorbilder*, Vol. I, Part II, pp. 102–3). Auguste
Kiss exhibited the figure groups at the
Academy in 1830. The fountain was made in
1831. In 1843 it was placed in its present
position in the vestibule of Schloss
Charlottenhof.

Lit.: Rave 1962, p. 350; Berlin 1980, 502;
Berlin 1981, 310, 326.

A.W.

147.

Made by Johann Friedrich Dannenberger,
    Berlin, after a design by Schinkel

Printed cotton, 445 × 535

Kunstgewerbemuseum, SMB (KGM 68, 2606)

The material with its rich, almost naturalistic
floral pattern, is from a folio of printed cotton
samples made to designs by various Berlin
architects. The volume was presented by the
Dannenberger factory soon after the
Kunstgewerbemuseum (Museum of Applied
Arts) was set up in Berlin. A note states that
this and a material with rich acanthus borders
was designed by Schinkel in 1829, 'on the
occasion of an extension to the Crown Prince's
residence'.

   J.F. Dannenberger, like many of his fellow
industrialists, received scientific support from
the chemist of the Technische Deputation für
Gewerbe, Sigismund Hermbstädt. He founded
his own company in 1810 with very little
money but much skill and energy. Like
Hossauer (cat. 138), he combined a feeling for
art with an understanding of the latest
technical developments such as cylinder
printing machines. This combination of
technical development and aesthetic sensitivity
was the basis of the high standard of cotton
printing in Berlin at the beginning of the
nineteenth century.

Lit.: Berlin 1980, 471.

                                        A.W.

148.

TEXTILE DESIGN

Lettered at bottom left: *Gezeichnet von C.
    Boetticher* (Drawn by C. Boetticher) and at
    bottom right *Gedr.: v. J. Storch in Berlin*
    (Printed by J. Storch in Berlin)

Colour lithograph, 410 × 550

Vorbilder für Fabrikanten und Handwerker. Vol
    II, part III, plate 10.

Kupferstichkabinett, SMB (KK. B 2060 IIa)

Textile patterns take up a lot of space in the
Vorbilder, making up one third of both
volumes, with 10 and 33 plates respectively.
This undoubtedly reflects the universally high
regard for ornament in the nineteenth century.
Unlike the other two parts of the *Vorbilder* the
stylistic range in these surface decorations is
very great. Tending to abandon classical
models, Schinkel became strongly influenced
by Islamic ornament and European decorative
motifs from the Middle Ages to the late
eighteenth century, anticipating the accurate
historicism of the second half of the nineteenth
century.

   In Volume II, published in 1837, part III

opens with a design by Schinkel; all the other textiles were historical examples drawn by the architect Carl Boetticher during a tour through North Germany ordered by Beuth and Schinkel. According to the accompanying text, the plate depicts a 'gold and velvet textile. A church vestment from Brandenburg Cathedral'. It is probably Italian and late fifteenth or early sixteenth century. This commission presumably had a decisive influence on Boetticher's subsequent work. In 1834 he became a tutor in ornament drawing at the Gewerbe-Institut, and between 1834 and 1844 he published a highly influential book on ornament.

The technique used in the production of this sheet is also important. Some plates in the de luxe edition were, as here, produced with extreme care by the technique of colour lithography developed by Alois Senefelder, in 1817, but not fully developed until the 1830s.

A.W.

149.

DESIGNS FOR GLASS VESSELS.   1829

Inscribed lower centre: *Schinkel. erfunden.*
  (designed by Schinkel)

Pencil, 512 × 342

Nationalgalerie, SMB (SM 43a.31)

Drawing for the *Vorbilder*, Part II, Plate 5

Schinkel cultivated the use of historical form and techniques in his designs for glass vessels. The design for the tall slender glass shown here derives from Venetian reticulated glass. The process was still unknown when the *Vorbilder* were published, and in 1839 the Association for the Promotion of Industry in Prussia announced a competition for the rediscovery of the Venetian net glass technique. It was won in 1842 by Franz Pohl, a former pupil of the Berlin Gewerbe-Institut and director of the Gräflich Schaffgottsche Josephinenhütte in Schreiberhau. Dutch-German Renaissance rummers with the characteristic nubs of berries fused on to them served as models for the wine goblet on the right. A similar, larger vessel from the Gernheimer Hütte run by the Schrader brothers, to which reference is made in the text volume of the *Vorbilder*, is in the Kunstgewerbemuseum, SMB (Inv. No. 1976, 233). The heavy footed bowl in the centre of the picture has Biedermeier features, and is embellished with a diamond-cut pattern in the English manner. The network of parallel lines is broken by four round medallions; this view shows Europa on the bull. The pear-shaped vase with deep, curved handles recalls Venetian vessels of the sixteenth and seventeenth centuries. The piece also has a unique mixture of decorative elements from different periods. The fluting on the lower part is borrowed from antique clay vessels. Next come leaf ornamentation in the antique manner, pearl bands, a diamond-cut pattern on the slender neck and a wavy, turned-down rim. The design is not known to have been executed.

The three profile designs on the lower half of the sheet are clearly related, in shape and design, to work in precious metals. Both the variety of the cut patterns and the clean lines of the vessels suggest that they were intended to be made in pressed glass.

Lit.: Berlin 1980, 464; Berlin 1981, 318b.

C.M.

150.

DESIGN FOR A PICTURE FRAME

Friedrich Wilhelm Schwechten (1796–1879) after Schinkel

Colour lithograph 465 × 313

Lettered lower left: *Erfunden u. gez. v. Schinkel* (designed and drawn by Schinkel) and at the centre: *gedr. v. Prêtre* (printed by Prêtre) and at the lower right: *gest. v. Schwechten.* (engraved by Schwechten.)

Kupferstichkabinett, SMB (KK B2060IIa)

Vorbilder, Part II, Plate 10

Schinkel received the commission to design a large number of picture frames for the Royal Museum (the Altes Museum) in Berlin between 1824 and 1830. All missing and damaged frames were to be replaced, and in view of the short time and limited funds available this was an immense task. The first design drawings were presumably made only after Schinkel returned from England in 1826. Since pictures of various kinds and sizes were to hang beside each other, he proposed three different types of frame, which would fit most pictures, simple in design and differing only in their decoration. The simplest was made from the design shown here. The moulded wooden frame with its decorative strips has cast-zinc ornamentation consisting of tendrils, spirals and palmettes, which extend beyond the profile of the frame. The corner motif is repeated in smaller and varied form midway along the sides. The use of series-produced cast-zinc parts, instead of the usual carved wood, is typical of Schinkel's concern to promote the use of this material, which had found its way into art manufacture in the early 1830s.

Lit.: Sievers 1950, pp. 75–85; Berlin 1980, 458; Berlin 1981, 321.

C.M.

151.

CUP WITH LID.   1854–9

Johann George Hossauer (1794–1874) after a design (*c.* 1830) by Schinkel

Engraved on the inner side of the lid: *Hossauer Berlin*, and stamped with a bear with an 'L' (for J.W.D. Friedrich, first Assay Master) and 'D' in a circle (for L.Th. Wendelboe, second Assay Master), *12 Löth*

Silver, stamped, embossed, cast, chased, cup and lid gilded on the inside, h. 470

Kunstgewerbemuseum, SMB (1990, 496)

From the 1820s onwards, once the Prussian economy had recovered after the Wars of Liberation, presentation cups became the favourite gift for many occasions. Needless to say, Schinkel was most often asked to design these, having had experience in this field through his *Vorbilder für Fabrikanten und Handwerker*. His most productive collaboration was with Berlin's leading goldsmith, Johann George Hossauer, who left an album – destroyed in 1945 – of over 60 silver designs, mainly by Schinkel.

In 1830 Schinkel designed a cup for General von Roder's jubilee year in office, which was made by Hossauer in 1831 and shown with a similar cup at the 1836 Exhibition of the Berlin Academy. The cup depicted here matches the 1830 drawing in overall structure and in several details. In 1846, Hossauer adapted his 1830 design into a giant cup 84 cm tall as a celebration gift for Field Marshal Graf Wrangel, and this cup is a great deal more opulent and cluttered. Interestingly, in the 1850s Hossauer went back to the austere classical style of his early designs. Schinkel always recommended that his general designs be treated as a basis for variations. As with much of Schinkel's silver, this design has a strong English feeling.

B.G.

152.

VASE PAINTED WITH A PANORAMA SHOWING THE
FRIGATE ROYAL LOUISE.   1836

Royal Porcelain Manufactory (KPM), Berlin.
The vase form after a design by Schinkel.
The decoration designed by Prof. Friedrich
Wilhelm Ludwig Stier and carried out by
Hermann Looschen. The panorama painted
by Carl Emanuel Koch

Mark: underglazed blue sceptre. Painter's
mark: imperial orb over KPM in red
overglaze

Porcelain in three parts, enamelled and gilt
with gilt bronze handles. h.875

Reproduced by Gracious Permission of
Her Majesty the Queen

The vase was a present from Friedrich
Wilhelm II in return for the model frigate
Royal Louise, which King William IV of
England had presented to the Prussian king for
the Pfaueninsel (Pheasant Island) on the Havel
in the summer of 1832. This sailing yacht was
described by the *Nautical Magazine* in June
1832 as 'a most beautiful model of a 32-gun
frigate', with the following dimensions: 'Her
length is 55⁶ feet, breadth 12 feet, depth in
hold 8¹⁰ feet. Her registered tonnage 30 tons.'
The *Royal Louise* was not only used by the
Royal Family for occasional sailing parties, but
also 'offered a virtually irreplaceable decorative
feature in the landscape', as had its predecessor,
a gift from the Prince Regent which had
arrived in Berlin in 1814 and survived until
1930. The *Royal Louise* was released by the
British naval authorities for scrap in 1945 as
unseaworthy, in ignorance of her origins.

The work on this vase, decided upon by the
Prussian king at a relatively late date, began in
the winter of 1835. On 3 February 1835 Georg
Frick, Director of the KPM, wrote to the
court gardener of the Pfaueninsel asking him
to allow the frigate to be drawn.

On 6 September 1836 the finished vase
reached London. On 8 October the King of
England expressed his gratitude from Windsor
Castle in the following lines: 'I need not assure
Your Majesty, that I shall always feel a pride in
preserving Your Majesty's splendid present in
my family, as a specimen of the perfection to
which this manufacture has been carried in
Your Majesty's Dominions, under Your
Majesty's fostering care, and as a memorial to
Your Majesty, and of the friendship by which
we have long been united.'

The view is taken from the ideal standpoint
for such a panorama, the tower of the
Kavalierhaus at the centre of the Pfaueninsel.
With its fantastic decoration derived from
antique motifs, but giving a general impression
of lithographs of orientalising textile designs,
the vase is an excellent example of this
ornamental period. Emblems which refer to
the Pfaueninsel or its situation – such as
mussels, tridents, dolphins, swans, pheasants,
monkeys, otters and other creatures – as well
as twelve different small views of buildings on
the Pfaueninsel in fan-shaped shields, round off
its rich appearance. The twelve allegorical
scenes painted under the lip, after designs by
August von Klöber, are assembled from two
different series. Their thematic significance is
not clear.

This form of vase was designed by Schinkel
in 1830 for the use of the KPM, where it was

known as the 'Schinkelsche Sorte' (Schinkel Type). Schinkel's drawing was lost from the Schinkel Museum in 1945; the designs for the ornament on this example are in the KPM-Archiv.

Lit.: Pachomova-Göres 1985, 701 (a); Berlin 1987 II, cat. P2.

W.B.

153.

DESIGN FOR A TABLE AND FLOWER-STAND: PLAN, PERSPECTIVE AND FULL-SIZE DETAILS.   *c.*1837

Pencil and watercolour, 556 × 625

Nationalgalerie, SMB (SM 43a.86)

The design shows a garden table doubling as a flower-stand, which Schinkel had drawn for the veranda of the summer villa owned by his friend Peter Christian Beuth in Schönhausen. It was presumably meant to be executed in Berlin cast iron, but the piece itself has not survived.

This design occupies a special place in the field of Schinkel's furniture. It is possible that ideas emerged from the personal and intellectual bond between client and artist. Like Schinkel's later architectural Utopias, it exemplifies the Romantic-Classical outlook of a cerebral, idealistic art. The table's supporting frame is made up of several individual elements derived from medieval architecture. The motif of twisted rope and the gargoyle-like animals tearing their quarry apart might be intended to symbolise the warding off of evil. They are matched by the sunflowers symbolising good fortune and the tree symbolism of the slender branch-like brackets supporting the table-top.

The symbol of the tree of life acts as an actual and metaphorical link between the natural order below and human artistic and creative order above. Two rows of flowerpots are arranged on the elongated oval top which is framed by a gallery. The pots surround the figure of a flower-girl holding a basket, which is taken from Johann Friedrich Drake's statuette of 'The Vintager,' as noted by Michael Snodin.

Drake had completed his first version in plaster in 1834, and a second one three years later in marble. The marble statuette (900 mm high) was shown in 1838 at the Exhibition of the Berlin Academy, where it was greatly admired. In 1840 the Verein der Kunstfreunde (Association of Art-lovers) in Berlin raffled the marble statuette of 'The Vintager' and a cast bronze copy. We do not know whether Beuth owned the statuette. A cast-iron copy of the table-top sculpture after Drake's original may also have been made as envisaged in the design. The plan of the table top shows the statuette in the top third, which suggests the possibility of a matching arrangement with another statuette at the other end.

Lit.: Berlin 1987 III, F 98.

C.M.

Utopian Visions

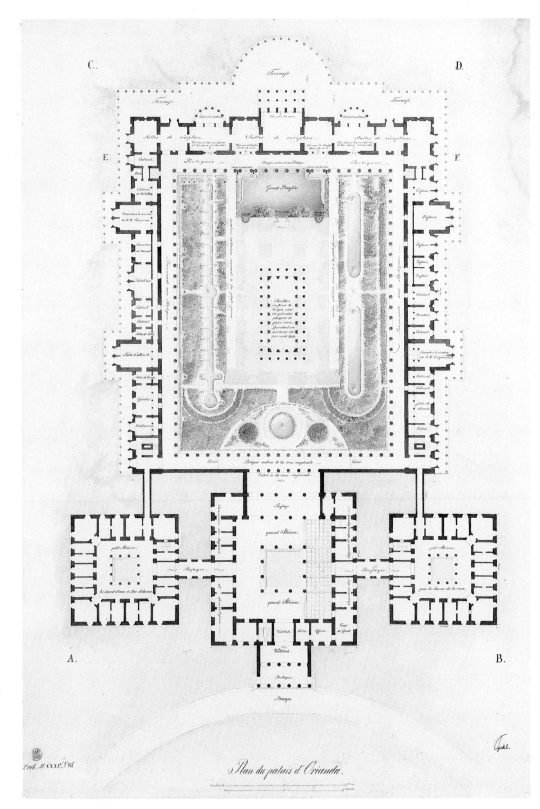

154.

PROJECT FOR A PALACE AT ORIANDA:
GROUND PLAN.   1838

Inscribed at the bottom: *plan du palais
d'Orianda* and with notes on structural
components. Signed bottom right: *Schinkel*

Pen and ink and watercolour, 886 × 610

Nationalgalerie, SMB (SM 35.45)

Elévation de la façade C.D. du plan.

Elévation de la façade A.B. du plan.

Coupe selon E.F. du plan.

155.

PROJECT FOR A PALACE AT ORIANDA: ELEVATIONS
OF THE SEA AND LAND FRONTS AND A SECTION
THROUGH THE IMPERIAL (GARDEN) COURT. 1838

Inscribed: *Elévation de la façade C.D. du plan*
(Elevation of the façade C.D. of the ground
plan); *Elévation de la façade A.B. du plan*
(Elevation of the façade A.B. of the ground
plan); *Coupe selon E.F. du plan* (Section
according to E.F. of the ground plan).
Signed bottom right: *Schinkel*

Pen and ink and watercolour, 473 × 604

Nationalgalerie, SMB (SM 35.47)

156.

PROJECT FOR A PALACE AT ORIANDA: PERSPECTIVE
VIEW OF THE GREAT ATRIUM.   1838

Pen and ink and watercolour, 372 × 665

Nationalgalerie, SMB (SM 35.49)

157.

PROJECT FOR A PALACE AT ORIANDA: PERSPECTIVE
VIEW OF THE IMPERIAL (GARDEN) COURT. 1838

Pen and ink and watercolour, 446 × 459

Nationalgalerie, SMB (SM 35.56)

158.

PROJECT FOR A PALACE AT ORIANDA: PERSPECTIVE
VIEW OF THE TERRACE BY THE SEA.   1838

Pen and ink and watercolour, 485 × 494
Nationalgalerie SMB (SM 35.57)

159.

PROJECT FOR A PALACE AT ORIANDA: PERSPECTIVE
VIEW OF THE MUSEUM OF THE CRIMEA AND
THE CAUCASIAN PROVINCES.   1838

Inscribed at the bottom: *Musée de la Crimée et des provinces Caucasiennes dans le soubassement du temple au milieu du château d'Orianda, residence d'été de Sa Majesté imperiale l'Imperatice de la Russie en Crimée.* Signed bottom right: *Schinkel*

Pen and ink and pencil and watercolour,
944 × 602

Nationalgalerie, SMB (SM 35.52)

In 1838 Crown Prince Friedrich Wilhelm's sister, who had become Tsarina in 1825, asked her brother to design with Schinkel a summer residence near Orianda on the Crimean coast. The Crown Prince and Schinkel, greatly inspired by the concept and potential of the project, and by its rocky site high above the sea, threw themselves into the task. They soon went beyond the Princess's desire for 'something like Siam' (i.e. Charlottenhof), produced a Gothic design and finally, in 1838, a stupendous dream palace intended to symbolise, in Schinkel's own words to the Princess, 'the greatest Imperial House on earth'. Like Schinkel's scheme for a palace for King Otto I on the Acropolis, the plan was rejected as too ambitious and a modest house was built.

The symmetrical plan (cat. 154) is aligned with the land side at the bottom. Entering through a portico flanked by service blocks, the visitor passes through the great formal atrium (cat. 156) to the vast enclosed Imperial (or garden) court, in the centre of which is a tall podium planted with trees and carrying a pavilion in the form of an Ionic temple. Incorporating plate glass panels which would make it almost transparent, it appears to float above the rest of the palace.

The garden court, filled with fountains and plants, is entirely surrounded by a shaded walk of octagonal columns decorated with startling geometric and plant patterns in mosaic (cat. 157). The podium itself, visible on the left of the drawing, also employs stones of different colours, but used structurally.

The state rooms on the sea side of the garden court lead out on to the dazzling terrace by the sea (cat. 158), with a central portico supported by caryatids modelled on those of the Erectheum on the Acropolis in Athens. Also taken from the Erectheum are the Ionic columns of the semicircular side bays which, like the temple pavilion, are filled with plate glass in bronze frames.

MUSÉE DE LA CRIMÉE   ET DES PROVINCES CAUCASIENNES
dans le soubassement du temple au milieu du château d'Orianda, résidence d'été de Sa Majesté impériale l'Impératrice de la Russie en Crimée

Inside the temple podium is a cool grotto-like walk intended to be a museum of classical antiquities (cat. 159). Its great piers and stepped vaults are consciously archaic and far larger than would be required to support the temple above. An important element of almost all sections of the project is the use of colour, much of which (for instance in the garden court) is anti-classical. Schinkel was, however, no doubt also influenced by the late classical studies such as Hittorf's *L'architecture polychrome chez les Grecs* (1830) and Gottfried Semper's *Vorläufige Bemerkungen über bemalte Architektur und Plastik bei den Alten* (Interim Observations upon Painted Architecture and Sculpture among the Ancients), (1834). Posthumous publication in the *Werke der höheren Baukunst* was the only lasting result of these designs by Schinkel in which he was totally committed to the idea of absolute architecture.

Lit.: Schinkel 1840–8; Berlin 1980, 645–51; Berlin 1981, 96; Kuhn 1989.

M.S. and G.R.

160.

BLICK IN GRIECHENLANDS BLÜTE.   1846

Wilhelm Witthöft (1816–74) after an oil painting (1825) by Schinkel

Engraving, 317 × 775

Kupferstichkabinett, SMB (KK 959–95)

The painting *Blick in Griechenlands Blüte* (A View of Greece in its Prime) was created by Schinkel in 1825 for the Magistrate of Berlin. The large picture (940 × 2350) was intended as a gift from the City of Berlin on the betrothal of Princess Luise of Prussia, the king's youngest daughter, to Prince Frederick of the Netherlands. In 1826 the Crown Prince ordered a copy, which was hung in the waterside pavilion of the Roman Baths at Charlottenhof in the same year, and in 1836 a further full-size copy was made. This last, by Wilhelm Ahlborn, is the only one to have survived the Second World War (Nationalgalerie, SMPK). With this reproduction, an engraving produced in 1846 for the Association of Friends of Art in the Prussian State, the work reached a wider public. The idealised but instructive panorama of a Greek city, a polis, is spread before the onlooker, with builders and artists in the foreground, constructing a harmonious temple. The picture was the culmination and peak of Schinkel's activity as an easel-painter. Bettina von Arnim described the composition in a letter to Goethe from Berlin in the summer of 1826:

'. . . a landscape by Schinkel, presented to the king's youngest daughter by the town on her marriage, is arousing general amazement and admiration . . . [The foreground] is taken up by the building of a temple, the viewer is on a level with the workmen on the first floor, who have finished a bas-relief. A second line of columns, is already partly erected on the right, between which is fixed a tent roof under which the sculptors have set up their workshop and are at that moment busy making the tympanon; the treetops at our feet and the row of capitals of the first floor, distinguishable behind the scaffolding and the machinery, make this clear. Up here a mountain range leads the eye from left to right into the distance, holding it with its graceful forms and lines, with which it flatters the horizon, almost preventing one from noticing the fine middle ground, occupied by a new Athens, devised with all the sense of place of one imbued with the customs and spirit of Greece. The Temple of Jupiter rises at the very centre between its forecourts on an eminence, surrounded by palm trees, which absorb into themselves the gift of the sun. Colossi, academies and a circus surround it, then come the markets, suburbs arising on all sides, cool rustling grottoes, and fountains, shooting their pearls into the air. And one confesses that the artist knows how to make common cause with the ceremonial and significance of Greek public life . . . . Mists steal out between mountain clefts along the sea that washes round them and, adorned by a few pennants, it is stirred to life, only to be flooded by the grace of the spirit of peace, and be once again extinguished. One could enlarge for ever on green-washed islands, settled on the heights above the sea – on pleasure grounds, on lonely fishermen's inlets in the distant rocky coves, on the most distant points, where one feels: there people must live, or there I would wish to live, and find that one being who unfolds such deep and powerful feeling for nature in the depiction of an imaginative creation.'

Lit.: Berlin 1980, 642; Berlin 1981, 204.

G.R.

Chronology

1781

Born 13 March in Neuruppin (Mark Brandenburg), son of Superintendent Johann Cuno Christian Schinkel and Dorothea, née Rose. The second of five children.
Publication of The Critique of Pure Reason, *Immanuel Kant's major work.*
Birth of Achim von Arnim and Peter Christian Beuth.

1782

The first steam-engine built by James Watt.

1786

Death of Friedrich II (Frederick the Great) King of Prussia. Succeeded by Friedrich Wilhelm II (1744–97).
Revival of the Kgl. Preussischen Akademie der Künste und Mechanischen Wissenschaften (Royal Prussian Academy of Arts and Mechanical Sciences).

1787

Death of his father on 25 October after rescue work during the great town fire of Neuruppin.
Johann Wolfgang von Goethe: Iphigenia on Tauris.

1788

David Gilly arrives in Berlin.

1789

Beginning of the French Revolution.

1791

First competition for a memorial to Frederick the Great.
Karl Gotthard Langhans: Brandenburger Tor (begun in 1788).
Wolfgang Amadeus Mozart: The Magic Flute, Requiem Mass.

1792

Attends Neuruppin Gymnasium (grammar school) (to 1794).

1793

Louis XVI and Marie Antoinette guillotined.

1794

His family moves to Berlin.
Attends the Graue Kloster Gymnasium there (to 1798).

1795

Earliest known drawing: *The ruins of a Greek temple.*

1796

Start of the Napoleonic Wars.

1797

Exhibition of Friedrich Gilly's design for the memorial to Frederick the Great in the Academy inspires Schinkel to become an architect (cat. 5).
Draws and paints landscapes.
Friedrich Wilhelm III (1770–1840) succeeds as King of Prussia.
Development of lithography by Alois Senefelder.
Friedrich Gilly: Design for a memorial to Frederick the Great.

1798

Leaves school 'to devote himself to architecture' and becomes a pupil of David Gilly with whom he lives.
Gilly's son Friedrich becomes his main teacher.
First design: *a three-storey residence (cat. 6).*
First landscape composition: *Landscape with lake.*
Designs for Eckardstein faience factory (also 1799).

1799

Attends the newly-founded Bauschule (School of Architecture) known as the Bauakademie: instructors David and Friedrich Gilly, Karl Gotthard Langhans, Heinrich Gentz, Friedrich Becherer, Johann Albert Eytelwein, Aloys Hirt.
Friedrich Gilly gives him his first designing jobs.
First design of a memorial: *To a sailor.*

1800

Death of Friedrich Gilly at Karlsbad.
Leaves the Bauakademie and completes Friedrich Gilly's projects:
Haus Steinmeyer Berlin (until 1802) (Dem.), industrial buildings in Haselberg, Quilitz, Bärwinkel (until 1801).
Design for the Pomona Temple on the Pfingstberg at Potsdam: first building executed according to his own design (completed 1801).
Designs for unexecuted projects: a museum, a veterinary college, a residential park by the pavilions in the Berlin Zoo.
First furniture and porcelain designs, made intermittently until 1803 (cat. 8).
Heinrich Gentz: New Mint building in Berlin.

1801

Travels to Köstritz and Karlsbad, meeting at the grave of Friedrich Gilly the philosopher Karl W.F. Solger, through whom he also encountered the philosophical work of Friedrich Wilhelm Schelling.
Designs for a country house by the water, a church and a mausoleum (none executed).

1802

Becomes acquainted with the philosophical teachings and writings of Johann Gottlieb Fichte.
Travels to Köstritz and Jena.
Design for the conversion of Schloss Buckow, including a summerhouse (completed by 1803) (Dest.).
Designs for Schloss Köstritz (designs completed 1803, not built) (cat. 9).
Designs for Schloss Elley in Courland (not built).

Design for scenery for *Iphigenia in Aulis*, shown at the Academy.
Karl Gotthard Langhans: Theatre on the Gendarmenmarkt.

1803

Leaves for Italy on 1 May (via Dresden, Prague and Vienna) with Gottfried Steinmeyer the Younger; visits Trieste, Istria, Venice, Padua, Bologna, Florence.
Arrives in Rome in October (staying until May 1804) (cat. 11).
Meets, among others, Wilhelm von Humboldt and Joseph Anton Koch.

1804

Travels to Naples and Sicily. Returns via Pisa, Livorno, Genoa, Milan. Arrives in Paris.
Plans for a work on architectural theory with medieval Italian examples, given up on the death of the Berlin publisher Johann Friedrich Gottlieb Unger.
Foundation of the Berlin Royal Iron Foundry, with the building of a cupola furnace on the English pattern (required for precision casting).
Ludwig van Beethoven: Eroica.

1805

Returns to Berlin in March via Strasbourg, Frankfurt, Weimar.
Journey to Neu-ruppin – and Kränzlin.
Designs (for Gilly) Tilebein Manor near Stettin (built 1805–6) and for Schloss Owinsk on the Warthe.
Design for a monument to Luther.
(*c.*) first painting, a gouache: *Antique town on a mountainside.*
Alliance of England, Russia and Austria against Napoleon I.
Napoleon's victory at Austerlitz.
Death of Schiller.

1806

Drawings for Ernst Friedrich Bussler's *Verzierungen aus dem Alterthum* (Ornaments from the Antique), publ. 1806–29
Napoleon's victories over Russia and Prussia at Jena and Auerstedt, 27 October. Napoleon's entry into Berlin (occupied until 1808). Continental blockade until 1813.
Philipp Otto Runge: Copperplate engravings, Times of day.

1807

Starts work on 'perspective optical' paintings for Wilhelm Gropius's Diorama, with geographical and historical themes, including Italy, the East, 'Wonders of the World' (over forty designs up to 1815).
Executes numerous drawings, paintings, lithographs.
Designs a candelabrum to be made by the sculptor Johann Gottfried Schadow; the first of a large number of such commissions for Schadow, especially for metalwork.

Prussia signs the peace conditions dictated by Napoleon.
Beginning of Prussian reforms under Freiherr von Stein.
Johann Gottlieb Fichte: Reden an die Deutsche Nation (Addresses to the German Nation), against Napoleon.

1808

Panorama: *View of Palermo.*
Joins the household of the Gropius family.
Continues to paint.
Designs for the Höhler and Feilner stove manufactory, Berlin (fig. 59).
Designs a silk screen for the Gabain textile manufactory, Berlin.
Design for the refurbishing and furnishing of the Chamois Room in the Königliches Palais, Berlin (cat. 33) (Dest.).
Reform of the army in Prussia.
Goethe: Faust, Part I.
Death of David Gilly.

1809

Marriage to Susanne Berger (1782–1861) in Stettin on 17 August. Their children are: Marie (b.1810), Susanne (b.1811), Karl Raphael (b.1813) Elisabeth (b.1822, marries Schinkel's commentator Alfred Freiherr von Wolzogen). Until 1814 they live on the Alexanderplatz, Berlin.
Joins the Berlin Romantic literary circle which includes Achim and Bettina von Arnim, Friedrich Karl von Savigny, Clemens von Brentano.
Meets and befriends Peter Christian Beuth.
Design for extension of the Prinzessinen Palais (with Heinrich Gentz).
Designs (and in 1810) beds for Potsdam and the bedroom and furnishings for Queen Luise at Schloss Charlottenburg (made 1810) (cat. 34–6).
Painting: *Landscape with motifs of the coast of Genoa.*
Painted scenes presented before the Royal Family, introduced to Queen Luise.
Mural for Zimmermeister Glatz: a Gothic church and groups of trees.
First Institute of Lithography in Berlin (G. Decker).
Royal family returns to Berlin.

1810

Appointment, through the mediation of Wilhelm von Humboldt, as Geheimer Oberbauassessor (Senior Assessor of Public Works) with the Technische Oberbaudeputation, responsible for supervising the design of public, royal and religious buildings in Prussia, and architectural preservation.
Design for conversion and apartments of the Königliches Palais (Kronprinzen Palais) (built 1810–11) (cat. 37).

Commission: 'Public Grand Buildings', Court Buildings.
Designs (with Heinrich Gentz) a Doric mausoleum for Queen Luise in Charlottenburg (cat. 15).
Ideal design for a Gothic mausoleum for Queen Luise in Charlottenburg, with a memorandum on Gothic architecture (cat. 16).
First design for the Petrikirche Berlin (domed building, not built).
Lithograph experiments: *Landscapes* (cat. 17).
Death of Queen Luise. Friedrich Wilhelm (now Humboldt) University, Berlin, opens under the direction of Wilhelm von Humboldt, with Johann Gottlob Fichte as first rector.
Caspar David Friedrich exhibits at the Academy.

1811

Becomes full member of the Prussian Royal Academy of Arts.
Meets the sculptor Christian Daniel Rauch.
Travels with his wife via Dresden, Murkau (with Count Pückler), Prague, Bukowan (with Clemens von Brentano) to the Salzkammergut.
Creates a series of landscape drawings there (cat. 18).
Further design for Berlin Petrikirche, published (not built).
Design for gothicising Schloss Ehrenburg, Coburg (until 1815, built 1812–40).
Designs for the cast-iron memorial to Queen Luise in Gransee and a Luise Gate in Paretz (latter not built).
Pair of drawings: *Morning* and *Evening* (dest.).
Stage design for *Vestalin* (unexecuted).

1812

Design for the Singakademie (Choral Academy) and for the conversion of the Academy building (neither carried out).
Designs for the reconstruction of Strasbourg Cathedral and Milan Cathedral.
Designs first scheme for remodelling the Prince Heinrich Palais for the University. Scheme of 1813 executed.
Optical perspective picture: *The Fire of Moscow* (cat. 27).
Designs decorative work and silver for Schadow.
Painting: *Landscape with Salzburg motifs.*
Napoleon invades and is defeated in Russia.

1813

Joins the Prussian *Landsturm* (conscript wartime militia).
Design for the rebuilding of the Nationaltheater (National Theatre) on the Gendarmenmarkt (not built).
Design for reconstruction of the Klosterkirche, Berlin.
(*c.*) Designs the Iron Cross (cat. 20).
Paintings: *Medieval town by the water, Morning and Evening* (as a pair), *Landscape with weeping*

willow, Landscape with pilgrims, cycle of Times of day.
Optical picture series: *The Seven Wonders of the World.*
Alliance with Russia.
Wars of Liberation. Napoleon decisively defeated in the Battle of the Nations at Leipzig.

1814

Moves to 99, Grosse Friedrichstrasse, there until 1822.
Designs for a cathedral as memorial to the Wars of Liberation (not built) (cat. 21).
Design for a memorial fountain for the Schlossplatz (not built).
Designs for festive decorations for the victory celebrations at the Brandenburger Tor and Unter den Linden.
Revised design in Gothic form for the Petrikirche, Berlin (not built).
Design for the furnishings of the Hardenberg Palace, Leipziger Strasse.
Design for Neuhardenberg village church (building continued until 1817).
Design for a monument to Hermann of the Cherusci (to 1815, not built) (cat. 24).
Painting: *Cathedral on a hill by the water, Sunset in a rich region of the Italian countryside.*
General conscription in Prussia. The Allies march into Paris.
Napoleon exiled to Elba.
Opening of Congress of Vienna.

1815

Promoted to Geheimer Oberbaurat (senior Councillor in charge of the Berlin office) and made a member of the Technische Oberbaudeputation.
Design for a 'Valhalla' in a competition, for King Louis I of Bavaria (not built).
First designs for the Neue Wache (New Guardhouse), Berlin. Final scheme of 1816 executed 1817–18 (cat. 42, 43).
(*c.*) Designs for a cast-iron candlestick (cat. 129).
Report on 'Principles for the maintenance of old monuments and antiquities in our country'.
Set designs for *The Magic Flute* (performed January 1816) (cat. 28, 29).
Starts working for the Nationaltheater, designs for over forty plays and operas up to 1830.
Paintings: *A medieval city on a river* (cat. 22), *Greek town* (as a pair).
Foundation of the German Federation.
Battle of Waterloo: final abdication of Napoleon.
Exhibition in Berlin of returned Prussian art treasures stolen by Napoleon; first demand for a public national museum of art.
Christian Daniel Rauch: Queen Luise's tomb.
Johann Gottfried Schadow made Director of the Academy of Arts.

1816

Travels via Weimar (visit to Goethe) and

Heidelberg (to try to obtain Boisserée collection for Prussia), to the Rhineland, Antwerp and Amsterdam.
Designs for the interiors and furniture of Prince August's Palace in Wilhelmstrasse (building continued to 1817) (cat. 38) (dest.).
First designs for the alteration and rebuilding of the interior of Berlin Cathedral (executed 1816–17, dest.).
Design for the Army Medical College ('Pépinière', not built).
Design for the 'Grosser Stern' (a traffic circle) in the Tiergarten (partially built after 1841).
Designs iron monuments, including war memorial in Spandau, Berlin.
Designs a sword (cat. 26).
Designs a medallion for Blücher (cat. 25).
First report 'On the condition of the Cathedral in Cologne'
Designs for sets for *Undine* (E.T.A. Hoffmann) and *Faust* (Goethe, private performance arranged by Prince Radziwill).
Plan for illustrations for Clemens von Brentano's fairy tales (not executed).
The Nazarenes (Wilhelm Schadow, Peter von Cornelius, Friedrich Overbeck) begin on the frescoes for the Casa Bartholdy in Rome.

1817

Journey to Pomerania.
Designs for alterations to the Berlin Town Hall (not built).
Design for the barracks of the training squadron in Lindenstrasse (built 1818, dest.).
First town plan for Berlin (not realised).
Designs remodelling of interior of Prince Friedrich's Palace, Berlin (dest.).
Designs parish churches for the Oberbaudeputation (and in following years).
Takes part in the rebuilding of the Marienburg and Cologne Cathedrals.
Designs for memorials for battlefields of the Wars of Liberation.
Paintings: *Triumphal Arch for the Great Elector and Frederick the Great, On the bank of the Spree at Stralau.*
Design for set for *Alceste.*
The first steamships in Germany on the Weser and between Berlin and Potsdam.
Nationaltheater on Gendarmenmarkt gutted by fire, destroying many of Schinkel's sets.

1818

Design for the theatre on Gendarmenmarkt, the Schauspielhaus (building completed 1821) (cat. 45–7).
Designs for residential buildings in Wilhelmstrasse and urban development plans for the surrounding area (partially built by 1822, dem.).
Design for the cast-iron memorial on the Kreuzberg (the Kreuzberg monument) (building dedicated 1821) (cat. 23).
Design for the Civilian Casino in Potsdam

(partially built by 1824, dest.).
Designs church for Gross-Beeren (built 1818–20).
Set designs: *Fernando Cortez* (cat. 31), *Maid of Orleans* (cat. 32).
Beginning of collaboration with Christian Daniel Rauch, after his return from Carrara.
Submits proposals for 'Reform of state architectural education' at the Bauakademie, Berlin.
G.W. Friedrich Hegel moves as Professor of Philosophy from Heidelberg to Berlin.

1819

Becomes a member of the Technische Deputation für Gewerbe (Trade and industry) in the Ministry of Trade, Industry and Construction (Director Beuth), responsible for its aesthetic aspects.
Journey to East Prussia, Danzig (Gdansk), Marienburg (Malbork): report for Hardenberg on their reconstruction.
Design for the Schlossbrücke (building completed 1824) (cat. 49).
Designs for the Gertraudenkirche on the Spittelmarkt (not built) (cat. 101–2).
Design for remodelling the façade of Berlin Cathedral (building completed 1822, dem.).
Issue of the first part of the *Sammlung architektonischer Entwürfe* (28 parts up to 1840).
Publication (by L.W. Wittich) of Schinkel's theatre designs (until 1824). (cat. 28).
Friedrich Tieck carves Schinkel's bust (cat. 1).

1820

Schinkel made member of the Senate of the Academy of Arts as 'Professor of Architecture'.
Journey with Tieck and Rauch to Weimar (visits Goethe) and Jena (equipment of library).
Design for conversion of Schloss Tegel for Wilhelm von Humboldt (building completed 1824).
Design for conversion of Schloss Neuhardenberg (formerly Quilitz) (building completed 1823).
Design for Gabain Manor in Charlottenburg (not built).
Design for the furnishing of Radziwill Palace by the Brandenburger Tor.
Designs for the observatory and anatomical institute in Bonn (building completed 1822).
Design for Scharnhorst's tomb at the Invaliden Friedhof, Berlin (building completed 1833).
Design of the setting for the 300th anniversary of Raphael's death, in the Academy of Arts.
Prepares the 'Lalla Rookh' festivities at Königliches Schloss (Jan. 1821) (see cat. 142).
Design for a standard silver cup (cat. 137).
Begins preparing drawings and text for the unpublished *Architektonisches Lehrbuch* (cat. 124–6 and pp. 47–55).

1821

Moves to 4a Unter den Linden (stays until 1836).

Visits Stettin, Pomerania and Rügen.
Design for the Singakademie (Choral Academy) (not built).
First designs for the Friedrich-Werder Kirche (in the classical style, not built) (cat. 103, 104).
Design for the Nikolaikirche in Magdeburg (building completed 1824).
Design for a theatre in Düsseldorf (not built).
Design for Prince Louis Ferdinand's tomb at Saalfeld.
Design for a Swiss cottage on the Pfaueninsel.
Second report on Cologne Cathedral.
Painting: *Stubbenkammer auf Rugen*.
Begins work with Beuth on *Vorbilder für Fabrikanten und Handwerker;* about forty plates by Schinkel by 1837, others in accordance with his instructions (cat. 133).
Opening of the Schauspielhaus, with prologue by Goethe, and his *Iphigenie auf Tauris*.
Foundation of the Association for the Encouragement of Industry in Prussia and foundation of the Gewerbe-Institut (Institute of Trade) by Peter Christian Beuth.
Foundation of Egell iron foundry in Berlin.
Carl Maria von Weber: Der Freischütz *(première in the Schauspielhaus, with Schinkel scenery.)*

1822
Design for the museum on the Lustgarten, now called the Altes Museum, Berlin (work starts, building opened 1830, frescoes, 1841–64).
Design for the School of Artillery and Engineering in Berlin (dem).
Designs for the interior installation of the Gewerbe-Institut in Klosterstrasse.
Designs for the theatre and Elise Fountain at Aachen (built 1824–6).
First design for a memorial to Frederick the Great (as a quadriga, not built).
Designs for the extension of the Schloss at Murkau (not built).
Design for the Hunting Lodge at Antonin near Posen (Poznan) (built by 1821) (fig. 10, 11).
Design for a Swiss house as a ducal country house in Alexisbad.
Report on the architectural training at the Düsseldorf Academy.
First Prussian Trade and Industry Exhibition in Berlin (176 exhibitors, 998 exhibits).

1823
Designs for the layout of Leipziger Platz and Potsdamer Tor, Berlin.
Design for Behrend Manor, Charlottenburg (dem.).
Designs for Schloss Belriguardo at Potsdam (not built).
First design for the extension of the fortress ruin of Stolzenfels (not executed).
First report on Cologne Cathedral (reconstruction begins 1826).
Designs for the castle (not built) and church (built by 1844) in Krzeszowice.

Designs for the Hardenberg tomb in Neuhardenberg (Marxwalde) (built in simplified form).
Design for Gothic version of the Friedrich-Werder Kirche, Berlin (built 1825–30, cat. 105).
Painting: *Arcadian landscape*.
Ludwig van Beethoven: Ninth symphony ('To Joy').

1824
Second Italian journey with Gustav Friedrich Waagen, Henri-François Brandt and August Kerll, via the Rhineland and Switzerland; main stopping places, Rome, Naples, Venice; duration June to December (cat. 2).
Member (Associé étranger) of the Institut de France.
Honorary Member of the Royal Academy of Fine Arts in Copenhagen.
Designs for the Crown Prince's and Princess's apartment (including Drawing Room, Star Room, Tea Salon, Library) in the Königliches Schloss (completed by 1827, cat. 64–8).
Design for partial remodelling (including chapel) of the Königliches Palais (executed 1825–6, dest.).
Designs for picture frames for the royal collection (to 1830) (cat. 149).
Design for the Neue Pavillon (New Pavilion) in the park at Schloss Charlottenburg for Friedrich Wilhelm III, now called the Schinkel Pavillon (completed by 1825) (cat. 61–2).
Design for a Schloss and Casino, Klein-Glienicke (completed by 1827) (cat. 57, 60).
Design for Scharnhorst memorial (completed by 1833).
Design for the Kavalier or Danziger Haus on the Pfaueninsel (Pheasant Island) incorporating an old Danzig façade (completed by 1826).
Foundation of the Berlinischer Gewerbeschule (Berlin College of Trade and Industry).
Foundation of the Society of Architects and Engineers in Berlin.
Robert Smirke: building of the British Museum in London (completed 1847).

1825
Honorary Member of the Accademia di San Luca in Rome.
First designs for the Packhof (Customs House) buildings on the Kupfergraben.
Design for guardhouse buildings at the Teltower Tor in Potsdam.
Design for Gesellschaftshaus (Company House) in Magdeburg (completed by 1829).
Design for Arkona lighthouse (completed by 1827) (fig. 3).
Design for the theatre in Hamburg (built 1825–7)
Painting: *Blick in Griechenlands Blüte* (cat. 160).

1826
Journey to Britain with Peter Christian Beuth, having spent some time in Paris: studies

building and industry in England, Wales and Scotland (cat. 109–12).
Design for the Neue Packhof (New Customs House) (completed by 1832) (cat. 117).
Designs for remodelling of Prince Karl's Palais, Berlin (executed 1827–8, dest.) (cat. 84–8).
Designs for five residential town buildings (not built).
Designs for Schloss Charlottenhof (completed by 1828) (cat. 69–74).
First designs for Nikolaikirche in Potsdam (cat. 107–8).
Design for Kolberg (Kołobrzeg) Town Hall (completed by 1832).

1827
Member of Berlin Architectural Association, founded in 1824.
Designs for the rebuilding of Berlin Cathedral (not built).
Designs for a memorial to Frederick the Great (up to 1830, not built).
Design for a bazaar on Unter den Linden (not built) (cat. 114).
Design for the Royal Stables on the Kupfergraben, Berlin (not built).
Design for the extension of the Gewerbe-Institut in Klosterstrasse (built in 1829, dest.).
Design for the Jägerhof (hunting lodge) in Glienicke Park (completed by 1828).
Design for a 'standard church' (as a pattern for small, rural churches).
Design for conversion of the Schloss in Friedersdorf (completed by 1828).
Designs for the Schloss in Putbus.
Design for the Schloss in Rossla/Unstrut (built in modified form).
Report on the reconstruction of the Marienkirche in Frankfurt on Oder.
Gas lighting installed in Berlin by an English company, at Schinkel's suggestion.
Second Prussian Trade Exhibition in Berlin (208 exhibitors, 1659 exhibits).
Death of Ludwig van Beethoven.

1828
Design for extension of Prince Wilhelm's Palais (Army corps headquarters), Unter den Linden (completed by 1829).
Design for conversion of the Palais Redern on Pariser Platz, Berlin (completed by 1830, dest.) (cat. 118).
Design for a town house for Tobias Feilner (completed by 1829, dest.) (cat. 115–16).
Designs for churches in the northern suburbs of Berlin (not built) (fig. 24, 25).
Designs for the layout of the Lustgarten (cat. 48).
Designs of settings for the Dürer Festival at Singakademie (Choral Academy) and the Naturforscherfest (Festival of Natural Scientists) at the Schauspielhaus.
Designs for frescoes for the vestibule of the Altes Museum (by 1831, painted 1841–64,

dest.) (fig. 16).
Customs Association of Central and South Germany and Prussia-Hesse founded.
Dresden Technical College founded.

1829
Designs for Prince Albrecht's Palais in Wilhelmstrasse (completed by 1833, dest.) (cat. 87–93).
Designs for Prince Wilhelm's Palais in Pariser Platz and Opernplatz (not built).
Fresh designs for a memorial to Frederick the Great (not built).
Second design for Nikolaikirche, Potsdam (cat. 107).
Design for the Swiss House and Palm House (interior) on Pfaueninsel (Pheasant Island) (completed by 1830).
Design for the Gärtnerhaus (Court Gardener's House) at Charlottenhof (completed by 1830) (cat. 76–77).
Design for the extension of the Moritzburg in Halle as a university (not built).
Design for a chapel in the Peterhof Alexander-Park (completed by 1833).
Design for a bronze fountain for the courtyard of the Gewerbe-Institut (made 1831, in Charlottenhof since 1843) (cat. 146).
Scenery and design for a commemorative cup for the 'Festival of the White Rose' in the Neues Palais, Potsdam (cat. 145).
Peter Christian Beuth made Director of the Bauakademie.

1830
Schinkel promoted to Geheimer Oberbaudirektor, taking over the direction of the Oberbaudeputation.
Travels via Rhineland and Switzerland to northern Italy.
Dedication of the Museum on the Lustgarten on 2 August, the King's 60th birthday.
Design for the observatory in Charlottenstrasse (built 1832–5, dest.).
Completion of the Friedrich-Werder Kirche.
Design for the Pavillon at the Gärtnerhaus, Charlottenhof (cat. 75).
Design for a vase for the Royal Porcelain Manufactory (cat. 153).
Design for Jenisch Manor in Othmarschen near Hamburg (modified design carried out by 1833).
July Revolution in Paris, unrest in Germany.
Liverpool–Manchester Railway (beginning of the modern railway system).
Leo von Klenze: completion of Glyptothek (Sculpture Gallery) in Munich (begun in 1816).

1831
50th birthday, honoured with a special festival.
Travels to Marienbad.
Design for the building to house the Allgemeine Bauschule (Bauakademie) and the Oberbaudeputation (completed by 1836, dest)

(cat. 119–23).
Design for conversion of the Royal Library (not built).
Design for Glienicke Bridge at Potsdam (completed by 1834, dest.).
Design for the Hauptwache (main guardhouse) in Dresden (completed by 1833).
Design for Leipzig University (built in modified form by 1836).
Cholera (deaths of Hegel, Gneisenau and Clausewitz).

1832
Honorary Member of the Royal Bavarian Academy of Fine Arts.
Official journey through Silesia, in Cracow and Krzeszowice.
Designs for four Berlin suburban churches: St Elisabeth (Rosenthal suburb), Nazareth (Wedding), St Paul (Gesundbrunnen), St John (Moabit) (completed by 1835).
Fresh design for Prince Wilhelm's Palace, Unter den Linden (not built).
Report on the extension of the Abbey Church in Cappenberg.
Death of Goethe, publication of Faust, *Part II.*

1833
Official visit to the provinces of Saxony, Westphalia and Rhineland.
Fresh town plan for Berlin.
Design for the Römische Bäder (Roman Baths) an extension to the Gärtnerhaus at Charlottenhof (completed by Persius by 1840) (cat. 77, 80, 81).
Design for Schloss Babelsberg (built 1834–49) (cat. 94–7).
Designs for a 'Villa of Pliny' at Charlottenhof (not built).
Design for the memorial to Frederick the Great in the form of a tower (not built).
Design for the Stock Exchange building in Stettin (built 1834).
Designs for a mausoleum for King Gustav Adolf in Lützen (completed by 1837).

1834
Honorary Member of the Academy of Fine Arts, Petersburg.
Official journey through Pomerania, East and West Prussia, the province of Posen.
Design for a residential palace on the Acropolis for King Otto I of Greece (von Wittelsbach) (not built).
Plan for complete reconstruction of Cologne Cathedral.
Design for the renovation of the Martinsstift in Erfurt.
Designs for the Niebuhr Mausoleum in Bonn (completed by 1841).
Design for a memorial to Field Marshal Schwerin in Prague.
Reconstruction of Burg Stolzenfels (completed 1847) (cat. 100).

German Customs Union under the leadership of Prussia.

1835
Honorary Member and correspondent of the Royal Institute of British Architects in London.
Official tour of the Altmark, Western Pomerania, Uckermark; stays in Hamburg, Kiel, Lübeck and Mecklenburg.
Plan for the reorganisation of the square at the Brandenburger Tor, and of the Tiergarten.
Designs for a library building for Berlin (not built) (cat. 127).
Designs for the Dichter Zimmer (Poets' Room) in Weimar Schloss (built in modified form by 1840).
Designs for the Fürstliche Residenz (Residence of a Prince) as the last stage of the uncompleted *Architektonisches Lehrbuch*.
Designs a Pavilion (Grosse Neugierde) at Schloss Glienicke (built to 1837).
Designs street signs for Berlin.
Designs reconstruction of Pliny's Villa Laurentina.
First part of Ludwig Lohde's *Schinkels Möbelentwürfe* (furniture designs) (until 1837).
First German railway line from Nuremberg to Fürth.
The books of Junges Deutschland (Young Germany) prohibited, together with all Heine's works.
Death of Wilhelm von Humboldt.

1836
Honorary Member of the Austrian Imperial Academy of Fine Arts in Vienna.
Moves into an apartment on the upper floor of the Bauakademie when it opens in that year.
Cure in Bad Gastein, travels to Silesia.

1837
Cure in Carlsbad and Teplitz, as well as in Silesia.
Design for the theatre in Gotha (built in modified form by 1840).
August Borsig sets up his iron foundry and machine factory in Berlin.

1838
Promoted to Oberlandesbaudirektor in recognition of his lifelong service to Prussia.
Travels via Silesia (Kamenz), Prague and Carlsbad to Bad Kissingen (for the cure) and the Rhineland.
Design for Schloss Kamenz (built in modified form by 1873).
Design for the observatory in Bonn (completed by 1845).
Assists in designs for university buildings for Christiania (Oslo) (built from 1839).
Designs for Schloss Orianda, Crimea (not built) (cat. 155–60).
Design for a memorial temple to Frederick the

Great on the Mühlenberg in Potsdam (not built).
First monograph by Franz Kugler, published as a book in 1842.
Opening of the first Prussian railway line between Berlin and Potsdam.

1839
Cure in Bad Kissingen, stays in Munich and Kamenz.
Report on the expansion of the library and on the Veterinary College.
Report on the reconstruction of the Klosterkirche in Berlin and the Nikolaikirche in Spandau.
Onset of symptoms of paralysis.

1840
Last journeys: Kamenz, Bad Kissingen, Munich, Bad Gastein.
Last design: conversion of a residence for the sculptor Kirchmayer in Munich (not built).
Start of publication of *Werke der höheren Baukunst* (Works of higher architecture) with plates after designs for Orianda and the Acropolis (until 1848).
9 September: stroke and beginning of coma.
Accession of Frederick William IV (1795–1861) as King of Prussia.
Deaths of Caspar David Friedrich, Karl Blechen and Niccolo Paganini.

1841
Death, on 9 October, in his residence in the Bauakademie.
Burial at the Dorotheenstadt Cemetery in Berlin on 12 October.

1842
Friedrich Wilhem IV orders that Schinkel's artistic legacy be purchased by Prussia. Annual Berlin *Schinkelfest* instigated (continues).

Select Bibliography

This bibliography has been selected from the vast body of literature on Schinkel, chiefly written in German. A great expansion was prompted by the bicentenary of 1981 producing, most notably, the great Berlin catalogues of 1980 (east) and 1981 (west). These have joined the *Lebenswerk* series, Wolzogen's *Nachlass* publications, and the *Sammlung* as the key works of reference. Good short treatments in English are in Hitchcock 1971 and Watkin and Mellinghof 1987. Berlin 1980 contains the most thorough bibliography so far, based on others of 1935, 1962 and 1965. Shorter bibliographies are in Pundt 1972, Zadow 1980, Berlin 1981, Hamburg 1982, Watkin and Mellinghof 1987 and Szambien 1989. The short references here are to the *Bibliography of works cited* (pp. 216–18).

PUBLICATIONS OF SCHINKEL'S WORKS IN HIS OWN LIFETIME

Dekorationen auf der Königlichen Hoftheatern zu Berlin, 1819–24 (Schinkel 1819–24). Aquatint plates after designs for theatre sets.

Sammlung architektonischer Entwürfe, 1819–40 (*Sammlung*). This collection of plates illustrating 50 executed and projected buildings, accompanied by descriptions, is the chief contemporary source of Schinkel's buildings.

Vorbilder für Fabrikanten und Handwerker, 1821–37 (*Vorbilder*). See cat. 133.

Schinkels Möbel-Entwürfe, 1835–7 (Lohde 1835–7). Coloured plates after the furniture designs.

Werke der höheren Baukunst, 1840–8 (Schinkel 1840–8). Coloured plates after the designs for the palaces on the Acropolis and at Orianda.

In Schinkel's lifetime his drawings were also published as book decorations and in Büssler 1806–29 and Berlin 1835–6. Prints after his designs were published after his death in Gropius 1869–72; Geiss 1849 shows objects made to his designs.

LETTERS, DIARIES AND MANUSCRIPTS

Autograph sources are particularly valuable in the study of Schinkel, partly because so much of his theoretical material, such as that leading to an *Architektonisches Lehrbuch* (cat. 124 and pp. 47–55), was unpublished in his lifetime, and also because a major biography remains to be written. The travel diaries (with sketches) are also important. The most useful publications include Wolzogen 1862–3, Wolzogen 1864 I, Mackowsky 1922, Meier 1967, Riemann 1979, Riemann 1986 and Wegner 1990.

MONOGRAPHS AND BIOGRAPHICAL AND CRITICAL ACCOUNTS

Of particular importance are the early works by Kugler (1842), Waagen (1844 and 1847), and Wolzogen (1864 II). Szambien 1989 (in French)

is one of the best modern monographs; other works include Gruppe 1842, Hittorf 1858, Eggers 1867, Ziller 1897, Grisebach 1981 (reprint of 1924), Lorck 1937, Rave 1953, Hitchcock 1971 (in English), Zadow 1980, Ohff 1981, Forssman 1981, Volk 1982, Betthausen 1983, Watkin and Mellinghof 1987 (in English) and Haus 1987.

KARL FRIEDRICH SCHINKEL: LEBENSWERK

This great series was begun under the editorship of P.O. Rave and was published in Berlin. Since 1968 it has been edited by Margarete Kühn and published in Berlin and Munich by Deutscher Kunstverlag.

Hans Kania, *Potsdam, Staats- und Bürgerbauten*, 1939.

Günther Grundmann, *Schlesien*, 1941.

Paul Ortwin Rave, *Berlin: Bauten für die Kunst, Kirchen, Denkmalpflege*, 1941 (reprinted 1981).

Johannes Sievers, *Bauten für den Prinzen Karl von Preussen*, 1942.

Paul Ortwin Rave, *Berlin: Stadtbaupläne, Strassen, Brücken, Tore, Plätze*, 1948 (reprinted 1981).

Johannes Sievers, *Die Möbel*, 1950.

Hans Vogel, *Pommern*, 1952.

Johannes Sievers, *Bauten für die Prinzen August, Friedrich und Albrecht von Preussen*, 1954.

Johannes Sievers, *Bauten für den Prinzen von Preussen*, [*i.e.* for Prince Wilhelm, later King and Kaiser], 1955.

Hans Kania and Hans-Herbert Möller, *Mark Brandenburg*, 1960.

Paul Ortwin Rave, *Berlin: Bauten für Wissenschaft, Verwaltung, Heer, Wohnbau und Denkmäler*, 1962 (reprinted 1981).

Eva Brües, *Die Rheinlande*, 1968.

Ludwig Schreiner, *Westfalen*, 1968.

Goerd Peschken, *Das architektonische Lehrbuch*, 1979.

Margarete Kühn (ed.), *Ausland, Bauten und Entwürfe*, 1989.

Reinhard Wegner, *Die Reise nach Frankreich und England im Jahre 1826*, 1990.

While much of the other literature on particular buildings or areas of Schinkel's work is contained in periodicals, the following recent works should be mentioned: Pundt 1972 (Berlin), Wiederanders 1981 (churches), Schmidt 1981 (cast iron), Springer 1981 (the Schlossbrücke), Vogt 1985 (*Blick in Griechenlands Blüte*), Günther 1985 (on Lenné), Kunst 1987 (the Neue Wache), Berlin 1987 I (Schloss Glienicke), Hempel 1989 (furniture) and Börsch-Supan 1990 (stage designs).

MONOGRAPHIC EXHIBITION CATALOGUES

Berlin 1980, Berlin 1981, Berlin 1981 I, Berlin

1981 II, Potsdam 1981, Hamburg 1982, Venice and Rome 1982 (in Italian). Berlin 1979 and 1987 I–III are also important.

NON–GERMAN LITERATURE

Listed here is some of the literature on Schinkel in languages other than German. Unless otherwise mentioned it is in English.

Allies 1979, Binney 1979 & 1981, Börsch-Supan 1977, Börsch-Supan 1979 (French), Börsch-Supan 1990, Carter 1979, Clelland 1980 & 1983, Crimp 1987, Edwards 1914, Ettlinger 1945, Filler 1984, Forster 1983, Himmelheber 1979, Hitchcock 1971, Huth 1977, Jullian 1979 (French), Lebherz 1988, Lipstadt & Bergdoll 1981, Pevsner 1952, Pevsner 1972, Posener 1972, Posener 1983, Pundt 1972, Pundt 1983, Richardson 1912, Stirling 1980, Szambien 1989 (French), Ungers 1981, Vann 1977, Watkin 1979, Watkin & Mellinghof 1987.

(Allies 1979) Bob Allies, 'Schinkel's poetry', *Building Design*, 15 June 1979, pp. 18–19.

(Behr 1984) Adalbert Behr, 'Griechenlands Blüte und die "Fortsetzung der Geschichte". Zur Kunsttheorie Karl Friedrich Schinkels', in H. Gärtner (ed.), *Schinkel-Studien*, Leipzig, 1984, p. 16ff.

(Berlin 1835–6) *Grundlage der praktischen Baukunst*, published by Kgl. Technischen Deputation für Gewerbe, Berlin. Vol. I *Vorlageblätter für Maurer* (1835), vol. II *Vorlageblätter für Zimmerleute* (1835), vol. III *Vorlageblätter für Maurer und Zimmerleute* (1836).

(Berlin 1846) *Amtliche Bericht über die allgemeine Deutsche Gewerbe-Ausstellung zu Berlin im Jahre 1844*, Berlin, 1846.

(Berlin 1856) *Amtlicher Bericht über die allg. Pariser Ausstellung von Erzeugnissen der Landwirtschaft, des Gewerbefleisses und der schönen Kunst im Jahre 1855*, Berlin, 1856.

(Berlin 1881) *Das Kunstgewerbe-Museum zu Berlin: Festschrift zur Eröffnung des Museumsgebäudes*, Berlin, 1881.

(Berlin 1979) *Berlin und die Antike*, exhibition catalogue, Deutsches Archäologisches Institut and SMPK, Berlin, 1979.

(Berlin 1980) *Karl Friedrich Schinkel, 1781–1841*, exhibition catalogue, Staatliche Museen zu Berlin (Altes Museum), Berlin, 1980–1.

(Berlin 1981) *Karl Friedrich Schinkel; Architektur, Malerei, Kunstgewerbe*, exhibition catalogue, Staatliche Schlösser und Gärten and Nationalgalerie (Schloss Charlottenburg), Berlin, 1981.

(Berlin 1981 I) *Karl Friedrich Schinkel. Werke und Wirkungen*, exhibition catalogue, Senat von Berlin (Martin Gropius Bau), Berlin, 1981.

(Berlin 1981 II) *Karl Friedrich Schinkel. Werke und Wirkungen in Polen*, exhibition catalogue. Senat von Berlin (Martin Groupius Bau), Berlin, 1981.

(Berlin 1986) *Galerie der Romantik*, Nationalgalerie, SMPK, Berlin, 1986.

(Berlin 1987 I) *Schloss Glienicke, Bewohnur-Künstler-Parklandschaft*, exhibition catalogue, Staatliche Schlösser und Gärten (Schloss Charlottenburg), Berlin, 1987.

(Berlin 1987 II) *Carl Daniel Freydanck*, exhibition catalogue, Verwaltung der Staatliche Schlösser und Gärten (Schloss Charlottenburg) and KPM, Berlin, 1987.

(Berlin 1987 III) *Kunst in Berlin*, exhibition catalogue, Staatliche Museen zu Berlin (Altes Museum), Berlin, 1987.

(Berlin 1987 IV) *Das Denkmal auf dem Kreuzberg von Karl Friedrich Schinkel*, exhibition catalogue, DEU Kunstamt Kreuzberg, Berlin, 1987.

(Betthausen 1983) Peter Betthausen, *Karl Friedrich Schinkel*, Berlin, 1983.

(Binney 1979) Marcus Binney, 'The Peacock Island, Berlin', *Country Life*, vol. CLXVI/4295 & 6 (1 & 8 Nov. 1979), pp. 1506–9, 1622–6.

(Binney 1981) Marcus Binney, 'Schloss Stolzenfels, near Koblenz', *Country Life*, vol. CLXIX/4352 & 3 (15 & 22 Jan. 1981), pp. 118–21, 190–4.

(Börsch-Supan 1977) Eva Börsch-Supan, 'Schinkel as a universal man', *Apollo*, vol. CVI/186 (Aug. 1977), pp. 134–41.

(Börsch-Supan 1979) Helmut Börsch-Supan, 'Caspar David Friedrich et Carl Friedrich Schinkel', *Revue de l'Art*, 1979, pp. 9–20.

(Börsch-Supan 1990) Helmut Börsch-Supan, *Karl Friedrich Schinkel: Bühnenentwürfe, Stage Designs*, 2 vols, Berlin, 1990 (text in English and German).

(Brües 1968) Eva Brües, *Die Rheinlande*, Berlin and Munich, 1968 (in the Schinkel Lebenswerk series).

(Büssler 1806–29) Ernst Friedrich Büssler, *Verzierungen aus dem Altertume*, (21 parts), Potsdam and Berlin, 1806–29.

(Carter 1979) Rand Carter, 'Karl Friedrich Schinkel's project for a royal palace on the Acropolis', *Journal of the Society of Architectural Historians*, vol. XXXVIII/1 (Mar. 1979), pp. 34–46.

(Clelland 1980) Doug Clelland, 'From Calm Poetry to Failed Epic—Some Notes on Karl Friedrich Schinkel 1781–1841', *Architectural Design*, 7/8 (1980) pp. 106–13.

(Clelland 1983) Doug Clelland and others, 'Berlin: an architectural history', *Architectural Design*, vol. 11/12 (1983), pp. 1–88, 144ff.

(Clochar 1809) P. Clochar, *Palais, Maisons et vues d'Italie*, Paris, 1809.

(Crimp 1987) Douglas Crimp, 'The end of art and the origin of the museum', *Art Journal*, XLVI/4 (winter 1987), pp. 261–6.

(Dinsmoor 1950) W.B. Dinsmoor, *The Architecture of Ancient Greece*, (3rd ed.), London, 1950.

(Durand 1799–1801) Jean-Nicholas-Louis Durand, *Recueil et Parallèle des édifices de tout genre. . .dessinés sur une même échelle*, Paris, 1799–1801.

(Durand 1817–19) Jean-Nicholas-Louis Durand, *Précis des Leçons d'Architecture données a l'École polytechnique*, 2 vols, Paris, 1817 (vol. II) & 1819 (vol. I); (1st ed. 1802–5); reprinted Uhl, 1975.

(Durand 1821) Jean-Nicholas-Louis Durand, *Partie graphique des cours d'Architecture*, Paris, 1821; reprinted Uhl, 1975.

(Durm 1910) J. Durm, *Die Baukunst der Griechen*, 3rd ed., Leipzig, 1910.

(Eagleton 1990) Terry Eagleton, *The Ideology of the Aesthetics*, Oxford, 1990.

(Edwards 1914) A.T. Edwards, 'Karl Friedrich Schinkel', *Architects and Builders Journal*, 40 (1914), pp. 45–7, 80–2, 96–9.

(Eggers 1856) Friedrich Eggers, 'Die Zinkgiesserei von Moritz Geiss in Berlin', *Deutsches Kunstblatt*, 7 (1856).

(Eggers 1867) Friedrich Eggers, 'Erinnerung an Schinkel', *Vier Vorträge aus der Neueren Kunstgeschichte*, Berlin, 1867, pp. 57–82.

(Ettlinger 1945) Leopold Ettlinger, 'A German Architect's Visit to England in 1826', *Architectural Review*, 97 (1945), pp. 131–4.

(Filler 1984) Martin Filler, 'Schinkel: the restless Romantic', *House and Garden*, vol. 156/2 (Feb 1984), pp. 156–72, 174.

(Forssman 1981) Erik Forssman, *Karl Friedrich Schinkel. Bauwerke und Baugedanken*, Munich and Zurich, 1981.

(Forster 1983) Kurt W. Forster, 'Schinkel's panoramic planning of central Berlin', *Modulus: the University of Virginia School of Architecture Review*, vol. 16 (1983), pp. 62–77.

(Geiss 1849) Moritz Geiss, *Zinkguss-Ornamente nach*

Zeichnungen von Schinkel, Stüler, Persius. . .Ausgeführt Berlin, Berlin, 1849.

(Gentz 1803–6) Heinrich Gentz, *Elementar-Zeichenwerk: Lehrbuch für die Kunst- und Gewerbe-Schulen in Preussen*, 1803–6.

(Giedion 1922) Sigfried Giedion, *Spätbarocker und romantischer Klassizismus*, Munich, 1922.

(Greifenhagen 1963) Adolf Greifenhagen, 'Nachklänge griechische Vasenfünde im Klassizismus', *Jahrbuch der Berliner Museen*, 5 (1963), pp. 84–105.

(Grisebach 1981) August Grisebach, *Karl Friedrich Schinkel (Architekt, Städtebauer, Maler)*, Munich, 1981 (first published Leipzig, 1924).

(Gropius 1869–72) Martin Gropius, *Karl Friedrich Schinkel. Dekorationen innerer Räume*, 1869 and 1872.

(Grundmann 1941) Günther Grundmann, *Schlesien*, Berlin, 1941 (in the Schinkel Lebenswerk series).

(Grunow 1871) Carl Grunow, 'Schinkels Bedeutung für das Kunstgewerbe. Festrede gehalten bei der Schinkel-Feier am 13 März 1871', *Zeitschrift für Bauwesen*, 21 (1871), p. 403.

(Gruppe 1842) Otto Friedrich Gruppe, 'Karl Friedrich Schinkel', *Allgemeine Bauzeitung*, 7 (1842), pp. 147–70, 275–86.

(Guadet 1901–4) J. Guadet, *Éléments et Théorie de l'Architecture*, 4 vols, Paris, 1901–4.

(Günther 1985) Harri Günther, *Joseph Peter Lenné, Gärten, Parke, Landschaften*, Stüttgart, 1985.

(Hamburg 1977) *Hohe Kunst zwischen Biedermeier und Jugendstil-Historismus in Hamburg und Norddeutschland*, exhibition catalogue, Museum für Kunst und Gewerbe, Hamburg, 1977.

(Hamburg 1982) *Karl Friedrich Schinkel, Eine Ausstellung aus der Deutschen Demokratischen Republik*, exhibition catalogue, Hamburg Architektenkammer und Kunsthalle, Berlin, 1982.

(Hampel 1989) Frithof Detlev Paul Hampel, *Schinkels Möbelwerk und sein Voraussetzungen*, Bonn, 1989.

(Haus 1987) Andreas Haus, *Karl Friedrich Schinkel. Bauten, Gemälde, Industriedesign, Buhnenbilder*, Munich, 1987.

(Himmelheber 1979) Georg Himmelheber, 'Biedermeier', *Connoisseur*, vol. CCI/807 (May 1979), pp. 2–11.

(Hirt 1809) Aloys Hirt, *Die Baukunst nach den Grundsätzen der Alten*, Berlin, 1809.

(Hitchcock 1971) Henry-Russell Hitchcock, *Architecture: Nineteenth and Twentieth Centuries*, Harmondsworth, 1971.

(Hittorf 1858) Jacob-Ignaz Hittorf, 'Geschichtliche Bemerkungen über C.F. Schinkel', *Zeitschrift für Bauwesen*, 8 (1858), pp. 98–106.

(Huth 1977) Hans Huth, 'Palaces in Potsdam and Berlin', *Apollo*, vol. CVI/186 (Aug. 1977), pp. 98–111.

(Johnson 1962) Philip Johnson, 'Schinkel and Mies', *Program* (Columbia University, School of Architecture), Spring 1962, pp. 14–34.

(Jullian 1979) Philippe Jullian, 'Schinkel', *Connaissance des Arts*, March 1979, pp. 78–85.

(Kania 1939) Hans Kania, *Potsdam, Staats- und Bürgerbauten*, Berlin, 1939 (in the Schinkel Lebenswerk series).

(Kania & Möller 1960) Hans Kania and Hans-

Herbert Möller, *Mark Brandenburg*, Berlin, 1960 (in the Schinkel Lebenswerk series).

(Korth 1978) Thomas Korth, *Stift St. Florian: die Entstehungsgeschichte der barocken Klosteranlage*, Nürnberg, 1978.

(Kugler 1842) Franz Kugler, *Karl Friedrich Schinkel. Eine Charakteristik seiner künstlerischen Wirksamkeit*, Berlin, 1842. (first published in the *Hallesche Jahrbücher*, 1838, also in *Kleiner Schriften und Studien*, vol. 3, Stuttgart, 1854, pp. 306–61). (Reprint in *Architektur der D.D.R.*, 10 (1982), pp. 41–57).

(Kühn 1989) Margarete Kühn, *Ausland, Bauten und Entwürfe*, Berlin and Munich, 1989 (in the Schinkel Lebenswerk series).

(Kunst 1987) Hans-Joachim Kunst, *Schinkels Neue Wache*, Worms, 1987.

(Lebherz 1988) Hermann Lebherz, 'Schinkel and industrial architecture', *Architectural Review*, vol. 184/1098 (Aug. 1988), pp. 41–6.

(Lipstadt & Bergdoll 1981) Helene Lipstadt and Barry Bergdoll, 'Architecture as alchemy: Karl Friedrich Schinkel', *Progressive Architecture*, vol. 62/10 (Oct. 1981), pp. 72–7.

(Lohde 1835–7 Ludwig Lohde, *Schinkels Möbel-Entwürfe, welche bei Einrichtungen prinzlicher Wohnungen in den letzten zehn Jahren augeführt wurden*, 5 parts, Berlin, 1835–7 (2nd ed. 1852, 3rd ed. 1861).

(Lorck 1937) Carl von Lorck (ed.), *Deutschland in Schinkels Briefen und Zeichnungen*, Dresden, 1937 (2nd ed. as *Reisen in Deutschland*, Essen, 1956).

(Lübke 1851) Wilhelm Lübke, 'Berliner Beiträge zur Londoner Industrie-Ausstellung', *Deutsches Kunstblatt*, 2, 1851.

(Mackowsky 1922) Hans Mackowsky (ed), *Karl Friedrich Schinkel, Briefe, Tagebücher, Gedanken*, Berlin, 1922 (reprinted Frankfurt am Main, 1981).

(Mah 1990) Harold Mah, 'The French Revolution and the Problem of German Modernity', *New German Critique*, 50 (Spring/Summer 1990) p. 3ff.

(Meier 1967) Hans Meier (ed.), *Karl Friedrich Schinkel, aus Tagebüchern und Briefen*, Berlin, 1967 (2nd ed. 1969).

(Middleton 1982) Robin Middleton (ed.), *The Beaux Arts and Nineteenth Century French Architecture*, London, 1982.

(Mieck 1965) Ilja Mieck, *Preussische Gewerbepolitik in Berlin 1806–1844*, Berlin, 1965.

(Montclos 1976) J.M. Pérouse de Montclos, 'De la villa rustique d'Italie au pavillon de banlieue', *Revue de l'Art*, 32 (1976).

(Ohff 1981) Heinz Ohff, *Karl Friedrich Schinkel*, 1981.

(Pachomova-Göres 1985) Vasilissa Pachomova-Göres, 'Schinkels Wirken für die Königliche Porzellanmanufaktur Berlin', *Staatliche Museen zu Berlin: Forschungen und Berichte*, 25 (1985), pp. 154–67.

(Pérez-Gómez 1983) Alberto Pérez-Gómez, *Architecture and the Crisis of Modern Science*, Cambridge, Mass, 1983.

(Peschken 1979) Goerd Peschken, *Das architektonische Lehrbuch*, Berlin and Munich, 1979 (in the Schinkel Lebenswerk series).

(Pevsner 1952) Nikolaus Pevsner, 'Schinkel', *Journal of the Royal Institute of British Architects*, 59 (Jan 1952), pp. 89–96 (reprinted in *Studies in Art,*

Architecture and Design, London, 1968).

(Pevsner 1972) Nikolaus Pevsner, *Some Architectural Writers of the Nineteenth Century*, Oxford, 1972.

(Pevsner 1976) Nikolaus Pevsner, *A History of Building Types*, Princeton & London, 1976.

(Podro 1982) Michael Podro, *The Critical Historians of Art*, New Haven and London, 1982.

(Posener 1972) Julius Posener, 'Schinkel's English Diary', *From Schinkel to the Bauhaus, five lectures on the growth of Modern architecture*, New York, 1972.

(Posener 1983) Julius Posener, 'Schinkel's eclecticism and "the architectural"', *Architectural Design*, 11–12 (1983), pp. 32–9. (Also published in Doug Clelland (ed.), *Berlin: an architectural history*, New York, 1983).

(Potsdam 1981) *Schinkel in Potsdam: Ausstellung zum 200. Geburtstag, 1781–1841*, exhibition catalogue, SSG Potsdam-Sanssouci, Potsdam, 1981.

(Pundt 1972) Hermann G. Pundt, *Schinkel's Berlin: A Study in Environmental Planning*, Cambridge, Mass., 1972 (German ed. Berlin and Vienna, 1981).

(Pundt 1983) Hermann G. Pundt, 'Karl Friedrich Schinkel: a living legacy of excellence in architecture', *Space Design*, July 1983, pp. 3–22.

(Raczynski 1841) Athanasius Graf Raczynski, *Geschichte der neueren deutschen Kunst*, Berlin, 1841.

(Rave 1941) Paul Ortwin Rave, *Berlin: Bauten für die Kunst, Kirchen, Denkmalpflege*, Berlin, 1941 (in the Schinkel Lebenswerk series; reprinted 1981).

(Rave 1948) Paul Ortwin Rave, *Berlin: Stadtbaupläne, Strassen, Brücken, Tore, Plätze*, Berlin, 1948 (in the Schinkel Lebenswerk series; reprinted 1981).

(Rave 1953) Paul Ortwin Rave, *Karl Friedrich Schinkel*, Munich and Berlin, 1953 (2nd ed., Eva Börsch-Supan (ed.), Munich, 1981).

(Rave 1962) Paul Ortwin Rave, *Berlin: Bauten für Wissenschaft, Verwaltung, Heer, Wohnbau und Denkmäler*. Berlin, 1962 (in the Schinkel Lebenswerk series).

(Richardson 1912) A.E. Richardson, 'Karl Friedrich Schinkel', *Architectural Review*, 31 (Feb. 1912), pp. 60–79.

(Riemann 1979) Gottfried Riemann (ed.), *Reisen nach Italien. Tagebücher, Briefe, Zeichnungen, Aquarelle*, Berlin, 1979 (2nd ed. 1982, 3rd ed. 1988).

(Riemann 1986) Gottfried Riemann (ed.), *Reisen nach England, Schottland und Paris im Jahre 1826*, with an introduction by David Bindman, Berlin and Munich, 1986.

(Robertson 1969) D.S. Robertson, *Greek and Roman Architecture*, Cambridge, 1969 (2nd ed.).

(Sammlung) Karl Friedrich Schinkel, *Sammlung architectonischer Entwürfe*, 174 plates with accompanying commentary, first published in 28 parts in Berlin 1819–40. Later editions were 1843–7, 1852 (collected), 1857–8, 1866, 1872 (collected). Facsimiles have been published in 1980 (Leipzig), 1981 (Chicago), 1982 (London), 1984 (Chicago), 1989 (Guildford and Princeton).

(Schadow 1849) Johann Gottfried Schadow, *Kunstwerke und Kunstansichten*, Berlin, 1849 (reprint Berlin 1980).

(Schinkel 1819–24) Karl Friedrich Schinkel, *Dekorationen auf den königlichen Hoftheatern zu Berlin*, 5 parts, 32 plates, Ludwig Wilhelm Wittich, Berlin, 1819–24, vols 1–3 coloured, (later eds.

1847–9, 1861, 1874).

(Schinkel 1840–8) Karl Friedrich Schinkel, *Werke der höheren Baukunst, für der Ausführung erfunden*; part 1 (Akropolis), 10 plates, Berlin 1840–2, part 2 (Orianda), 8 plates, Berlin 1845–8. (later eds. 1850, 1861–2, 1878, 1986 (part)).

(Schmidt 1981) Eva Schmidt, *Der preussische Eisenkunstguss; Technik-Geschichte-Werke-Kunstler*, Berlin, 1981.

(Schreiner 1968) Ludwig Schreiner, *Westfalen*, Berlin and Munich, 1968 (in the Schinkel Lebenswerk series).

(Scully 1969) Vincent Scully, *The Earth, the Temple and the Gods*, New York, 1969 (2nd ed.).

(Seheult 1821) F.-L. Seheult, *Recueil d'architecture dessiné et mesuré en Italie dans les années 1791, 1792 et 1793. . . .*, Paris, 1821.

(Semper 1834) Gottfried Semper, *Vorläufige Bemerkungen über bemalte Architektur und Plastik bei den Altën*, Altona, 1834.

(Semper 1989) Gottfried Semper (trans. H.F. Mallgrave and W. Hermann), *Gottfried Semper: The Four Elements of Architecture and Other Writings*, Cambridge, 1989.

(Sievers 1942) Johannes Sievers, *Bauten für den Prinzen Karl von Preussen*, Berlin, 1942 (in the Schinkel Lebenswerk series).

(Sievers 1950) Johannes Sievers. *Die Möbel*, Berlin, 1950 (in the Schinkel Lebenswerk series).

(Sievers 1954) Johannes Sievers. *Bauten für die Prinzen August, Friedrich und Albrecht von Preussen*, Berlin, 1954 (in the Schinkel Lebenswerk series).

(Sievers 1955) Johannes Sievers, *Bauten für den Prinzen von Preussen*, Berlin, 1955 (in the Schinkel Lebenswerk series).

(Springer 1981) Peter Springer, *Schinkels Schlossbrücke. Berlin Zweckbau und Monument*, Berlin and Vienna, 1981.

(Stirling 1980) James Stirling, 'Winners in the Shinkenchiku Residential Design Competition 1979. Theme: a house for Karl Friedrich Schinkel; judge: James Stirling', *Japan Architect*, vol. 55/2 (Feb. 1980), pp. 7–52.

(Straube 1933) Hans Joachim Straube, *Die Gewerbeförderung Preussens in der ersten Hälfte des 19. Jahrhunderts*, Berlin, 1933.

(Stuart & Revett 1787) James Stuart and Nicholas Revett, *The Antiquities of Athens*, London, 1787.

(Szambien 1984) Werner Szambien, *Jean-Nicolas-Louis Durand, 1760–1834: De l'imitation à la norme*, Paris, 1984.

(Szambien 1989) Werner Szambien, *Schinkel*, Paris, 1989.

(Ungers 1981) Oswald Mathias Ungers, 'Five lessons from Schinkel's work', *Cornell Journal of Architecture*, (1981), pp. 118–9; and in *Quaderns*, March/April 1982, pp. 104–5.

(Vann 1977) James Allen Vann, 'Karl Friedrich Schinkel; Berlin as the City Beautiful', *Classical America*, vol. IV (1977), pp. 174–182.

(Venice and Rome 1982) *Schinkel, l'architetto del Principe*, exhibition catalogue, Venice (Museo Correr) and Rome (Palazzo dei Conservatori), Venice and Rome, 1982.

(Veseley 1985) Dalibor Veseley, 'Architecture and the conflict of representation', *AA Files*, 8 (January 1985), pp. 21–38.

(Vitruvius 1931–4) Vitruvius (trans. Frank Granger), *On Architecture*, 2 vols, Cambridge, Mass., 1931–4.

(Vogel 1952) Hans Vogel, *Pommern*, Berlin, 1952 (in the Schinkel Lebenswerk series).

(Vogt 1985) Adolf Max Vogt, *Karl Friedrich Schinkel, Blick in Griechenlands Blüte: ein Hoffnungsbild für 'Spree-Athen'*, Frankfurt, 1985.

(Volk 1982) Waltraud Volk, *Karl Friedrich Schinkel; sein Wirken als Architekt*, Stuttgart, 1982 (Berlin 1984).

(*Vorbilder*) Kgl. Technische Deputation für Gewerbe, *Vorbilder für Fabrikanten und Handwerker*, published in parts 1821–37 by the Kgl. Technische Deputation für Gewerbe. First collected ed. 1830, 2nd collected ed. 1837. Reissued 1863 with descriptive text (see cat. 133).

(Waagen 1844) Gustav Friedrich Waagen, 'Karl Friedrich Schinkel als Mensch und als Künstler', *Berliner Kalender*, 1844, pp. 305–428.

(Waagen 1847) Gustav Friedrich Waagen, 'Einige Äusserungen Schinkels über Leben, Bildung, und Kunst' (Schinkel-Festrede 1846), *Allgemeine Bauzeitung*, 2 (1847), p. 261ff.

(Waagen 1854) Gustav Friedrich Waagen, 'Über das Verhältnis Beuths zu Schinkel' (Schinkel-Festrede 1854), *Zeitschrift für Bauwesen*, 4, 1854.

(Watkin 1979) David Watkin, 'Karl Friedrich Schinkel: royal patronage and the picturesque', *Architectural Design*, vol. 49/8&9 (1979), pp. 56–72.

(Watkin & Mellinghof 1987) David Watkin and Tilman Mellinghof, *German Architecture and the Classical Ideal: 1740–1840*, London, 1987.

(Wegner 1990) Reinhard Wegner, *Die Reise nach Frankreich und England im Jahre 1826*, Berlin and Munich, 1990 (in the Schinkel Lebenswerk series).

(Wesenberg 1987) Angelika Wesenberg, 'Johann Georg Hossauer 1794–1874. Führender Berliner Goldschmied des 19. Jahrhunderts', *Staatliche Museen zu Berlin: Forschungen und Berichte*, 26 (1987), pp. 213–40.

(Wiebenson 1969) Dora Wiebenson, *Sources of Greek Revival Architecture*, London, 1969.

(Wiederanders 1981) Gerlinde Wiederanders, *Die Kirchenbauten Karl Friedrich Schinkels*, Berlin, 1981.

(Wiegand 1941) T. Wiegand, *Das Didyma*, vol. 1, Berlin, 1941.

(Wiegand & Schrader 1904) T. Wiegand and H. Schrader, *Priene: Ergebnisse der Ausgrabungen und Untersuchungen in den Jahren 1895–8*, Berlin, 1904.

(Wittkower 1962) Rudolf Wittkower, *Architectural Principles in the Age of Humanism*, London, 1962 (1st ed. 1949).

(Wolff 1968) Hans Christian Wolff, *Oper Szene und Darstellung von 1600–1900, Musikgeschichte in Bildern*, vol. IV, Leipzig, 1968.

(Wolzogen 1862–3) Alfred Freiherr von Wolzogen, *Aus Schinkels Nachlass, Reisetagebücher, Briefe und Aphorismen*, 3 vols, Berlin, 1862–3 (reprint 1981 and Munich 1985).

(Wolzogen 1864 I) Alfred Freiherr von Wolzogen, *Katalog des kunstlerischen Nachlasses*, Berlin, 1864 (vol. 4 of 1862–3).

(Wolzogen 1864 II) Alfred Freiherr von Wolzogen, 'Schinkel als Architekt, Maler und Kunstphilosoph', *Zeitschrift für Bauwesen*, 1864, p. 61ff and *Zeitschrift für bildende Kunst*, 3, 1868.

(Zadow 1980) Mario Zadow, *Karl Friedrich Schinkel*, Berlin, 1980.

(Zedlitz 1834) Leopold Freiherr von Zedlitz, *Neustes Conversationshandbuch für Berlin und Potsdam*, Berlin, 1834.

(Zick 1990) Gisela Zick, 'Zwei wiederaufgefundene Werke von Rauch und Tieck die Vendée-Kandelaber', *Jahrbuch der Berliner Museen*, 32 (1990), pp. 237–267.

(Ziller 1897) Hermann Ziller, *Karl Friedrich Schinkel*, Bielefeld and Leipzig, 1897.

86. Schinkel's grave (1841) in the Dorotheenstadt
cemetery, Berlin, c.1930. The stele was designed by
Schinkel in 1833 for the grave of Sigismund
Hembstaedt, the bronze parts being modelled by
August Kiss and made in the Gewerbe-Institut. The
medallion was modelled by Christian Daniel Rauch
in 1836. A wreath is laid during the annual Schinkel
Festival.